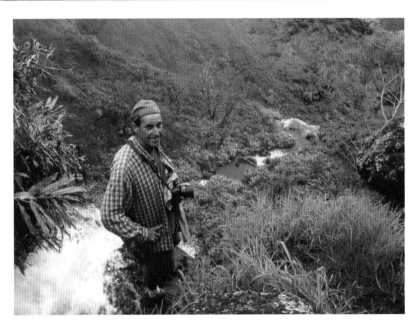

In memory of
David Boynton
(August 30, 1945 to February 10, 2007)

The
KAUA'I
Movie book

ISBN: 978-1939487-13-1 softcover
    Library of Congress Control Number: 2013944387

Cover landscape photograph © Susan Boynton

First Printing, October 2013
Printed in Taiwan

Mutual Publishing, LLC
1215 Center Street, Suite 210
Honolulu, Hawai'i 96816
Ph: (808) 732-1709
Fax: (808) 734-4094
email: info@mutualpublishing.com
www.mutualpublishing.com

Though extensive research was undertaken in producing *The New Kaua'i Movie Book,* inadvertent omissions or errors may have occurred.

Location filming for *Outbreak* at Kamokila village on the banks of the Wailua River.

Proceeds from *The New Kaua'i Movie Book* will benefit the Wilcox Health Foundation. The Wilcox Health Foundation supports the Wilcox Memorial Hospital's non-profit mission to provide quality healthcare to residents of and visitors to the island of Kaua'i.

Wetland taro fields in Hanalei Valley.

Table of Contents

Acknowledgments

The Wilcox Hospital Foundation Board ◆ Lourdes Alba ◆ Christine Alvezios ◆ Carlos Andrade ◆ Linda Antipala ◆ Peter Bart ◆ Jack Bean and Mitzi Gaynor ◆ Nick Beck ◆ Sue Boynton ◆ DeSoto Brown ◆ Bill Budd ◆ Camera Lab ◆ Ruth Cassel ◆ Michael Ching ◆ Terry and Maureen Chung ◆ Sally Clark ◆ Davy Cook ◆ Evelyn, Christian, and David Cook ◆ Lynne Costner ◆ Charlie Cowden ◆ Myrah Cummings ◆ David Cunningham ◆ Ken D'Attilio ◆ Mary Daubert ◆ Rita De Silva ◆ Gerald Dela Cruz ◆ DiscMaker ◆ Judy Drosd ◆ Alan Fayé ◆ Chris Fayé ◆ John Ferry ◆ Brian Frankish ◆ Dennis Fujimoto ◆ Pancho Graham ◆ Joel Guy ◆ Bethany Hamilton and family ◆ Laird Hamilton ◆ Rick Hanna ◆ Mike Harmon ◆ Duncan Henderson ◆ Jane Hopkins ◆ Payton Hough ◆ Bennett Hymer ◆ Bob Kajiwara ◆ Stanley Kaluahine ◆ Sue Kanoho ◆ Kaua'i Community College Library staff ◆ Kaua'i Historical Society ◆ Brian Kennelly ◆ Alekai Kinimaka ◆ Titus Kinimaka ◆ Dr. William Klein, Jr. ◆ Howard W. Kock ◆ Mayor Maryanne Kusaka ◆ Robert Lemer ◆ Janet Leopold ◆ Ken Levine ◆ Marvin Levy ◆ Lihu'e Public Library staff ◆ Margaret Lovett ◆ Myles Ludwig ◆ Greg MacGillivray ◆ Rick and Amy Marvin ◆ Brian McNulty ◆ Andy Melamed ◆ Claire Morris ◆ Maureen Morrison ◆ Vida Mossman ◆ Ed Naha ◆ Galen Nakamura ◆ Nakatsukasa Family ◆ Candyce Ogino ◆ Richard Palumbo ◆ David Penhallow ◆ Marion Penhallow ◆ James Pflueger ◆ Luis Reyes ◆ Alan Rietow ◆ Tim Ryan ◆ Akiko Senda ◆ Haunani Seward ◆ Michael Singer ◆ Joey Skaggs ◆ Anthony Sommer ◆ Stephanie Spangler ◆ Stephen Spaulding ◆ Steve Stafford ◆ Jeff Stott ◆ Tom Summers ◆ David Talisman ◆ Angela Tillson ◆ Art Umezu ◆ Damien and Liz Victorino ◆ Mike, Susie and Matt Wellman ◆ Wil Welsh ◆ Chipper Wichman ◆ Gaylord Wilcox ◆ Carol Young

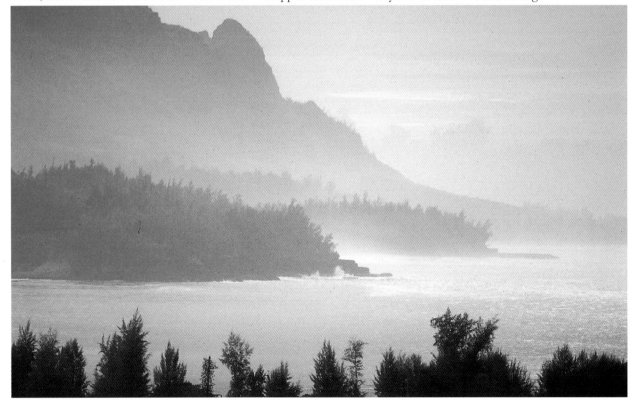

Misty Hanalei Bay, with Mount Makana in background. The landmark mountain became Bali Hai in the film *South Pacific*.

Preface

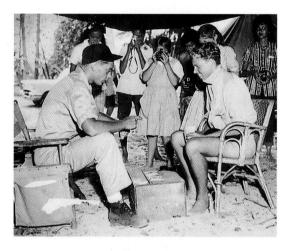

John Kerr plays cards with Kaua'i's David Penhallow, his double, during the Kaua'i location filming of *South Pacific*.

There is a theory that the red dust that hovers in the atmosphere above Kaua'i, when filtered through the lens of a camera, makes the colors of this island even more vibrant than what is seen in reality.

Whatever the theory, whatever the call, that brings film people to this island, Kaua'i is found to be magical. Kaua'i is magical because of its outrageous beauty. God compacted this magical island into a 550-square-mile, almost perfectly round island. Kaua'i is magical because of its mythical nature spirits that reside by 1,000 waterfalls streaming down purple mountainsides. Kaua'i is magical because the people of this island, bronzed by the sun, have smiles that radiate like a wave hitting a Na Pali cliff that breaks into a cascade of sparkling diamonds. Kaua'i is magical because, within a 40-minute driving radius, it seems as though you are in Africa, Australia, England, Tahiti, Vietnam, Arizona, and Bali Hai.

My first recollection of a film being made on Kaua'i was *Pagan Love Song*. I grew up on Kaua'i, learning about life from the films that I saw at the Lihue, Roxy, Kealia, Kilauea, Koloa, Star, Hanapepe, Kaua'i, Aloha, Pono, Waimea and Kekaha theaters. I could barely believe it when the cast and crew from MGM, the premier film factory of Hollywood, landed on Kaua'i to make a movie. The reality of it hit me the day I was trying to catch a glimpse of MGM filmmaking on the Coco Palms property. I ran smack into Esther Williams. In my mind, and in the minds of millions of people in 1950, Esther Williams was a true film goddess. She was the reigning queen of MGM's musicals, which were often set in a mammoth swimming pool. Watching her stride toward me that day with her long tapered athletic legs, I couldn't recall having seen a human creature more perfect or more beautiful. To my young mind, she was more dazzling in person than any Technicolor camera had ever captured her. I stood absolutely still and was dumbfounded. When she passed by and said hello to this mooning, slack-jawed adolescent, I knew the stars had come down from heaven and blessed this young acne-faced mortal. My fantasies of the movies suddenly turned into reality that day.

Kaua'i was made for Technicolor film because the beauty and lushness of this island is so unbelievable. I don't think there is a sound stage or an art director in the film industry that could create or duplicate the "magic" found on Kaua'i. The obsidian-blue ocean found in Hanalei, green and purple mountain ridges of Wai'ale'ale, Makaweli red-dirt cane fields, the slippery-slide falls above Anahola, or the upper wet cave at Ha'ena that boasts of a turquoise water cavern that rivals Capri—all are awesome originals.

This book documents those dreams that Kaua'i made come true by such filmmakers, actors, and technicians as Steven Spielberg, Josh Logan, Lyle Wheeler, Rita Hayworth, John Wayne, Richard Chamberlain, Frank Sinatra, and Howard W. Koch. Within the pages of this book, the reader will discover the known and many more unknown films made here. This book is a legacy to the many local people who were part of Kaua'i's film history. Kaua'i stands crowned as the island that has had more films shot on it than any other neighbor island.

My most memorable experience with films on Kaua'i was when I was a stand-in for John Kerr in *South Pacific*. I don't believe there was a group of filmmakers as well liked or as well known by local residents. They lived with us for almost five months. Mitzi Gaynor and Jack Bean, Rossano and Lydia Brazzi, John Kerr, France Nuyen, Josh and Nedda Logan, Ray Walston, Lyle and Donna Wheeler were among those that became *'ohana* (family) and friends to many of us. *South Pacific,* based on the book by James A. Michener and produced by 20th Century Fox, gave to the world a romantic musical film that had serious overtones of racial prejudice. This was a first. The film was also doubly blessed with the memorable music of Rogers and Hammerstein. It is still seen and loved by millions of people throughout the world.

The song "Bali Hai" can still haunt a movie dreamer when Bloody Mary (Juanita Hall), looking out to the cliffs of Ha'ena, sings:

> "Bali Hai may call you,
> Any night, any day, in your heart you'll hear it call you…
> Come away, come away…"

As movie dreamers sit in darkened theaters and hear the calling of Bali Hai, their own dreams begin:

FADE IN:

Two lovers holding hands as the sun sets behind a darkened cloud, a wave crashes on a white sandy beach, the sky turns crimson, lovers and coconut trees are silhouetted black against the red panorama…the music swells…

FADE OUT:

Kaua'i.

This book is about dreams. This book is dedicated to all those who love the movies and who love Kaua'i.

–David Penhallow

Howard Keel, co-star of *Pagan Love Song,* and kama'aina Maureen West Morrison on Kaua'i, 1950.

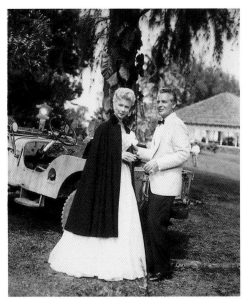

Mitzi Gaynor and Rossano Brazzi, in evening dress, with an authentic World War II Jeep, at the old Birkmyre Estate at Princeville.

Casually dressed Esther Williams and Howard Keel (left) are guests at a high society party supposedly held in Papeete. It's actually Kaua'i kama'aina acting as French officials, planters, and local residents on Tahiti; the location is the garden of the Horner mansion, which once stood on the beach at Wailua.

Introduction

The gates to Jurassic Park were built along a plantation road deep in the island's interior near the base of Mt. Wai'ale'ale.

Most beautiful, most blessed Kaua'i.
Serene she rests, rising from the sea
To lift the leaf-bud of her mountain Wai'ale'ale to the sky,
There to flower
In forty-thousand radiations of celestial light …
From an ancient chant of the Island

This Hawaiian chant, hundreds of years old, still evokes the essence of Kaua'i: the beauty of the Island's miles of white-sand beaches; its towering, verdant pinnacles and deep, mysterious valleys; the pure, vivid sunlight and moonlight that strike the Island in literally tens of thousands of hues. It is this allure that has drawn filmmakers to Kaua'i's shores to make over 60 feature films since 1933.

Filmmakers have dressed the Island's locations as Vietnam, an idyllic South Sea island, outback tropical Australia, an island off the coast of Costa Rica, a Fantasy Island, the misty domain of the great King Kong, Peter Pan's Never-Never Land, plague-ridden Africa, and a South Pacific World War II battleground.

Beyond the visuals, though, Hollywood's love affair with Kaua'i goes further than what the camera sees. The simple *aloha* shown directors and film stars – from Hollywood's first woman director Lois Weber during filming at Waimea for *White Heat* in 1933, to Steven Spielberg, who filmed *Raiders of the Lost Ark* in 1980 and returned in 1992 for *Jurassic Park*, to George Clooney playing a kama'aina landowner in 2011 in The Academy Award-winning *The Descendants* – is key to Kaua'i's success as the leading location for feature films made in the Hawaiian Islands.

Complementing the stories are behind-the-scenes movie stills and photographs of the locations as they appear today. A film-by-film list of feature films, major television productions, and surfing movies offers the most comprehensive research ever attempted on Kaua'i location filmmaking.

The brainchild of Claire Morris, former public relations director for Wilcox Memorial Hospital, *The Kaua'i Movie Book* was created by the late noted Kaua'i photographer David Boynton, and Kaua'i author and historical researcher Chris Cook in collaboration with the Kaua'i Film Commission and the Kaua'i Visitors Bureau. The "Producers" of the first edition of the *The Kaua'i Movie Book* were: Marion Penhallow, Wilcox Hospital Foundation's Vice President; Judy Drosd, Kaua'i's first Film Commissioner, who also provided significant editorial assistance; and Lourdes Alba, Judy's assistant film commissioner. Chris Cook returned to write and gather materials for this new, updated edition with the help of Kaua'i Visitors Bureau Executive Director Sue Kanoho and Kaua'i Film Commissioner Art Umezu. All involved hope they have honored the Island and its people and the filmmakers and actors who have brought Kaua'i to life on the big screen for almost a century.

1996-2012 KAUA'I MOVIES

2011

Pirates of the Caribbean: On Stranger Tides
Disney Pictures, Director: Rob Marshall

Just Go With It
Sony Pictures, Director: Dennis Dugan,
Production: Happy Madison Productions

The Descendents
Fox Searchlight, Director: Alexander Payne

Soul Surfer
Sony Pictures, Director: Sean McNamara

2010

Avatar
20th Century Fox, Director: James Cameron

2009

Dinocroc Vs. Supergator (for SyFy Channel)
Roger Corman Films, Director: Jim Wynorski

2008

High School Reunion Season 5
TV Land, Producer: Mike Fleiss

Perfect Getaway
Rogue Films, Director: David Twohy

Tropic Thunder
Dreamworks/Red Hour Productions, Director:
Ben Stiller

2006

Supergator (for SyFy Channel)
Rodeo Productions, Director: Brian Clyde,
Producer: Roger Corman

2005

Band Of Pirates, Buccaneer Island
Mercury Productions, Producer: Bruce Mercury

Komodo Vs. Cobra (for Syfy Channel)
Barking Sand Productions, Director: Jim
Wynorski

2002

Dragonfly
Universal Pictures

Lilo & Stitch
Disney Pictures

2001

Jurassic Park III
Amblin/Universal Pictures

Manhunt
United Paramount Network

Moolah Beach
Fox Family Worldwide

The Time Machine
Dreamworks LLC & Warner Bros.

2000

To End All Wars
Argyll Film Partners, LLC

Dinosaur
Disney Pictures

The Testaments
LDS Church

1998

Six Days Seven Nights
Touchstone Pictures

Mighty Joe Young
Walt Disney Pictures

1997

George of the Jungle
Walt Disney Pictures

The Lost World: Jurassic Park
Amblin/Universal Pictures

The Descendants

The 2011 Fox Searchlight film version of author Kaui Hart Hemmings 2007 book *The Descendants* is said to be the most accurate portrayal ever captured on film of what day-to-day life is actually like in Hawai'i for local residents.

The Descendants cast and crew, with Academy Award-winning actor George Clooney in the lead role as Matt King, the leader of a wealthy kama'āina major land-owning family, filmed several scenes on location on Kaua'i, with the bulk of the film shot in and around Honolulu.

Kaua'i filming took place in May 2010 and preceded three weeks of shooting in Honolulu.

Author Hart Hemmings' fictional story focuses on a large ocean-front valley the King family owns on Kaua'i, symbolically said to be the last parcel of undeveloped land on the Island. The land has been handed down to the "descendants" from their missionary family banker ancestor who fortunately married a Hawaiian princess who was heir to lands of Kamehameha.

The plot has the family facing two life-changing crises that must be resolved within days.

One has to do with land and power. Matt has the final say on whether the land, which is portrayed in the film by the Alexander family's isolated and private Kipu Kai valley located in the southeast corner of Kaua'i, is to be sold to one of the developers bidding on its purchase, or whether the family will keep the rare parcel in its native, undeveloped state. Due to reformed banking laws the family must take action within days.

Complicating the land sale drama is Matt's personal drama—an adventurous wife slowly dying and in a coma in Queen's Hospital in Honolulu following a boating accident, and his having to step in as the lead parent in a tenuous relationship with his two daughters: Alexandra a partying Punahou-type teenager sent away to prep school on the Big Island; the other Scottie, an impressionable ten year old who is getting in trouble as a reaction to her mother's state.

Troy Cook, the muscular, young surfer-boat racer involved in the boating accident, is played by big wave surfing legend Laird Hamilton. Laird grew up on the North Shore of Kaua'i, the stepson of 1960s-1970s era surfing legend Bill Hamilton.

The Kaua'i scenes focus on a twist in the story where Matt discovers his wife had been in an affair with Kahala Realtor Brian Speer, who happens to be vacationing at the King's beach home on the bay at Hanalei. He packs up his girls and Alexandra's alienated teenage boyfriend of sorts, Sid, for a trip to Kaua'i to confront Speer.

Kaua'i King cousin Hugh, played by Beau Bridges who does actually hang out at Tahiti Nui while at his home on Kaua'i, picks the family up at Lihu'e Airport, adding yet another familiar local touch to the film.

The Kings and crew go for a look-see at Kipu Kai, which is located on the other side of the Island in the film, causing local movie goers to feel jerked around as the family drives around Kaua'i. They have a meal and drinks at Tahiti Nui with Koko Kaneali'i and his band, and where a portrait of Tahiti Nui's late founder Lousie Marston and her son Christian Marston loom behind Clooney in one scene.

Musician Koko Kaneali'i led the local band playing at the Tahiti Nui in *The Descendants*.

Kaua'i Mayor Bernard Carvalho Jr. proudly stands with *The Descendants* author Kaui Hart Hemmings at a media reception held in recognition of her novel and its adaptation into an Academy Award-winning film in February 2012 by the County of Kaua'i and the Kaua'i Visitors Bureau in Beverly Hills.

Spectators watch closely as *The Descendants* film crew sets up for a shot outside the Tahiti Nui on Kuhio Highway in Hanalei.

The family walks the beach at Hanalei with the Hanalei Pier in one shot. Look for Kaua'i surfer Titus Kinimaka in the beach scenes at Hanalei, where he runs a surfing school.

A scene where Clooney as Matt King peeking over a beachfront hedge has become an iconic Descendants moment in the film for local residents and visitors. And they stay at the St. Regis-Princeville where the ties between Matt, the girls and Sid deepen.

The filmmakers apparently noticed how the ubiquitous Kaua'i chicken ties into setting the scene correctly when filming on Kaua'i. A report from Kilauea had Island visitors upset by the trapping of chickens along the rural road out to Kilauea Lighthouse. The chickens were released in small groups during a series of takes during the filming of the Kings walking down Weke Road. After ten takes or so, Weke Road homeowner Doug Blackburn recalls, there were quite a few chickens running around his yard. He approached the film crew and asked when the chickens who were roosting in a tree in his yard would be removed, and was told they were at home, for they were Hanalei chickens.

A second-unit crew filmed road scenes along Kuhio Highway at Wailua and other locations.

The North Shore filming was based at the Wilcox family's landmark Kauikeolani Estate located on the mauka side of Weke Road near Black Pot Beach Park. Scenes where Matt confronts Brian Speer and meets Speer's wife were filmed at the Nalu Beach Cottage located along Hanalei Bay, also near the beach park.

Director Alexander Payne invested time in making sure *The Descendants* had the feel of modern-day, and historic, Hawai'i, spending eight months on O'ahu. He employed Hawai'i history author Gavan Daws and University of Hawai'i law professor, and Bishop Estate break-up expert Randall Roth, as consultants.

"It's very unique out there. Capturing a sense of place is very important to me," Payne told NPR radio. "By the time I got to doing *The Descendants*, I really wanted to show—almost with the eye and sensibility of a documentarian—the right feeling, physically and rhythmically, of Hawai'i."

Early on, author Kaui Hart Hemmings imagined Clooney playing Matt King. In her 2007 novel young Scottie wears T-shirts with humorous, quirky sayings, one says "Mrs. Clooney." Once Payne and *The Descendants* producer Jim Burke began work on the film the author suggested that Clooney play Matt King. Hart Hemmings told *The Guardian* newspaper in England, "A few weeks after my suggestion Alexander had met with George in Toronto. Alexander emailed: "We got your man."

In *The Guardian* piece she described filming at

The Descendants crew sets up a camera track along Weke Road in Hanalei.

Beau Bridges as Hugh and George Clooney as his cousin at the Tahiti Nui bar.

Kaua'i-raised waterman Laird Hamilton rides a stand-up paddleboard (SUP) off of Honopu Beah on Na Pali. Hamilton appears in *The Descendants* as Troy Cook, a friend of Matt King's wife Elizabeth who was involved in the speed boat accident that critically injured Elizabeth. Hamilton and fellow big wave surfer Dave Kalama pioneered the re-introduction of the ancient Hawaiian sport of paddle surfing in the modern era of surfing, as well as playing leading roles in launching tow-in surfing in huge waves at Maui's Peahi - Jaws surf break.

Hanalei with Clooney, who was wearing board shorts and a surf shirt, with her six-year-old daughter playing at the beach serving as an extra. "They looked equally related to the place I call home. I was watching my life, my memory, a movie star and my book collide."

In the acknowledgements section of *The Descendants* novel, Hart Hemmings writes: "...a note on Hawai'i's present and past. I was inspired by historical facts and current events, yet this book is a marriage of reality and fiction, and fiction wears the pants in this family."

These quotes reference in part the author's own descendants story, for she is a descendant of Kaua'i missionary son, businessman, landowner and philanthropist Albert Spencer Wilcox. A.S. Wilcox's legacy of donated land and funding is a foundation for many Kaua'i institutions including Kaua'i Community College, the G.N. Wilcox Hospital, the Mahelona Hospital, and in Honolulu the Kapiolani Children's Hospital. He was also an owner of the Princeville Plantation in the late 1800s. He moved to the Puhi area in 1898 to his livestock ranch, the lands of which today make up the Kilohana estate.

Her first name is a family tie to Emma Kauikeolani Napoleon Wilcox, A.S. Wilcox's Native Hawaiian ali'i wife who enjoyed stays with him at their family estate in Hanalei. His father and mother, American Board of Commissioners Congregational missionaries Abner and Lucy Wilcox from Connecticut, raised him at the Wai'oli Mission House that is open for tours today in Hanalei.

In an interview with the *San Francisco Chronicle*, the author described her family ties to Hanalei, which includes her aunt Patricia "Patsy" Sheehan.

"It was very fun to see my real life and this fictional life merge into one. I always felt a little bit of an outsider, especially, because I grew up on O'ahu. This film almost made me get acquainted with that side of the family, and my cousins. I introduced them to Alexander and we used their properties."

Spending for the Kaua'i filming tallied up to an estimated $15 million-plus. Over 200 extras were hired on-island for all the scenes, with 45 alone being used for the Tahiti Nui scene.

Director-screen play writer Alexander Payne won his second Academy Award for Best Adapted Screenplay for his work on *The Descendants*; his first was for the California wine country film *Sideways*. *The Descendants* was nominated for Oscars in five categories including best picture and best actor for George Clooney. The award was notable for Kaua'i. Kaua'i made films had won Academy Awards, but in technical categories such as Best Sound − *South Pacific* in 1958 and *Jurassic Park* in 1994.

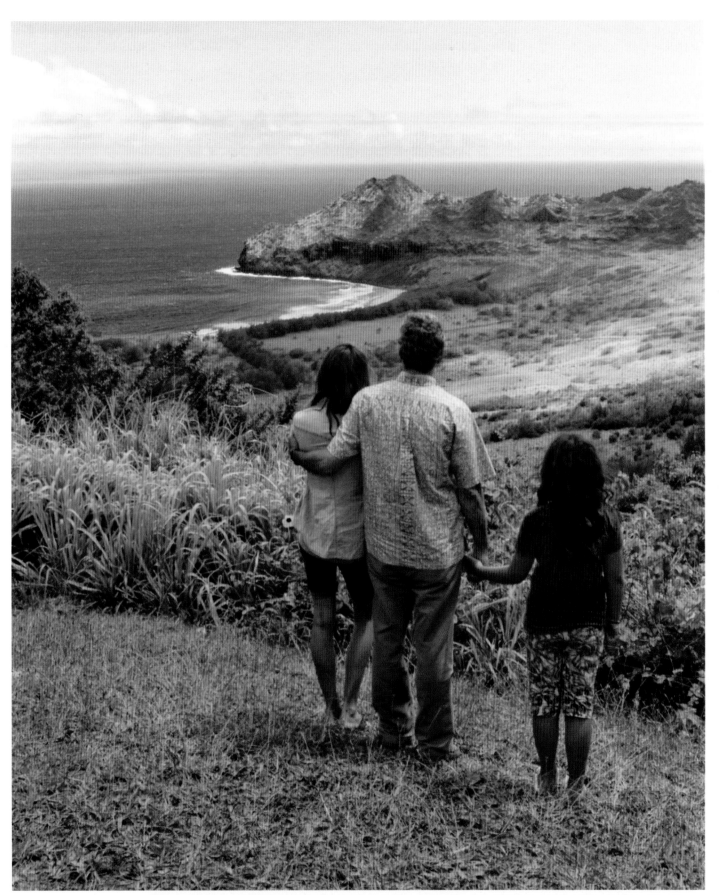

George Clooney as Matt King in *The Descendants* looks out over Kipu Kai with his screen daughters Shailene Woodley as Alexandra and Amara Miller as Scottie. The Alexander family property is at the center of the film's plot as the last large track of undeveloped coastal land remaining on Kaua'i.

Pirates of the Caribbean: On Stranger Tides

"That's an entrance, eh?" says Johnny Depp – dressed in his full Captain Jack Sparrow the pirate rig – as he shuffles in his tall pirate boots across the wide white sand of Honopu Beach on Na Pali while exiting a Blue Hawaiian charter helicopter, the landmark Honopu Arch looming in the background with pinnacles taller than skyscrapers on its flanks.

This scene in a Walt Disney Pictures' promo for *Pirates of the Caribbean: On Stranger Tides* marked the opening moments of the first day (June 14, 2010) of shooting for the fantasy adventure family film that would draw a $1 billion global box office.

But on this day, the film's cast and crew were absorbed with the adventure of filming on a pristine Kaua'i wilderness beach on a beautiful blue sky warm day, not with financial projections.

Director Rob Marshall landed at Honopu in moderate surf, transitioning off a board towed in behind a jet ski. Strict state Department of Land and Natural Resources rules forbid boats to land at Honopu. The valley is located west, around a headland, from Kalalau Beach and the Kalalau Trail, and is inaccessible except by helicopter or by sea, towed in behind a jet ski.

"Yep, we are definitely back on a *Pirates of the Caribbean* movie," producer Jerry Bruckheimer recalled of the kick-off location filming day at remote Honopu in the Disney Editions' book *The Art of Disney Pirates of the Caribbean*. "It was set transportation, POTC style: boarding a Zodiac craft on one side of the island, and then disembarking several yards offshore on the other, before literally being dragged through pounding surf on a floating sled behind a jet ski doing its utmost to evade the waves, but not quite succeeding. Johnny Depp and I were a little drier than most of the crew, as we were dropped off onto the sands of the incredibly beautiful and secluded Honopu Beach – tucked into the magnificent Na Pali Coast of Kaua'i – by the only other means possible: helicopter. And it was quite a sight to see Johnny, fully attired as the now legendary Captain Jack Sparrow, emerge on that beach, as excited as the rest of us to set sail on another *Pirates of the Caribbean* epic."

The cast and crew came to Kaua'i following months of pre-production work in California.

Though the first location filming for *On Stranger Tides* is here at Honopu, Kaua'i appears well into the movie, and doubles as the tropical Caribbean site of Ponce de Leon's fabled Fountain of Youth.

In production notes released by Disney for *On Stranger Tides,* the film's production designer John Myhre explained Kaua'i's role in the overall plot.

"The film kind of divides into three chapters: the opening in London, the middle section on the 'Queen Anne's Revenge,' and the last third is a trek through the jungle in search of the Fountain of Youth," he said, "Looking for those thick, dense, gorgeous jungles brought us to Kaua'i and O'ahu in Hawai'i, then a huge set for the mermaid sequence in Los Angeles, on to Puerto Rico for a tiny island and historic Spanish fort, and finally to the United Kingdom for London exteriors and a large number of sets built at Pinewood Studios."

Producer Bruckheimer notes that, "Although we filmed the first three 'Pirates' movies mostly in the actual Caribbean, for 'On Stranger Tides' we

Hanging out with pirates on the set of *Pirates of the Caribbean: On Stranger Tides* are (from left) County of Kaua'i Office of Economic Development Director George Costa and wife Krystal Costa, Regina Carvalho and Mayor Bernard Carvalho and Kaua'i Visitors Bureau Executive Director Sue Kanoho.

This Pirates of the Caribbean: On Strange Tides set uses elements of Kaua'i's environment also with the magic-making of prop makers to create Ponce de Leon's fabled Fountain of Youth.

The Makauwahi Cave Reserve near Po'ipu provided another setting and viewpoint for the Fountain of Youth scenes in *Pirates of the Caribbean: On Stranger Tides*. The ancient sinkhole is providing a wealth of information on the pre-history of Kaua'i.

The look of oil lamps in the evening jungle in a grove of Kaua'i coconut trees lent a romantic air to this *Pirates* scene.

The Honopu Arch on Na Pali was one of the first locations used by *Pirates* director Rob Marshall during Kaua'i location filming.

Hundreds of hopefuls vying to be hired as extras for *Pirates of the Caribbean: On Stranger Tides* lined up at the Kaua'i War Memorial Convention Center.

The "Blue Room" is located inside the Waikapala'e "Wet Cave" at Ha'ena. The entrance to the cave and the colorful pool were used as Fountain of Youth locations in *Pirates of the Caribbean: On Stranger Tides.*

required landscapes so beautiful they're almost otherworldly."

His location scouts found that areas they found on Kaua'i – and on O'ahu – were the best choices.

"Both islands, especially Kaua'i, have these extraordinary jungles, mountains and shorelines," director Marshall explains in the production notes. "They're so lush, oversized and just stunning. O'ahu also has beautiful landscapes, and we also did all of our shooting at sea there of Blackbeard's ship, the 'Queen Anne's Revenge.'"

The lure of being in a pirate movie, and on top of that a blockbuster *Pirates of the Caribbean* sequel from Walt Disney Pictures, drew hundreds of local pirate wannabes to the Kaua'i War Memorial Convention Hall on Hardy Street in Lihu'e in late April 2010.

A *Honolulu Star-Advertiser* reporter described the scene, "Some sported British sailing attire, some wore pirate-like bandanas, earrings and necklaces, and others just came in board shorts and tank tops."

The broadside for the casting call sought real pirate types, "authentic-looking scavenger-types…ages 18 to 60s, all ethnicities, especially extreme character types – thin, tall, short, emaciated, odd features, huge nose, eyes, ears, lazy eye, grizzled and wrinkled faces, odd body types, missing limbs, teeth, etc. MEN ONLY."

Sailor roles were also on the bill. The sailor's were to be…"Thin and average builds, from good-looking to extreme characters. British types, Spaniards or other ethnicities. Ages 18 to 50s MEN ONLY."

Photo-doubles and stand-ins were also cast.

A second round of casting sought a mermaid, Syrena, a "young Caucasian female with pale skin…very thin, around 5 feet 6 inches tall, with hair colored dark blond to brown." Casting agent Sande Alessi told *The Garden Island* that, "We found some great people at the men's open casting call."

With a careful look you can spot Kaua'i locals in the final print of *On Stranger Tides.* When the trailer for the film was released, young North Shore surfers hyped their coup in standing out as rousing, over-the-top pirates in one scene pictured.

Filming continued at Kaua'i locations beyond Honopu for about a month. Locations included the grounds of the National Tropical Botanical Garden in Lawa'i, Kipu Ranch, Grove Farm lands mauka of Lihu'e and Valley House in upper Kealia Valley. The Disney production notes report showed Kaua'i provided what Bruckheimer and Marshall needed for *On Stranger Tides,* "(Kaua'i) provided rich landscapes for thick jungle growth, rivers, chasms and cliffs, much of it ruggedly challenging for the cast and crew to access and film, especially with the two-camera 3D rigs."

Among the cameras brought to Kaua'i were the most technically advance ever use to film on the Island, enhanced models that built upon the technology director James Cameron used in filming his landmark film *Avatar,* which included Kaua'i background footage. The new cameras were smaller and thus more mobile, and able to be used on beaches and in rain forest jungle scenes during the Kaua'i filming.

One scene – with Depp, co-stars Penelope Cruz and Ian McShane, a crew of zombie pirates, and assorted sailors atop a waterfall on private mauka land and overlooking a tropical river on their quest for cave hiding the Fountain of Youth – features a spectacular leap by a stunt double Jack Sparrow, one likely deadly to any Island visitor or local trying to duplicate the feat.

Waikapala'e Cave, commonly known as the "Wet Cave," and located a bit back from Kuhio Highway at Ha'ena, was set as the cave entrance to the Fountain of Youth in *On Stranger Tides.*

Tears of a mermaid were part of the formula for the ceremony required in the Fountain of Youth, and devious, beautiful but demonic mermaids do battle with Blackbeard's men in the run-up to this cave scene. And here the filmmakers, probably unknowingly, crossed paths with a Native Hawaiian legend featuring mermaids.

Carlos Andrade—Kaua'i-born author, noted Hawaiian musician and songwriter, expert waterman and the holder of a doctorate in geography from the University of Hawai'i and now director of the Kamakakuokalani Center for Hawaiian Studies at UH – in his book *Ha'ena - Through the Eyes of the Ancestors*, relates this legend.

The Kapala'e of the place name Waikapala'e (freshwater of Kapala'e) is a kupua, a shape-shifter who can change her body form. She often appears as a beautiful woman, and would appear at the mouth of the cave combing her "long, lustrous, beautiful hair." Kapala'e, as tradition says, lured a handsome man to his death there. Violet Hashimoto Goto, a Ha'ena elder, shared her memories of Waikapala'e with Andrade.

"No, I've read those stories about that (mo'o), but they are just little stories. They used to say that they were mermaids that used to sit on the rock, but then even by grandma's place there used to be one mo'o. You know some people call the mo'o mermaids, but the old folks called them mo'o."

Further west, past Waikapala'e, the cast and crew moved the production to Ke'e Beach, the end of the road. A rainy North Shore day postponed filming. The time off was thriftily used to film Jack Sparrow in England in an interior 18th century paddy wagon set rigged together on Kaua'i. The delay set up a terrific cinematic pay off the next day.

"The next day, though, skies cleared enough to allow Depp and McNally to shoot an important sunset scene on the beach, with enough clouds moving in to suddenly create a perfect image with radiant light," according to the production notes for the film. "All agreed that with all of the technological advances in film made over the past few decades, and computer generated imagery capable of manifesting virtually anything, nothing could match the perfection which nature herself bestowed upon that landscape." Jerry Bruckheimer then comments, "That's why we go to such locations for exactly such moments as that."

"Kaua'i was phenomenally beautiful and perfect for us," actor Geoffrey Rush relates in the notes of the beach-and-sky scene that appears near the end of the movie and spotlights him and Depp at Ke'e Beach, "because we were shooting in really surreal-looking bamboo forests and finding wild and rugged cliff faces, and extraordinary jungle. It added so much to the film."

Closing out *On Stranger Tides* filming on Kaua'i fittingly found Depp and Rush tied with much rope to a coconut tree in the huge coconut grove at Coco Palms, Grace Guslander's shuttered grand resort on the coast at Wailua. It was noted

Adding a bit of a fantasy look to a Kaua'i lava rock outcrop, along with ship cable and beams, turned this location into a Fountain of Youth island location in *Pirates of the Caribbean.*

that hundreds of coconuts were trimmed to keep them from bombing down unannounced on the cast and crew.

Geoffrey Rush, who like many of the fans who travel to Kaua'i to honor the King is from England, invited friends to his hotel room for a showing of Elvis' *Blue Hawaii*, which was principally filmed on Kaua'i at the Coco Palms and nearby locations. "We re-cast every part in the film with actors from 'Pirates,'" recalls screenwriter Terry Rossio in the production notes, "and of course Elvis would be Johnny Depp!"

"Every film crew has it's own vibe when they shoot on Kaua'i," Kaua'i Visitors Bureau Executive Director Sue Kanoho says of her experiences helping out with location filming for *On Stranger Tides*. "I was pleasantly surprised at how the crew fit hand-in-glove with Kaua'i and her people. The production team was truly concerned about doing things the right way and wanted to be sure they were being respectful of our sacred areas.

"I was excited to see producer Jerry Bruckheimer tweeting photos of Kaua'i during their first few days of location shooting, and telling people where he actually was in the moment. We are so used to keeping location shoots a secret, and this new approach caught me off-guard. I was thrilled to see the video that was released on the making of the movie on Kaua'i showing Johnny Depp arriving via helicopter at Honopu Beach and director Rob Marshall coming in to Honopu Beach via a jet ski - how awesome is that?! I have watched that video several times since and it still puts a smile on my face."

The film *Pirates of the Caribbean: On Stranger Tides* is the fourth film in the Walt Disney Pictures series that broke many box office records upon release in May 2011, and is on the list of highest-grossing films of all time.

The Kaua'i Film Commission was presented with this *Just Go With It* poster signed "Much Mahalo" by Adam Sandler. The crew for the film employed a pontoon raft with poles for navigating for scenes filmed in the Kilauea Falls pool.

An elaborate jungle scene suspension bridge was constructed adjacent to Kilauea Falls for a comic scene of Adam Sandler and crew crossing over it in *Just Go With It*. Sabra Kauka poses at Kilauea Falls with child actors featured in the tropical jungle tour scenes in the film.

Just Go With It

Comic Adam Sandler's 2011 film *Just Go With It* is notable for his decision to move his film company lock, stock and jungle bridge from location filming on Maui to Kaua'i to use what he saw as the "perfect" tropical waterfall location in the Islands, a place known on Kaua'i as Kilauea Falls.

Kilauea Falls, located near a neighborhood of post-plantation era homes in Kilauea town, is now located on private property and inaccessible to the public. Kaua'i Film Commissioner Art Umezu assisted the crew of about 30 in scouting Kaua'i.

The $80 million Columbia Pictures-Happy Madison Productions film was released in the winter of 2011 and did well at the box office, with almost $20 million spent on the Kaua'i filming.

The Happy Madison production brought *Just Go With It* cast and crew to Kaua'i for three weeks of filming in May 2010. The stars stayed at the St. Regis Princeville hotel.

The film stars Sandler as a Beverly Hills plastic surgeon on a vacation trip to Maui. Jennifer Aniston plays his clinic assistant, whom he talks into playing his estranged wife after he discovers being married is an attraction for a younger woman played by blonde *Sports Illustrated* swim suit model Brooklyn Decker. The son and daughter of divorced Aniston will only go along with the act if the good doctor will taken them to Hawai'i.

The Kaua'i scenes occur as an interlude in a mixed-up family vacation to Maui funded by wealthy doctor Sandler. He takes everyone on the adventure tour hike and winds up at the scenic waterfall, which is dressed with rows of bright tropical flowers.

Aniston and Decker dive into the Kilauea Falls pool, and comic figure Nick Swardson, as Sandler's hanger-on cousin, or at least a stunt double, does a back flip into the pool from about 20 feet up from a dry cliff face.

Just Go With It is directed by Dennis Dugan, a long-time collaborator with Sandler on many hit films. Dugan and production designer Perry Andelin Blake scouted locations across Hawai'i about three months before the cast and crew arrived.

Production notes from Columbia for the film point out that the Kilauea Falls location is unique in Hawai'i as it is close to paved roads, the falls are moderately low and have a deep pool, allowing for safe stunt work, and the lush North Shore environment provides what filmmakers want for a tropical rainforest setting.

"We looked everywhere in Maui first, since we knew we'd be shooting there," Blake said in the production notes. "We looked on Hawai'i. We looked on O'ahu. And finally we found what we were looking for on Kaua'i. We walked around the corner and we saw this amazing waterfall. We had found the holy grail of waterfalls. We walked through the jungle about three miles – our guide said it was going to be about a half mile, and three miles later through the bugs in the jungle we came to this waterfall, which was just spectacular. After looking at so many different ones what was cool about this one was that it was cinematic – a lot of waterfalls are tall and have a lot of height and were spectacular, but for us we wanted something that spread across more in the format of a film screen. It wasn't a little thing coming down into a small pool – it was a massive wall of water coming into a big, beautiful pool. It was perfect.

"This is Adam's dream of a waterfall. In fact, when we showed him, he said, 'That's the one.'" Blake said in the notes.

Most impressive in the Kilauea Falls scenes is the rope suspension foot bridge set designers built. The foot bridge looks like it was modeled after the Hanapepe swinging bridge or the Kaipaia suspension bridge located just outside of Lihu'e.

"The filmmakers didn't find what they were looking for, and so a bridge had to be built," Blake explains in the production notes. "It seemed like the best solution – we could build it at the exact height we wanted, we could make it look rickety, and we could make it safe. So we found a great, huge mango tree, and on the other side, we anchored the bridge up into the rocks. We wanted it to look like it's been here forever, so once we built it, we aged it and threw plants all over it. It looks dilapidated, it looks dangerous, it looks scary, but it's completely safe."

Long-time Kilauea resident Gary Smith is the descendant of a line of Hawai'i sugar plantation managers, the son of Ernest Smith, who served as C. Brewer's plantation manager at Kilauea from 1960-1969, and grew up with his family in the Kilauea Plantation Managers home.

He recalls: "By the early 1900s, the Japanese plantation workers referred to the lower one as Takinoshita and the upper as Takinoue, literally lower and upper waterfalls. In our day – 1960s – we referred to the lower as Claro Falls, which we seldom went to other than fishing and exploring, and the upper (just off Kilauea Road) as Kilauea Falls; the general public and *The Garden Island* sometimes called it South Pacific Falls.

"Claro Duco was a Filipino plantation laborer who was into body building and his physique, he was known as the Filipino Tarzan! He had a garden along that valley and frequented the falls where he swam with a Speedo...unheard of in our day. At the close of the plantation Claro went back to the Philippines as the plantation was obligated to pay for their return if they so chose to go back."

Kilauea Falls in the early 1980s was an isolated swimming spot accessible through a jungle of bamboo, avocado trees and underbrush near the remains of an old plantation camp. Today the falls are off limits, with access only through permission of a private property owner.

Bethany is held by her father Tom when she was a toddler following a church service held by the Garden Island Christian Fellowship in the event room at the rear of the landmark Tahiti Nui Restaurant in the early 1990s. Her mother Cheri is to the left of Tom and with brothers Timmy and Noah foreground.

The Hamilton family on the beach pictured on the cover of Cheri's faith-based background account of her family, *Soul Surfer* and Bethany's fame: (from left) Noah, Tom, Bethany, Cheri and Tim. Bethany's Sharpei dog, Hana, is featured in the film as Ginger.

Becky (Baumgartner) Hamilton directed/produced the documentary film *Heart of a Soul Surfer*, released in 2007. It is a special feature on the *Soul Surfer* DVD, and likely the most successful ever film made on island by a local filmmaker. The Hamilton family's *Soul Surfer* clap board is signed by the film's cast and crew.

Soul Surfer

The 2011 film *Soul Surfer* is a dramatized account of a Kauaʻi story now known around the world. Kauaʻi-born surfer Bethany Hamilton – then 13 years old lost her left arm and 60 percent of her blood to a tiger shark attack at a surf spot known as Tunnels located offshore of Haʻena on Halloween Day 2003.

Bethany overcame her close call with death and loss of her arm through faith, family and the support of Kauaʻi's people and the local- and global-surfing community.

Soul Surfer is unique in that the storyline is about real Kauaʻi people, and in the use of off-island locations to replicate Kauaʻi settings.

The backstory of *Soul Surfer* portrays the tight-knit Kauaʻi surfing community, and the island's evangelical churches – the sources of the worldview of Bethany and her family (mom and dad Tom and Cheri Hamilton, brothers Noah and Timmy) and keys to her recovery and positive response to her personal tragedy.

Soul Surfer blends this timeless story with gorgeous backdrops filmed on Kauaʻi, Oʻahu and in Tahiti, and with some of the most authentic surfing scenes ever to appear in a Hollywood feature film. Bethany's older brother Noah, who worked as a producer on the film, took the lead in this, along with brother Timmy, who was an assistant to cameramen, and Noah's wife Becky (Baumgartner) Hamilton, also a producer, who was on the set daily to advise director Sean McNamara in keeping the entire film accurate.

Becky's 2007 documentary film *Heart of a Soul Surfer* told Bethany's story using years of family footage and was utilized to help land the major feature film deal for the Hamiltons through their agent Dutch Hofstetter.

The Hamiltons had gone through and rejected several potential scripts and film deals over the years mostly for thematic reasons before clicking with the Sony Pictures production.

The family says their desire was to present a female sports movie where adversity was overcome with God's inspiration and loving kindness.

Becky Hamilton was "side by side" with the director, Cheri Hamilton recalls, offering tips on Bethany's characteristics, dialogue, lifestyle, environment, and actions. For example how Bethany, using just one arm, cuts a grapefruit and does her hair. From the art and set direction to the wardrobe design, the filmmakers strived to give an accurate portrayal of the Hamilton family and their lifestyle. The film crew visited the family home on Kauaʻi taking pictures of the interior including Bethany's bedroom to use to replicate the home in the film.

The scenes featuring actual Kauaʻi locations in *Soul Surfer* were filmed in March 2010 by McNamara, who grew close to the Hamilton family during the production of the film.

A movie crew, including Noah Hamilton and his wife Becky as production help and consultants, was sent over from Oʻahu, trimmed down and able to easily move around the Island, away from the full-on production complex set up at Kawela Bay-Kahuku on the North Shore of Oʻahu. Their guide was Kauaʻi filming coordinator Eddie Abubo. They shot B-roll background footage at Haʻena, then up above Keʻe Beach on the leg of the Kalalau Trail that

Bethany Hamilton (right) and actress AnnaSophia Robb pose at Tunnels Beach at Haʻena during location filming for *Soul Surfer*. Robb portrays Hamilton in the film, and holds a replica of the surfboard the young Kauaʻi surfer rode on Halloween 2003, the day she lost her arm at Tunnels to a tiger shark.

leads to Hanakapiʻai Beach, and then to Hanalei Pier. Aerial photography was guided by Kauaʻi-raised helicopter pilot Jedrick Squyres.

A montage of Bethany's elementary school days, Bethany, her brothers Noah and Timmy and her best friend Alana Blanchard are pictured having fun as children. Look in the background for Hanalei School, the soccer field next door to the Waiʻoli Church, Hanalei Shopping Center, young Bethany and Alana surfing Kiddies just west of the Hanalei Pier and a scenic aerial shot looking east from the Mount Makana area near Keʻe Beach. Tim Hamilton, who has filmed and produced bodyboarding movies, lent his filmmaking skills in providing the footage. Footage from ten locations including Tunnels Beach appear in the montage for the key scene in the film – the shark attack.

A wide angle aerial of the lagoon at Keʻe Beach segues into a scene of Bethany and the Blanchards paddling in the ocean well offshore to lead up to the Tunnels shark attack scene. A helicopter birds-eye-view of waves rolling in at Tunnels look about the size of waves the day when the actual attack took place in 2003.

The shark attack is played subtly, not with great suspense, but still realistically. Bethany was adamant about that. CGI effects were overlaid on footage taken in the surf off of the Turtle Bay Hotel on Oʻahu. Renowned waterman-surfer and water photography advisor for the film Brian Keaulana yanks AnnaSophia Robb underwater during the sequence to replicate the thrust of the shark when it attacked. Tom Hamilton says the family wanted to keep the attack "PG," with the final print still "pretty much exactly as it happened."

Sony Pictures production notes details how sixteen-year-old actress AnnaSophia Robb, whom the Hamiltons believe was the perfect choice for the role, was transformed visually into Bethany. "More than 750 visual effects were also employed in post-production to transform AnnaSophia Robb's left arm into Bethany's distinctive, at-the-shoulder stump." They note that the film's visual effects team covered Robb's arm with a green sleeve throughout filming. They then digitally inserted the stump in every single shot where it was exposed.

The filming of the night scene with the hanging of a prop, but realistic, 14-foot tiger shark took place at a location in Laie mocked up as the beach at the Hanalei Pier. In Sony Pictures production notes for the film Bethany says, "It was weird for me to see for the first time how big and scary it really was. But I thought it was cool, too, because I also think sharks are really beautiful."

Bethany, who became a worldwide figure through her outspoken faithful response to the attack, also commented about her faith helping to save her life in the water at Ha'ena, "It was Jesus Christ who gave me peace when I was attacked by the shark. They had to get me to the beach, which took 20 minutes of paddling." She relates it to the Bible verse Philippians 4:7, which says, "The peace of God, which surpasses all understanding, will guard your hearts and your minds in Christ Jesus."

The Hamilton family worked closely with filmmakers in authentically portraying their Kaua'i-style Christian faith in the film.

Director McNamara attended services at churches that meet under tents on Kaua'i including the Hamiltons' home North Shore Christian Church, which meets under a large tent in a field off the road to Kilauea Lighthouse. Tom and Cheri

Hamilton were hired as extras for this scene and can be seen sitting in the congregation behind their film doubles Dennis Quaid and Helen Hunt.

Once it was discovered that Becky Hamilton sang worship songs in church she was added to the church singing group that includes Carrie Underwood playing Sarah Hill. Seeing the film congregation as too somber during filming, Bethany spoke up and told them, "This isn't a funeral, it's a time to rejoice and be happy," her mom recalls.

American Idol-winner country star Carrie Underwood chose to portray Bethany's youth Bible group leader Sarah Hill in part because of her own Christian faith.

Tom recalls the singer spent only five days on the set in O'ahu for her first acting role ever, and that the McNamara started her out in simple scenes to warm her up for the more complex scenes involving Bethany's youth group meeting and her counseling session with Sarah Hill.

This interweaving of the Hamiltons' story with the surfing community on Kaua'i can be seen throughout the film. Many of the family's friends and fellow surfers were hired as extras or stunt surfers.

Bethany's fictional surfing competition nemesis Malina Birch in *Soul Surfer* is played by Sonya Balmores Chung, a Kaua'i surfer from the champion Balmores surfing clan.

The first cut of *Soul Surfer* got a thumbs up from the Hamilton family except for its surfing footage. Noah and Bethany lobbied hard for McNamara to send a film crew with stand-ins to Tahiti to boost

Actors portraying Bethany Hamilton and the Blanchard family ready to paddle out at Tunnels are (from left) Kevin Sorbo as Holt, AnnaSophia Robb as Bethany, Lorraine Nicholson as Alana, and Jeremy Sumpter as Byron Blanchard.

Director Sean McNamara gathers his cast and crew for a scene at Makua (Tunnels) Beach at Ha'ena.

the quality and authenticity of the surfing in the film. McNamara and crew flew to the South Pacific four months after principal filming was completed, boarding with Tahitian families on the beach at the renowned Tahitian surf break Teahupo'o on the southwest coast of the island of Tahiti.

It was in Tahiti that Bethany was able to put on a great display of high-level female surfing and help to deliver the big wave performance surfing the Hamilton's new the film needed.

Adding a finishing touch to the film was its sound track. Family footage of Bethany & Alana during a school performance introduced the filmmakers to the traditional Hawaiian song "Hele on to Kaua'i." Enhancing the spiritual aspect of *Soul Surfer* are the Hawaiian chants recorded for the film

Tim, Tom and Bethany Hamilton (right) in Thailand in 2006 with the Nakatsukasa family of Kaua'i (Mark, Hans, Dorien and Seth). The Nakatsukasa founded and run an orphanage in southern Thailand near the site of the devastating Southeast Asia Tsunami. The orphanage is supported by Kalaheo Missionary Church and a network of Hawai'i-based supporters. World Vision sponsored Bethany and family's visit, which proved to be a turning point in her recovery from her shark attack, as shown in *Soul Surfer*.

by award-winning composer, and surfer, Marco Beltrami. Through a local connection Beltrami brought Hawaiian music artist Keali'i Reichel to his cutting-edge studio located above Malibu Beach to record the chants.

Out of all the movies made on Kaua'i, it's nice to see that one about a local family was done with respect and class, and saw success. "Yes, we're happy with the portrayal," Cheri says, who added the family admired director McNamara who they said went above and beyond his role in bringing Bethany's story to the big screen. Cheri shares more fascinating in-depth details in her book *Raising a Soul Surfer*.

The film provided publicity for the Friends of Bethany Hamilton Foundation. Among other charitable outreach, the organization sends our what her dad Tom calls encouragement packages to shark attack victims across the globe.

The film also delivered on their prayers for it serving to spread the gospel, Cheri says." Once we started shooting, the hand of God was on that movie; the Holy Spirit was on the set everyday."

Bethany, now in her early 20s, continues to share her faith across the world out of her home island. Young girls, and people of all ages, follow her on her website bethanyhamilton.com and through her books like *Soul Surfer*, which was co-written by South Shore Kaua'i pastor Rick Bundschuh soon after the shark attack. As of today, she also surfs in world-class surfing competitions in places like faraway Bali in Indonesia. Bethany's Christian faith is an on-going part of her life and that of her family.

Avatar

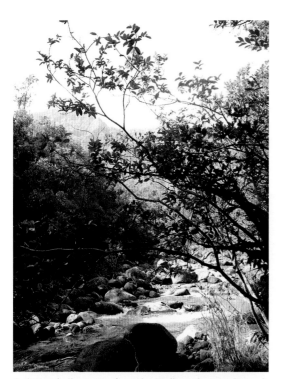

A stream in the area of mauka Wailua where actors were brought by *Avatar* director James Cameron to experience first-hand how to move about in a lush environment prior to filming inside a bare sound stage wearing digital rigs tied into Cameron's virtual CGI world of Pandora.

Underlying the fantasy jungle planet of Pandora in the epic sci-fi fantasy blockbuster *Avatar*, perhaps the most technically complex feature film ever made, is the very real rain forest located at the center of Kaua'i.

Kaua'i became an actor's training ground and source of background footage for *Avatar* when director James Cameron of *Titantic* fame saw he needed the human element in his cutting-edge film, which is about two-thirds digitally generated. His fantasy is set in the year 2154 at a time when Earthlings are on the faraway Pandora, a moon that orbits a giant planet called Polyphemus and located light years away from Earth, to extract valuable minerals. However, the mining is a danger to the delicate environmental balance of life for the native blue-skinned Navia who dwell in a lush, tropical world in Pandora.

"We went to Hawai'i because Jim wanted us to experience a real rain forest," says Sigourney Weaver in Twentieth Century Fox's "making of" featurette for *Avatar*. Weaver plays Dr. Grace Augustine in the film. Dr. Grace runs a program that blends human and alien DNA into "Avatars" – artificial bodies run by human "pilots."

This fictional procedure is symbolic of the techniques used by Cameron and his crew of 1,000 in blending live action with digital effects in brand new ways, using sensors to capture the nuances of even facial movements of the actors that guide the digital effects producers in animating the CGI characters. The director calls it "captured performance."

Weaver and other actors spent five days on Kaua'i, joined by Cameron. The Kaua'i trip for the actors was similar to the boot camp used by directors to bond actors and prepare them for roles in war films. Here, during daylight hours they built fires and ate around them as part of the training as well as experiencing the real rain forest prior to having to pretend to be in a jungle setting in an interior, non-landscaped stage. Back in Southern California the actors trained in hand-to-hand fighting, shooting guns, riding horses and shooting arrows.

The trip to Kaua'i for the cast came during the early days of filming in California in the spring of 2007. Cameron saw his actors needed to experience first-hand what it is like to hike in an actual rain forest before they played out scenes set on the faraway alien tropical jungle world of Pandora.

Cameron chose the physical experience of tromping through the damp rain forest floor located in the shadow of Wai'ale'ale mauka of Wailua in bringing the realism of human locomotion to the digitally-created world of Pandora.

Director Cameron told of being "way up in the mountains" in the center of Kaua'i with his cast members. The Kaua'i filming was "about making it real for the actors, in volume," Cameron said in the making of video.

Actor Joel David Moore compared how it felt putting your foot into the muddy floor of the rain forest in the mauka Wailua area to how it felt stepping on concrete, as he would feel when filming using Cameron's inventive, never before used techniques and film camera in making the hybrid digital-real life production.

Actor Sam Worthington plays a paralyzed marine veteran who regains his mobility when Dr. Grace's magic morphs him into a towering avatar Navia with a tail. Worthington pointed out the advantage of using the Kaua'i rain forest as a reference point for filming in front of a green screen.

Scenes from other locations woven into *Avatar* included the Hamakua Coast of the Big Island, rain forest locations in Brazil and Argentina and in director Peter Jackson's filming facilities in Wellington, New Zealand.

Avatar was released in December 2009. A 3D version could be viewed in IMAX theaters. The worldwide box-office gross for *Avatar* is estimated at an incredible $2.7 billion; its filming cost has been estimated at between $200 million and $300 million-plus. *Avatar* was nominated for nine Academy Awards including Best Picture and Best Director.

The Keahua Arboretum is near the staging area for the *Avatar* cast and crew's foray into the mauka rain forest world of Kaua'i. The state Department of Land and Natural Resources forestry showcase arboretum is easily accessible by driving mauka to the end of Kuamo'o Road in Wailua Homesteads.

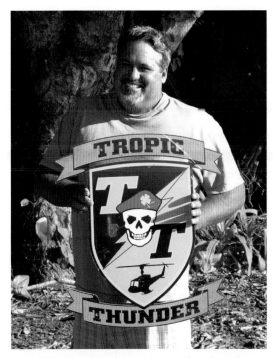

Cast-off movie props show up in Kaua'i yards and homes. A carved styrofoam idol from the first *Indiana Jones* film has been perhaps the most visible over the years. Here Payton Hough Sr. of Kapahi displays a *Tropic Thunder* shield he was given.

A helicopter view of the *Tropic Thunder* village set located in Grove Farm Co. property mauka of Lihu'e.

A major telecommunications array linked the Wailua base camp of *Tropic Thunder* with filmmakers during Kaua'i location filming in 2007. Kaua'i Film Commissioner Art Umezu said the highly visible site set up along Kuhio Highway, caused several people to call his office to ask if Kaua'i was being invaded by aliens.

Tropic Thunder

Ben Stiller loves Kaua'i. He owns a vacation home on the Island. He married his wife actress Christine Taylor in 2000 on the North Shore. And he went all out to secure Kaua'i as the main location for his adventurous Southeast Asian-set film *Tropic Thunder*.

Stiller directed, co-wrote and starred in his successful over-the-top film that spoofs Hollywood action filmmaking and overbearing Hollywood producers with an all-star cast he seems to have pushed to the edge on location in the spirit of Francis Ford Coppola's *Apocalypse Now*.

Tropic Thunder set a record for location film spending on Kaua'i and likely any neighbor island, according to Kaua'i Film Commissioner Art Umezu, bringing $64 million in spending to Kaua'i over 13 weeks in 2007 that provided paychecks for hundreds of extras and crew members, paid for months of hotel rooms for cast and crew, for rental cars, boosted sales at retail stores and suppliers across the Island.

The Film Commissioner remarked in an interview in *The Garden Island* on the extensive use of Kaua'i locations in *Tropic Thunder*. "What's astounding is that all the filming will be done on Kaua'i, with the exception of a few post and L.A. studio shots…That's quite amazing in this day and age of digitized film technology."

Tropic Thunder even improved Kaua'i's infrastructure, improving a road leading into the main set for the film, which is located on private Grove Farm Co. land.

Generous Hawai'i State tax incentives offered to Stiller and his film partners under the then newly-enacted Act 88 secured the deal to film in the Southeast Asian jungle-like interior. The legislation offered an extra five percent bonus for film productions traveling to the neighbor islands. Umezu cites passage by the Legislature of the key filmmaking support as a major reason for the filming of a series of big-budget films between 2007 and 2010.

The comic and action film star came up with the concept for *Tropic Thunder* while acting as an American POW in director Steven Spielberg's 1988 World War II-in-China film *Empire of the Sun*. He pictured a film focusing on actors who attend boot camp training to ready themselves for a war movie and come away thinking they'd actually been in military action.

Tropic Thunder evolved into a film where actors, cast in the most expensive war film ever made, unwittingly step into an actual war zone while filming a Vietnam era action movie in Southeast Asia. They face a gang of poppy-growing drug lords, led into trouble in the jungle by novice director Damien Cockburn, played by veteran British film and television comedian Steve Coogan who plays in Stiller's *Night at the Museum* films.

In the Kaua'i jungle warfare scenes in *Tropic Thunder*, Stiller plays fading action hero Tugg Speedwell, a role that satirizes the type of character played by Sylvester Stallone in *Rambo*. Method actor Robert Downey Jr. plays Sgt. Osiris/Kirk Lazarus, an Australian actor in black face playing an unrelenting jive-talking Vietnam Vet GI. Comedian Jack Black is deranged, drug and drink-addled comedian Jack Portnoy. Nick Nolte is cast as Four Leaf Tayback, the Vietnam vet author of the book behind the movie.

Actor Matthew McConaughey, who plays Tugg's agent back in Los Angeles, provides a link to Kaua'i's surfing world in the film. Prominently displayed in his hip LA office is a copy of the book *Bunker Spreckels: Surfing's Divine Prince of Decadence* by Art Brewer and C.R. Stecyk III. Spreckels was the heir to the Claus Spreckels sugar fortune, and stepson of Clark Gable. He burned out in the mid-1970s on the North Shore of O'ahu, and is noted for his surfing style as a young, adventurous, experimental surfer on Kaua'i during the late 1960s transition from longboards to short surfboards.

Besides production trailers there wasn't much sign of *Tropic Thunder* filming along Kaua'i's main highways. The filmmakers mostly used interior jungle locations in south-central Kaua'i and on the North Shore.

The Grove Farm set provided enough variety for the bulk of the filming with ponds of taro, a river running through the site, mountain backdrops in several directions and a variety of waterfalls. Secondary locations included sites in Hanalei, Lumaha'i Valley, Kilauea, the Kaua'i Ranch in Kealia Valley, and the Kaua'i Sands Hotel in Wailua, which became a town in Vietnam, much like sections of Kapa'a became a Central American town in *Jurassic Park*.

Director of photography John Toll described the advantage of filming a Vietnam-set film on Kaua'i in a post on a Kodak webpage. He said the on-again, off-again rainy interior, dense jungle look and a mix of terrains provided what was needed.

Ben Stiller scouted locations for *Tropic Thunder* beginning in 2004 over a six-week span traveling in a helicopter, on a quad and in boats. In Paramount's production notes for the film production designer Jeff Mann recalled spending 25 hours aboard a chartered helicopter searching for a location for the "Hot LZ (landing zone)" set that is dramatically blown up, and for the Flaming Dragon drug lord compound that looks like the run down remains of an abandoned sugar mill. "We were looking for mountain ranges and environments that didn't feel recognizably Hawaiian – without the red earth and vertical ridges of the Na Pali Coast," Mann reported. "We needed to discover someplace that felt more like the Golden Triangle."

"We wanted unique locations, places that hadn't been shot before," producer Eric McLeod said. "That required more work on our end, but in the end we found everything we needed and it was well worth the work."

Once Dreamworks gave the go-ahead for production in 2006, crew members worked for six months to prepare for the arrival of the stars and main crew.

Filming began in July 2007 with a major movie-within-a-movie battle scene at the Hot LZ site, which was as complex as battle scenes in big-budget war films, and capped off with huge pyrotech explosions.

The Flaming Dragon compound was located a few miles mauka of the LZ site.

The crew found pre-World War II hydroelectric plants that once powered now-shuttered sugar cane mills, which fortunately had roads running to them from a developed section of the Island.

Building a one-hundred-foot wooden suspension bridge leading into the compound took three months. The bridge is a key setting in the film.

Producer Stuart Cornfield, a key administrator for the filming, told *The Garden Island*, "never have I been able to work in such a naturally beautiful place – this island is spectacular."

Cornfield also complimented Kaua'i's people in a piece in *The Garden Island*, comparing the hundreds of extras hired locally to the typical extras used on films in Los Angeles. "The extras have been so amazing, really dedicated. Here, they all really want to be doing this and so it's all worked out very well."

A 21st century *Tropic Thunder* jeep sits idle alongside a Vietnam era jeep at the base camp set up in the empty lot in Wailua adjacent to the Kintaro Restaurant in July 2007.

The Kaua'i Premiere of *Tropic Thunder* at Kukui Grove Cinema was held for the local cast and crew. Ben Stiller made a special video mesage to be shown at the screening. Kaua'i Film Commissioner Art Umezu is at the mic speaking and is joined by (from left) Kaua'i Visitors Bureau Executive Director Sue Kanoho, Governor's Liasion Kaua'i Laurie Yoshida, Director of Office of Economic Development County of Kaua'i Beth Tokioka, and Kukui Grove Cinema Owner Marlene Blair.

'Dragonfly

Venezuelan Amazon Basin Indians portray themselves in a rainy North Shore valley during *Dragonfly* filming.

Princeville Airport was set as a regional Venezuelan airport located in the Amazon in *Dragonfly*.

In Universal Studio's 2002 supernatural romance film *Dragonfly*, starring Kevin Costner and directed by Tom Shadyac, the mauka forests deep in Wainiha Valley, Kealia Valley and the jungle mauka of Wailua are made to look like the Venezuelan Amazon basin.

Village scenes were filmed at Kaua'i Ranch, a private estate located by the Spalding Monument in Kealia. The cemetery scene featured at the climax of *Dragonfly* was filmed in the Blue Hole area located at the base of Wai'ale'ale Crater. Princeville Airport served as a regional Venezuelan airport. Kaua'i's interior landscapes are shown from a helicopter that transports Costner deep into the Amazon.

Honolulu-based film critic and film location chronicler Tim Ryan called *Dragonfly* "a sort of *Field of Dreams* meets *The Sixth Sense*."

Kaua'i Film Commissioner Judy Drosd, who worked closely with the film crew to find the right locations for *Dragonfly* told *The Garden Island*, "We're really looking forward to seeing this movie. Kaua'i has been many locales in many movies, but this is the first time we've doubled for deep in the heart of the Venezuelan jungle."

A location scout for the *Dragonfly* production had scouted extensively in South America for a village with a waterfall prior to the decision to film on Kaua'i. In the end, a CGI-enhanced waterfall is shown in the background of the village scene.

Costner plays Dr. Joe Darrow, who is head of emergency services at a Chicago hospital. His wife, a pediatric cancer specialist who is pregnant with their first child, is reported missing in the faraway Venezuelan jungle while on a medical mercy mission when the bus she is on loses control and careens over a steep cliff. Her body is not recovered and she is presumed dead.

The dragonfly theme comes from a symbol that ties the film together, appearing as a birthmark on the shoulder of Darrow's wife, a symbol that her terminally-ill young cancer patients in Chicago mysteriously draw over and over, and finally as a map symbol for a waterfall that helps lead Darrow to Venezuela. All seem to be messages from beyond, guiding the doctor to resolve the unknown events surrounding his wife's death. As Darrow travels to the Venezuelan jungle, Kaua'i locations are interspersed with footage from Coffeepot Rapids in the Middle Fork American River in Placer County near Lake Tahoe.

Dragonfly director of photography Dean Semler had filmed Costner in Waterworld, the high-budgeted apocalyptic sci-fi film made mostly on the Big Island in the mid-1990s with location filming at Kawaihae Harbor and Waipio Valley.

Location scouting for *Dragonfly* started in May 2000. The movie's cast and crew filmed at Kaua'i locations between February 2 and February 17 in 2001. Kaua'i Film Commission statistics show that 20 Kaua'i crew members worked a total of 500 days, and 50 Kaua'i extras put in a total of 650 days on the set. *Dragonfly's* producers spent $5.3 million while on Island for the film, which had a $60 million budget.

A most interesting highlight of the *Dragonfly* experience for Kaua'i residents was the arrival of Venezuelan Indian extras from that nation's Amazon Basin region, flown in to play themselves in the film.

Kaua'i casting director Angela Tillson of Whale of a Time Productions had cast scores of Kaua'i residents who were clothed and made up to look like village natives, but the producers wanted to add a mix of authenticity.

"They hired a private jet to fly about 115 Venezuelan natives from three different tribes, some as background and some as principal talent," Tillson recalls. "So I not only did the extras casting, but I was hired as a Spanish language translator. It was an awesome experience for me working with these people. We had to teach them how to use a real toilet, sleep on a bed, turn on lights etc…(Because it was February and the weather was colder on Kaua'i then they were used to) I asked the Kaua'i extras and crew to donate clothes for them…I got an overwhelming response by everyone to where we had enough clothes, books, toiletries and jackets for them and

nine other huge boxes of clothes for their villages and the studio paid to ship back with them."

People magazine reported on Costner joining local hunters on a Valentine's Day pig hunt to mark the final day of location filming on Kaua'i at the invitation of Jeff Rivera, manager of Kaua'i Ranch where the filming took place. The star was noted in local newspapers as enjoying mixing at everyday happenings with local residents. While making *Waterworld* on the Big Island, the popular star shot hoops with local players at a Kona gym. The magazine quoted Jeff Rivera, manager of Kaua'i Ranch, as saying of Costner, "'When he was told about the local style'—tracking the pigs with dogs, then stepping in with a knife for the kill—'he was pretty excited.'" During the hunt, according to the report, Rivera's son knifed the pig with Costner a ways away from the action.

The Venezuelan Amazon Basin village scenes were filmed at what is now called Kaua'i Ranch, a private estate located by the Spalding Monument in Kealia. Here Brazilian Indians, flown to Kaua'i from the Amazon region, threaten Dr. Joe Darrow, as played by the actor Kevin Costner, as Darrow searches for his long-missing wife in the Amazon.

Jurassic Park Lives On

Jurassic Park III film crew sets up a shot of the "Hero Boat" at the Wailua River marina. Angela Tillson from A Whale of a Time Productions stands besides the *Jurassic Park III* "Hero Boat" prior to dressing the boat for filming. Note the dinosaur cages on deck.

Two sequels to the Kaua'i-made 1993 blockbuster *Jurassic Park* – *The Lost World: Jurassic Park* and *Jurassic Park III* – featured Kaua'i in a few scenes. Together the three films brought in over $1.5 billion at the box office.

In the 1997 sequel *The Lost World: Jurassic Park,* the opening scene is set on Kipu Kai beach portraying a Costa Rican island of Isla Sorna where a wealthy family yachting outing turns into tragedy when a child is attacked by a bevy of knee-high dinosaurs known as Compsognathus, or compys, as the filmmakers called them during production.

Though a short scene, commentaries about the film point out that it was critical in establishing the believability of the dinosaurs on screen, and that it set the tone for the rest of the film.

This scene in *Lost World,* released as the big movie of summer 1997, was filmed on Kaua'i in December 1996, completing location filming for the movie. Other filming sites included Eureka, San Diego and Burbank in California.

Director Spielberg had planned to shoot this part of the movie in New Zealand, but at the last minute he opted to film it on Kaua'i. With Christmas around the corner and a tight deadline looming, plus the possibility of saving some budget money, an impromptu location scout was held and a four-day shoot planned. A small, but key, crew flew in including Spielberg, producer Jerry Molen and production designer Rick Carter. A second unit also filmed landscapes, to be used mostly as establishing shots. Special effects guru Stan Winston, who played a key role in all of the dinosaur effects in *Jurassic Park,* handled the puppet dinosaurs at Kipu Kai which were then brought to life on screen through computer graphics back in Los Angeles. Linda Antipala did the extras casting on Kaua'i.

"They wanted a completely new look for this film, and that was a challenge and a lot of work," Kaua'i Film Commissioner Judy Drosd told the *Honolulu Star-Bulletin's* Kaua'i reporter Anthony Sommer of her location scouting work with the film crew. "As with the other films, the Kaua'i locations were so remote and the crew so self-contained, it was hard to tell they were even on the island," Sommer reported. "They shot all over the island: the Wailua River, Kilauea, Princeville Ranch," Drosd commented.

Steven Spielberg celebrated his 50th birthday at a huge luau thrown in his honor at the Hyatt Regency Kaua'i. The hotel pulled out the stops with a feast for the senses and the eyes, with great food and beautiful Hawaiian dancing. Some of the Kaua'i cast and crew were invited.

Author Michael Crichton lived part-time on Kaua'i, having purchased a beach-front Hanalei Bay home, and wrote some of the *Jurassic Park* books while on the Island. He and his family were left alone by North Shore residents as is common for resident and visiting celebrities. Crichton, along with his friend, *ER* TV drama producer John Wells, co-staged a Turn of the Millennium New Year's Eve party featuring $20,000-plus fireworks at Well's beach house in Hanalei. North Shore resident Mary Paterson, who had served as Crichton's executive secretary at Hanalei, organized the party. Following the success of *Jurassic Park,* the author and producer developed *ER* together based on a 1974 Crichton screenplay.

Mighty Joe Young

In 1997 RKO Pictures filmmakers chose Kilauea Falls for a waterfall scene in the remake of the 1949 Merian C. Cooper film *Mighty Joe Young*. Cooper was also the producer of the 1933 production of *King Kong*, another film featuring a huge ape first updated in the mid-1970s using Kaua'i's Honopu Valley on Na Pali as a backdrop.

Cast and crew filmed most of the Hawai'i-based scenes in *Mighty Joe Young* in Kualoa Valley in Windward O'ahu. Both locations were set as the Pangani Mountains region of Tanzania in East Africa. The crew spent about a month total in filming in Hawai'i.

Using O'ahu and Kaua'i for the filming trumped actually going to Africa for the location filming, and followed the successful use of O'ahu and Kaua'i locations in the 1997 Disney film *George of the Jungle*. Director Ron Underwood and directors of photography Don Peterman and Oliver Wood found the Hawaiian foliage the right color and texture, and tropical mountain backdrop, to double as Tanzania.

Mighty Joe Young came to life on screen as an Animatronic gorilla built 15-foot tall, through computer graphics and through blue-screen techniques with actors. The ape was designed by Rick Baker, who also helped bring *King Kong* to life in Kaua'i scenes in the 1976 film.

Actress Charlize Theron, as Jill, the daughter of a gorilla researcher who loses her mother to poachers in the Pangani Mountains, bonds with baby Joe, whose mother is also killed in the same attack. They grow up and Joe becomes huge, weighing 2,000 pounds, but is still Jill's playmate.

Mighty Joe Young was released by Walt Disney Pictures in Christmas 1998.

The *Mighty Joe Young* poster from the collection of the Kaua'i Film Commission promoted the 1998 Christmastime release of the film.

This Kahili *Jurassic Ranch* (formerly the Mary Lucas Estate) pasture convincingly doubled for the Pangani Mountains region of Tanzania in East Africa for *Mighty Joe Young* filmmakers.

George of the Jungle

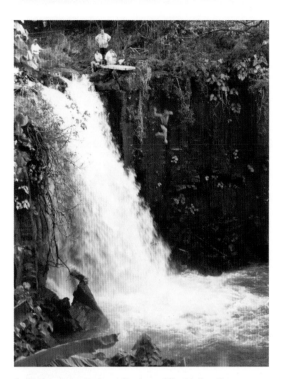

A stunt man leaps from the top of the Valley House waterfall for an action scene filmed for Disney's *George of the Jungle*.

George, played by Brenden Fraser, starts his life out as a baby who survives a plane crash in the Heart of Africa. The friendly, but accident prone George, face smashes into trees while swinging like Tarzan. He is raised by a wise, talking ape, in this comic, slapstick family-humor spoof of author Edgar Rice Burroughs' classic *Tarzan* story. The spirit of the Saturday morning cartoon *George of the Jungle*, created by animator Jay Ward, is woven throughout the film. The narrator of the film is a dead ringer for the voiceover heard in Ward's classic *Rocky & Bullwinkle* cartoon series.

In the $25 million film, released by Walt Disney Pictures in 1997, San Francisco heiress Ursula Stanhope, played by Leslie Mann, and her rich boy beau on safari stumble upon George of the Jungle's lair where apes talk and the wisest one, voiced by Monty Python actor John Cleese, mentor George. She later brings George home. After some madcap adventures in civilization, the couple return to the jungle.

George's location manager, Flip Wylly, was quoted in the *Honolulu Star-Bulletin* on the use of the Islands for a backdrop for jungle films. "They don't need to go anywhere else if they want jungle because all they need is right here." Filming in Australia, Puerto Rico and Mexico had been considered.

In a jungle-set scene, Kilauea Falls is used in *George of the Jungle* as a romantic setting for George and Ursula. The second-unit Kaua'i location scenes were filmed in summer 1996 and included aerial photography.

Lilo & Stitch

Lilo rides a longboard on a Kaua'i swell with big sister Nani and alien pet Stitch in this illustration from the film *Lilo & Stitch*.

The tropical watercolor palette that colors Walt Disney Pictures' 2002 animated action-comedy film *Lilo & Stitch* presents Kaua'i's places and people in warm, bright, friendly shades. Idealized, animated location shots of Kilauea Lighthouse, the waves of the North Shore, Hanalei landmarks, and especially the funky plantation-era buildings and streets of Hanapepe show clearly that *Lilo & Stitch* is a Kaua'i-set film.

Disney animators creating *Lilo & Stitch* drew on their studio's classic watercolor background animation style of the 1930s and 1940s, sourcing *Snow White and the Seven Dwarfs* and *Dumbo*, rather than the digital CGI magic of *Toy Story*. In fact, Disney had not used this type of animation in 60 years.

Kaua'i is spelt out in alien-looking lettering in this still from *Lilo & Stitch* that clearly identifies the landing spot for Stitch who comes to Earth after being labeled by the faraway Galactic Federation as an "illegal genetic" experiment gone bad.

Portrayed in this Territorial Era animation style, the Kaua'i scenes exude the exquisite, subtle beauty of the land, sea and sky that draws visitors from across the globe to the Garden Island. The classic Hollywood plot of *Lilo & Stitch* tells of an orphaned local girl, unpopular at school, adopting what she thinks is a pet dog to bring love and a close, unwavering friend into her life. However, the simple story line is but a storyteller's door into a tale of redemption that arguably could only be set on Kaua'i. Young Lilo's plight is resolved through the application of traditional Native Hawaiian cultural concept of family to real life as a salve to 21st century Hawaiian social problems. Or, as little, pudgy six-year-old Lilo so memorably explains to the world, "'Ohana means family. Family means no one is left behind – or forgotten."

Stitch is an odd-looking stray blue dog with huge pointed teeth she adopts from the Kaua'i Humane Society. He is really an alien set loose on Kaua'i, who is being hunted down by his fellow aliens, and he joins Lilo and older sister Nani's 'ohana. Stitch is super-strong, and can morph himself from a human-like alien into an ugly poi dog.

Lilo shares her life on Kaua'i with Stitch. The relationship benefits both, though fraught with problems they must both overcome. In the end the 'ohana and aloha of Kaua'i expressed in their lives wins out for the good.

Stitch can be seen as a symbol of the tourist, or malahini newcomer, who seeks a touch of paradise by traveling to Kaua'i. Lilo's reaching out of the cocoon of local 'ohana lifestyle to the "alien" who has landed on Kaua'i could represent that binding of cultures, an ideal visitor industry workers are taught to strive for on Kaua'i.

Disney's promotion of *Lilo & Stitch* tied into a marketing campaign launched by the Hawai'i Visitor and Convention Bureau following the film's release. *Lilo & Stitch* is "about bringing friends and family together even when they seem worlds apart," a Disney promotion for the film declared. "After crash-landing on Earth, Stitch wreaks havoc on the Hawaiian Islands, but he also learns about loyalty, friendship and 'ohana, the Hawaiian tradition of family," another promotion line reads.

The release of Walt Disney Feature Animation's *Lilo & Stitch* in U.S. theaters came in June 2002, just months after the tragic attacks of September 11, 2001. *Lilo & Stitch* was produced primarily at the animation studio located at Walt Disney World Resort's Disney-MGM Studios near Orlando, Florida.

In Disney's *Lilo & Stitch*, the young Kaua'i girl and mischievous alien look out over Kaua'i's North Shore from a peak west of Kilauea Lighthouse, just east of Secret Beach. The actual Kilauea Point is maintained by the U.S. Fish & Wildlife Service and is one of the Island's most popular visitor attractions, home to nesting Laysan albatross, iwa, boobies and other sea birds.

That black day caused Disney to reanimate a scene that had Stitch flying a 747 from Kaua'i into Honolulu to save Lilo. In the final cut of the film Stitch instead flies a space ship into the mountains of Kaua'i.

The upbeat Kaua'i 'ohana-and-aloha theme of the film did present hope and love at a time when the people of the world off island desperately needed it.

The on-screen fun, Academy Award-level animation, excellent song selections, and memorable cartoon characters Disney is so well known for are, of course, all there too.

Lilo & Stitch's story-behind-the-story begins with its creator, Disney's Chris Sanders, who co-directed the film. He dreamed up the adventurous alien antagonist dog Stitch as a sci-fi alien character doodling a 1980s kids book concept. Moving forward to the late 1990s, Disney was looking for a storyline for a feature-length animated film.

Chris saw the story of Stitch unfolding in a rural, isolated location in Kansas. He and Dean DeBlois, the co-directors and co-writers of the film, had recently worked on the Disney animated China-set epic, multi-character *Mulan*. They were ready for a simpler production. As development of the film advanced, Kaua'i, a somewhat isolated rural island, caught his eye on a map and a scouting trip was booked and soon Kaua'i was chosen as the setting for *Lilo & Stitch*.

The leap from heartland Kansas to a tropical Hawaiian Island would be groundbreaking in the animation world, too, for no feature-length animated film had ever been set in Hawai'i.

Lilo & Stitch came to life on their scouting trip. The Kaua'i locations were perfect backdrops. Most memorable, though, was the narrative of their tour guide who told of the 'ohana of Kaua'i, the extended families of the Island that weave together family and friends, bringing love, happiness, and security to the local communities.

Sanders and DeBlois, along with their co-creators at Disney Animation, brought great attention to detail in illustrating *Lilo & Stitch*. The teams' animated portrayal of Kaua'i accurately captures the Academy Award-nominated film's Kaua'i setting.

Scouting trips were undertaken in 1999, and described in Disney Editions' "Lilo & Stitch - Collected Stories from the Film's Creators."

"We had spent time in Hanalei and Hanapepe while on a research trip to Kaua'i, and these beautiful, sleepy little spots became the inspiration for Lilo's town," Dean DeBlois, recalls in the *Lilo & Stitch* film creators' book. Ric Sluiter, *Lilo & Stitch* art director, gained insight in how to portray Kaua'i's environment: "Our research trip to Kaua'i had taught us that the colors in Hawai'i are really turned up a notch, with the air being so clear and the islands getting pressure-washed almost daily."

The animators used this first-hand take on Kaua'i to capture the decor of Lilo and her sister Nani's plantation home in Hanapepe with surfboards and guitars stashed in the corner of the living room, single-wall construction interiors with family photos tacked on, 1940s plantation era rattan woven furniture, and much more.

Production designer Paul Felix in Hanapepe found the locale for Lilo's hometown.

"I found all the usual home details, ranging from rusted-out bridges to homemade mailboxes," he said. "In particular, I was interested to see how these details weathered in Kaua'i's unique climate…I certainly recall being impressed by the saturation of colors and the ever-changing moods of the skies and landscape."

Bob Stanton, background department head, found another setting for the film by heading north. "…driving to Hanalei in our rented vans, we began to see an older, more natural Hawai'i; small towns, red dirt roads, open lands. This was heaven. Right then and there, Ric Sluiter and I agreed we would try to spend as much of our time as possible painting this extraordinary landscape."

The voices are right too. Hawai'i resident cast members Tia Carrere and Jason Scott Lee advised the film makers on local pidgin usage.

Adding to the authenticity of the Hawaiian characters' body movements was highly considered too. Opening the film is a hula halau performance that captures the gentle flow of the hula. The filmmakers brought in Kumu Hula Mark Keali'i Ho'omalu the hula scenes. Ho'omalu, who contributed the opening sequence song, "He Mele No Lilo," a traditional place-naming song honoring Hawai'i's late monarchs, King Kalakaua and Queen Lili'uokalani, ties into the name Lilo. One meaning of the Hawaiian word lilo is to lose possession of something and here could imply the character of the young girl is in need of healing from the loss of her parents, who the story goes, died in an automobile crash, just as Lili'uokalani mourned the loss of her kingdom.

Rambunctious little Stich brings a tie to the web of interrelationships between Kaua'i's many feature films in his Elvis impersonator persona, recalling the King's filming of *Blue Hawaii* and *Paradise Hawaiian Style* on Kaua'i in the early 1960s. Several hit Elvis songs are featured in the film.

Disney and Kaua'i

The ties between Kaua'i and Walt Disney, and his renowned animation studio, go back to the first feature film made on Kaua'i, and to Disney productions filmed on location on the Island dating back to the 1960s.

Walt Disney traveled to Kaua'i in the mid-1960s, bringing his grandchildren to watch the filming at Po'ipu Beach of *Lt. Robin Crusoe* with Dick Van Dyke starring.

Roy Disney, vice-chairman of The Walt Disney Company when *Lilo & Stitch* was created, knew Kaua'i from summertime sojourns anchored in Hanalei Bay aboard his Trans-Pac sailboat following a post-race crossing from Honolulu. He recalled being told the story of *Lilo & Stitch* by Chris Sanders. "Then he told me that the story takes place on the Hawaiian island of Kaua'i. A rolling blue wave of warmth and nostalgia immediately washed over me as I recalled the time my wife Patty and I sailed from Honolulu…to Hanalei Bay, where we spent a tranquil week at anchor. We have been on Kaua'i several times, and it's without a doubt one of the most beautiful and romantic islands in the world. A true Bali Ha'i. I marveled that of all the places in which to set a movie, this astonishing little creature had found its way to my idea of heaven on earth."

The earliest link in the web of Kaua'i movie making to Disney Studios dates back to the making of the 1934 feature film *White Heat (Cane Fire)*. The creator of the story and scriptwriter for the Lois Weber-directed film was Jimmy Spalding Bodrero. Bodrero was born in 1900, the grandson of Captain Zephaniah Spalding, an owner of Kealia Plantation on the windward side of Kaua'i, and the builder of the famous Valley House in upper Kealia Valley. Bodrero's father was an Italian count who married one of Spalding's three daughters. His father and uncles were notorious on Kaua'i for spending their days as supposed plantation overseers who instead played polo. Interestingly, Hawaiian King David Kalakaua owned a quarter-share in the Spalding (then McKee) plantation during his reign in the 1870s-1880s, and the opening sequence song in *Lilo & Stitch* is written in Kalakaua's honor.

In 1938 cosmopolitan Bodrero was living in Southern California, likely then in tony Santa Barbara or Pasadena, and brought to Walt Disney a concept for creating an animated version of the British children's book *Wind in the Willows*. Bodrero was an expert at what's known in the animation trade as inspirational sketches. He was an expert sketcher and his work served as storyboards for Disney's landmark film *Fantasia*, in the Dance of the Hours segment, brought into the project by his friend Fantasia composer Leopold Stokowski. As a Disney artist, Bordrero joined Walt Disney on a trip to South America in 1941. The visit resulted in the making of the animated film *Three Caballeros*. In a direct tie to *Lilo & Stitch*, Bordrero worked on the Disney film *Dumbo*, a film that was one of the major influences on the watercolor background look of *Lilo & Stitch*. During Walt Disney's visit to Kaua'i in the 1960s, he mentioned in press interviews that his studio had a Kaua'i tie through Bordrero.

Jimmy Bodrero drew his own caricature in 1933 in Lihu'e still photographer W.J. Senda's *White Heat* scrapbook. The inserted photo pictures at a *White Heat* West Side location (from left) a local paniolo, Bodrero, actress Mona Maris as romantic interest Leilani and David Newell as West Side plantation owner William Hawkes.

The watercolor look of this circa 1934 *White Heat* lobby card reflects the Disney style cartoon backgrounds used in *Snow White* and other animated films that inspired *Lilo & Stitch* animators.

Following the publication of the first editon of *The Kaua'i Movie book*, W.J. Senda's gracious daughter Akiko Senda presented the author with a collection of Kaua'i film stills taken by her father from the 1930s into the 1960s including this movie-light-lit image of actress Virginia Cherrill, who rose to fame thanks to Charlie Chaplain casting her in a starring role in *City Lights* (1931). With Cherrill is English character actor Robert Stevenson. At the time she was a world-famous actress, and in 1934 she married then-young screen star Cary Grant.

To End All Wars

To End All Wars scenes from Koloa (Robert Carlyle, Kiefer Sutherland) and Akukini Pier (James Cosmo in blindfold foreground) are featured in this theater poster for the film.

A production assistant clicks the clapboard as *To End All Wars* cameras begin to roll in a Japanese POW camp parade ground roll call scene set at a mauka Koloa location. The POWs are mostly Kaua'i men costumed as British and American POWs. The sadistic camp sergeant Ito, kneeling in the foreground, is played by Sakae Kimura from the Akira Kurosawa troupe of film players.

A pocket valley located mauka of the old Koloa Plantation mill became a Japanese Army World War II POW camp in Thailand for the 2001 feature film *To End All Wars*, directed by David Cunningham.

To End All Wars is notable for being an award-winning feature film with Kaua'i locations in almost every frame of the film; for being directed by a Hawai'i-raised director; for in essence creating its own mini-railroad on location and building a complete replica of a thatch/bamboo Japanese POW camp; for the director's quest for authenticity through use of an international cast of leading actors from Japan, Scotland and America; and for the highly-visible role Kaua'i men played as bit players and extras during the filming in the late spring and summer of 2000.

The film stars Ciaran McMenamin as Scottish Capt. Ernest Gordon and Robert Carlyle of Full Monty fame as Maj. Ian Campbell, and Kiefer Sutherland as American POW Navy Lt. Jim "Yankee" Reardon.

Principal filming centered on the POW camp, which was accessible down former cane haul roads that run mauka from the site of the now-closed Koloa Plantation Mill, a few miles inland from Koloa town. On the outskirts of the compound, additional scenes were filmed including an interior of a rail car scene, POWs being marched through the hills to the camp, and POWs working alongside railroad tracks and railroad stock.

The long-abandoned Ahukini Pier on the south end of Hanama'ulu Bay, once a major sugar-loading dock and featured in the early 1950s film *Pagan Love Song*, was set as a dock in Sumatra where Allied escapees were brought after their escape sailboat was captured by the Japanese.

To End All Wars is based on the Argyll and Sutherland Highlanders Scottish commander Gordon's first-person survivor's account he titled "Through the Valley of the Kwai." The River Kwai was central to the Academy Award-winning 1957 film *The Bridge on the River Kwai*, based on French author Pierre Boulles' novel. In *To End All Wars*, the Hule'ia River becomes the POWs' river.

Gordon suffered for three and a half years while building the infamous Japanese Army's Death Railway, which was built by an estimated 16,000 POWs and tens of thousands of slave laborers through the center of Thailand north into Burma. The experience, and the redemption he experienced, led Gordon to become a Presbyterian minister; he served for 25 years as chaplain at Princeton University. He wrote his book as a response to what he saw as the inaccuracy of the 1957 film. Boulles' story focused on a conflict between a spit-and-polish British officer who goes along with Japanese Army orders to build the bridge on the Kwai versus other officers who plot to blow up the bridge to hinder the Japanese war effort.

The film tells of the fate of Gordon and his close-knit group of Scottish officers and how they cope with the brutality of the camp. Robert Carlyle as Campbell wants to kill the brutal, sadistic Japanese camp commander played by Masayuki Yui as Capt. Noguchi. Scottish character actor James Cosmo plays the stout hearted Lt. Col. Stuart McLean who dies a graphically brutal death onscreen after confronting Noguchi about the conditions in the camp. Mark Strong is serviceman Dusty Miller, a Christ-like figure who is crucified by the Japanese. Three of the lead Japanese actors are from the troupe of famed Japanese director Akira Kurosawa.

The men come to terms with their dire condition by going in the opposite spirit in forming a "jungle university" inside the camp morgue, a thatched building that the Japanese guards refuse to enter. Through Bible study, staging Shakespeare plays, studying ethics and other subjects in university-type classes taught from memory by fellow POWs, they cope and survive.

Their Japanese Army captors also reflect these conflicts, grappling with their allegiance to the militant Bushido Code versus their human compassion for the prisoners.

The POW camp is destroyed by Allied bombers, which brings the film to its climax, and the walls are figuratively torn down between the captors and captives, with dramatic results.

The technical highlight of *To End All Wars* is the appearance of two restored Grove Farm Homestead Museum narrow-gauge locomotives that once operated at Lihu'e Plantation, and later to haul Grove Farm Sugar Co. cane to be milled. Mike Fayé of Kikiaola Land Company used his house-moving rig and crew to transport 10-ton Paulo and 28-ton Wainiha from Grove Farm's warehouse in Puhi to the Koloa end of the Wilcox Tunnel in mauka Koloa. Museum director Bob Schleck told the *Honolulu Star-Bulletin*, "The board felt it was important to help the community through the making of this film."

The trains are still in operating condition thanks to the support of the late Miss Mabel Wilcox, the niece of Grove Farm founder G.N. Wilcox. Miss Mabel championed keeping the locomotives in working condition and warehoused to be preserved for display after cane haul trucks supplanted cane trains in the 1950s.

The filmmakers dressed the locomotives and a string of narrow-gauge boxcars as a Japanese Army work train. The 360 feet of track laid down in the Koloa valley was on loan from the O'ahu-based Hawaiian Railroad Society.

Scott Johnson, who has been a railroad supervisor for Grove Farm Homestead Museum since 1982, served as engineer during the filming, in a Japanese Army costume. He can be briefly seen in the cab of the train.

Johnson told the *Star-Bulletin* that the film's director Cunningham and his crew were "ecstatic" over having historic train locomotives in place and in operating shape on Kaua'i. "I saw a couple of photographs of the original engines (used by the Japanese in Thailand). They're close. Most people, unless they're real train buffs, won't notice."

Film director Cunningham grew up in Kailua-Kona, the son of the founders of the interdenominational missionary organization Youth With A Mission, or YWAM. Currently he is building new state of the art facilities called Lokahi Studios located on the YWAM-affiliated University of the Nations, Kona Campus. The studios will facilitate training along with professionally produced projects. Cunningham is in pre-production on a film trilogy with a working title Lion of War.

Cunningham earned a film and communications degree at the University of Southern California. He is also a graduate of Konawaena High School in Kona on the Big Island. His 1997 film *Beyond Paradise* presented his view of violence and drugs – and redemption – in a coming-of-age story told through the eyes of a Mainland haole student who attends Konawaena. Cunningham traveled to Kaua'i during the release of *Beyond Paradise* for a showing at Kukui Grove Cinema.

Returning in the spring of 2000 he began location filming on Kaua'i in mid-May, making a movie quite different than the Academy Award-winning 1957 film *Bridge on the River Kwai*, while addressing the same war time atrocities.

"I grew up on the Big Island of Hawai'i and had visited Kaua'i a number of times over the years," the director commented when asked about why he chose Kaua'i for *To End All Wars*. "Even as early as writing the screenplay for

The Grove Farm Homestead Museum locomotive Wainiha, built in 1915 for McBryde Sugar Co., was turned into a Japanese Railroad of Death locomotive in *To End All Wars*. Track for the train scenes was layed near the Koloa side of the Wilcox Tunnel.

To End All Wars director David Cunningham (left) goes over the shooting script with actor Kiefer Sutherland in the hospital hut built in mauka Koloa for the film. Sutherland plays an American sailor captured along with British soldiers.

A reunion of cast and crew at the Kaua'i premiere of *To End All Wars* at the Waimea Theatre in 2001 (from left) Teamster and film extra Robert "Bo" Jordan, David Maki of Hanapepe whose back (above) was featured in the film's paperback book cover and in one of its theater posters, Japanese actor Yugo Saso who played the prison camp interpreter and friend to the POWs, director David Cunningham, and Japanese actor Masayuki Yui, who played the POW camp commander Captain Noguchi.

Explosives blew up POW huts at the mauka Koloa camp in the climax of *To End All Wars* during a scene when Allied bombers target the railroad workers camp, not knowing POWs were being held there. The *To End All Wars* film and sound crew capture the action in a scene that replicates Sumatra where British troops were brought ashore after their escape sailboat was captured by the Japanese in the days following the fall of Singapore and prior to their imprisonment in Thailand.

To End All Wars, I knew I wanted to film the movie on Kaua'i. I had also spent quite a bit of time in Thailand (where the actual story took place) and saw what a great match Kaua'i could be for Thailand. The lush jungles, winding rivers and steep valleys made it a great cinematic choice. And to add to that – Kaua'i doesn't have snakes, malaria, the intense humidity of Thailand (and that it is a 40-minute plane ride from my home on the Big Island) and it was a no brainer!"

About 300 extras were hired during the more than two months of filming. Local casting director Angela Tillson of Whale of A Time Productions explained in a *Star-Bulletin* article, "The reason so many extras are needed is not because of many large crowd scenes. A recognizable extra like Laranio, who is photographed in a port in Sumatra, can't logically also show up again on the Kwai River," she said. "I can't have the same faces over and over," said Tillson who "conducted auditions all over the island – 'K-Mart, twice, Salt Pond Park, my house, the street, the malls, the stores' – and wasn't bashful about accosting people who never even considered extra work, if they had the right 'look.' She found an amazing number of skinny Caucasian men to play emaciated POWs."

Honey beekeeper David Maki of Hanapepe, his gaunt frame deeply tanned, stood out in the crowd of POWs played by local men. Cunningham and his team chose Maki to play a starved POW. Prior to filming Maki said he went on a mango diet to prepare for the part. A stylized photo of Maki taken to show off the taut skin of his back made for a striking movie poster for the film's first run.

To End All Wars was featured during the 2001 Hawai'i International Film Fetival. About 500 interested moviegoers, many of them extras and crew members bringing family and friends to see them on the big screen, attended the Kaua'i premiere at the Waimea Theatre on November 11, 2001, two months exactly after the 9/11 attacks.

"Two of the Japanese actors (Masayuki Yui, who played the camp commander, and Yugo Saso, who played the interpreter) received standing ovations when the film was over," *Honolulu Star-Bulletin* Kaua'i reporter Anthony Sommer reported.

Director Cunningham attended the screening. He told Sommer, "Since Sept. 11, people have been pushing to get it out earlier. It carries a message that deals with two totally opposing sides of thought that has become very timely."

The film premiered at Telluride and Toronto Film Festivals in 2001 and was sold to London based Goldcrest Films (*Killing Fields*, *The Mission*) and to 20th Century Fox. But due to the events of the 9/11 tragedy the USA theatrical release was reduced to a limited theatrical exhibition because of its war-related themes. It remains one of the more popular films on Netflix today and has received a cult following around the world.

Kaua'i Film Commissioner Judy Drosd praised Cunningham for his effort in making an independent film on Kaua'i during an era when independent films were coming into their own in the film world. "This is a fortunate break for local production crew and actors," Drosd told Sommer. "If we're able to attract this type of production, then more people can work more consistently in the film industry. Which will help us to truly build our local film industry."

Filming of *To End All Wars* gave a boost to the local economy with $5.5 million spent on island. About 65 local residents on average were at work each day of filming.

To End All Wars – Director's Cut is a reedited version of the film released in 2012 for special screenings in churches, schools and other settings where discussions are prompted to be held on redemption, loving your enemy no matter what and other issues prominent in the story. More information on the film plus a documentary film that features Kaua'i footage is available at www.toendallwarsthemovie.com.

"Mahalo Kaua'i!" Cunningham said in 2012 of his filmmaking on Kaua'i. "It was a joy to film on the very special Garden Isle and to work with such exceptional people."

Six Days Seven Nights

Here Harrison Ford flies a DeHavilland Beaver in the skies of Kaua'i during *Six Days Seven Nights* filming. "All the air-to-air and air-to-ground filming will be done from an American Eurocopter AStar helicopter, using a sophisticated, custom-built Flying Pictures USA Gyrosphere gyrostabilized camera attached to the right side. The chopper's agility and the Beaver's slow speed and stability make for a good match and allow shots that would be impossible to get from a fixed-wing camera ship. (From Steve Stafford's article "The Making of Six Days Seven Nights." For more on the aerial filming for the film read his account at www.studiowings.com/the-making-of-six-days-seven-nights.)

Harrison Ford returned to Kaua'i in 1997 for ten weeks to film the romantic comedy-adventure film *Six Days Seven Nights* from Disney's Touchstone Pictures.

The film is an interesting one in the history of Kaua'i filmmaking because of the use of a multitude of remote Kaua'i locations, and the return of Ford to Kaua'i, where the opening scenes featuring the actor in *Raiders of the Lost Ark* were filmed along the Hule'ia River back in September 1980.

Ford apparently felt right at home, often flying his personal Cessna from Princeville Airport to Lihu'e Airport on filming days, and riding his motorcycle along Kaua'i's scenic highways.

Ford plays Quinn Harris, a 50ish ex-patriate American pilot living in Tahiti who has seen better days. Anne Heche plays Robin Moore, a 20-something Manhattan magazine editor on a romantic wintertime getaway with her soon-to-be-husband Frank Martin, played by *Friends* star David Schwimmer.

Director Ivan Reitman, of *Ghostbuster* fame, choose to film along isolated Kaua'i beaches, in the wilderness valleys of the Na Pali coast plus and at Papa'a Bay where he constructed the South Pacific resort where much of the "civilized" action takes place in the film.

Six Days Seven Nights starts out in snowy Manhattan, where Robin is in a high-pressure job as editor of a *Cosmopolitan*-like women's magazine. Boyfriend Frank takes her to a Polynesian restaurant in Manhattan and surprises her with tickets to the resort island of Makatea.

This Polynesian place name was apparently chosen for how it sounds, a great name for a romantic South Pacific island concocted by Hollywood. The actual Makatea is a rugged phosphate-rich atoll in the Tuamotus, an island group in eastern French Polynesia, with a landscape vastly different than that pictured in the film. The Tuamotus are among the islands pictured on a wall map painted by movie scenics in the old Lihu'e Airport terminal used for the Tahiti arrival scene at the beginning of the film.

Flying into Tahiti, the couple look down and the film cuts to footage of the Sofitel Resort located on the island of Huahine in French Polynesia. They're flying aboard an Aloha Airlines jetliner, which dates the film a bit as the airline ceased flying passengers in 2008.

The yuppie Manhattanite couple weave through a Lihu'e Airport terminal crowded with hurrying passengers. Blue Kinney of Hanalei sweeps the floor in the scene; Blue's movie work dates back to an appearance in *South Pacific* in the 1950s and a stint as an outrigger canoe paddler at the Hawai'i pavilion during the 1964-65 World's Fair in New York City.

As in many Kaua'i-made films local residents familiar with the locations used as backdrops sometimes feel disoriented with the quick segues between unrelated locations. Here the couple step out of the new airport terminal into the old airport terminal at Lihu'e as if they were connected.

Robin and Frank walk out on the tarmac looking for the sleek inter-island jet pictured in their travel brochure for the flight from Papeete to outer-island Makatea. They find Quinn pulling a wrench on an oily De Haviland Beaver bush plane. Quinn tells them he's flying them because the scheduled

The DeHavilland Beaver aircraft starred in *Six Days Seven Nights*, an iconic element throughout the film that carried the plot along from Tahiti Island to Makatea and desert islands in between. Here one of the Beavers used in the filming sits crashed at Kipu Kai Beach.

Two versions of the DeHavilland Beaver aircraft used in *Six Days Seven Nights*. The Beaver on the left was flight-ready and flown by Harrison Ford. The Beaver to the left served as the Japanese WWII float-equipped prop in the lift-off scene filmed at Kipu Kai Beach.

aircraft is laid up in Fiji. "You're in luck!," he says to the couple looking on in shock. Once on the plane they are further amazed as Quinn's sexy Hispanic squeeze Angelica, played by Jacqueline Obradors, climbs over them to ride in the co-pilots seat.

The flight to Makatea is uneventful. Aerial footage of the Anahola Mountains and the resort nestled along a beach at Papaʻa Bay easily pass as their fictional Tahitian setting.

Once settled in, Robin visits the resort bar where a drunk Quinn makes a sloppy pass at her. Frank rescues her as Taj Mahal and his Hawaiian Blues Band play onstage. The internationally-renowned folk and blues singer moved to Kauaʻi in 1981 and now resides off-island after years of fishing Kauaʻi and adding his touch to the local music scene. Years earlier he put together a local band for a live broadcast of Garrison Keillor's popular Prairie Home Companion radio show from Honolulu. The band became Taj's Hula Blues Band, one of several bands he performs with. In this scene Kauaʻi musicians Carlos Andrade, Wayne Jacintho, Pat Cockett, Pancho Graham, and the late lap steel guitarist Fred Lunt of Honolulu – who together have recorded two albums as Na Pali.

In the film it appears the band was directed to appear more animated than usual while playing a Calypso tune with Taj in a brilliantly-colored aloha shirt.

After Frank proposes and Robin accepts his diamond ring, an emergency phone call from her magazine publisher creates a big twist in the film's plot. Robin must fly back to Papeete for a critical photo shoot, with celebrities crossing trans-Pacific flight paths there. Her only hope is to hire a hungover and reluctant Quinn, who finally accepts a $700 fee to fly her.

They depart at sundown from a grass strip actually located in the Aliomanu Beach area just south of Papaʻa Bay, a worker lighting oil pots to mark the rustic airstrip. About halfway to Papeete, after Robin gobbles sedatives and gets silly, Quinn flies into a CGI-imaged tropical lightning storm, the Beaver is hit by a bolt knocking out the radio and he decides to turn back to Makatea. He is unable to make it and crash lands on a desert island about 40 miles southeast of Makatea. The landing gear is demolished as the Beaver skids across a beach at Kipu Kai, a remote beach and valley located on Kauaʻi's isolated southeast coast. In the morning Robin stumbles out of the plane groggy from her medication and Quinn is asleep on the beach. The couple talks over their situation and she becomes a frantic. Meanwhile, back on Makatea Frank and an American helicopter pilot, conveniently based in Tahiti, go out to search for Quinn and Robin.

Back at the plane wreck, the survivors scout inland of the beach and discover a picturesque waterfall, actually Kilauea Falls, which in reality is located about 25 miles north of Kipu Kai. Returning they find peacocks lounging on the beach and Quinn kills one to barbecue.

Quinn and Robin begin to bond, and he tells a tale of a broken marriage and an escape from a much bigger business to the languor of Tahiti. In another geographical leap the couple hike to the scenic Na Pali coast. After a sink hole adventure, and even more bonding, Quinn decides they should look for a radio beacon that might connect them to the outside world. They reach a lookout, probably Nualolo Flats in Kokeʻe, and the camera scans eastwards for a spectacular view of the cliffs and valleys of Na Pali. In the distance a cruise ship turns toward the island. With possible rescue just below them – in fact down a deadly sea cliff face – they race down to the coast at Nualolo Kai and make it quickly back to the Kipu Kai beach, inflate a small orange life raft and take off a day-long paddle to Na Pali and the ship.

Coming up on the coast their binocular view reveals two ships – a millionaire's yacht and a grungy ocean-going fishing boat with the location Sumatra painted on the stern, referencing the pirates of Indonesia. A close up of the yacht shows the dark-skinned pirates shooting the aloha shirt clad yachties. Quinn reverses course and paddles at high speed. The pirates launch a motor-

These Kauaʻi men played a baggage handler, airplane mechanic, Papeete-based commercial airline pilot and gendarme in the first Kauaʻi scenes in *Six Days Seven Nights*. The map of French Polynesia behind the men was painted for the film on a wall of the old Lihuʻe Airport terminal. The real island of Makatea is located in the Tuamotu Archipelago.

A coveted film crew T-shirt from the Kauaʻi location filming for *Six Days Seven Nights*.

ized Zodiac, blow up Quinn and Robin's raft and catch up to them beached at Honopu with the wondrous Honopu Arch framing the background.

To film these Na Pali scenes director Reitman and crew were aided by the naval personnel stationed at Pacific Missile Range Facility. The navy provided an oversized raft and supporting vessels for the film crew. Harrison Ford made a memorable stop at the West Side base chatting with the crew out there, graciously signing an unopened Hans Solo action figure from the late 70s for a sailor Star Wars collector, greatly adding to the value of the piece.

According to production notes for the film, Ford did many of his own stunts including fighting with the pirates. Eventually he and Robin are captured and are about to be shot and killed. Robin concocts a tale of a gold cache back at their camp and lures the pirates into taking them back to the Kipu Kai location. Along the way the couple roll away down a sand dune thick with ironwood trees and come out at a death-defying diving rock located on the coast west of Kipu Kai. Ford and Heche "fake" jumped onto sand from a lower cliff at one of the tiny surfing beaches east of Mahaleupu. Frozen with terror, Robin is tricked into jumping by Quinn, saving them from the pirates.

Back at the resort, Angelica "consoles" Frank by luring him into spending the night with her in her cottage.

Quinn and Robin, energized by all the action to say the least, come together in a *From Here to Eternity*-style kissing in the surf on the beach scene.

Their discovery of a Japanese float plane crashed on the island during World War II presents a new opportunity. Quinn manages to free the floats and they walk the khaki colored metal pieces down a stream on the Wailua River and then through a wider stream at the bottom of Kilauea Falls, eventually hurling down another waterfall and landing safely at the bottom. This was set at the Slipper Slide in Kilauea, the location used for the "Happy Talk" scene in *South Pacific*. Ford was reportedly scrapped up pretty good during take after take of him falling down the waterfall with the pontoons.

Back at the resort, a despondent Frank reacts to news that the search for the Beaver has been called off.

But at the Kipu Kai location, Quinn ingeniously, with the help of Robin, rigs a bamboo frame that attaches the aged floats to the listing Beaver, replacing the smashed landing gear. The pirates show up just as Quinn is ready to rev the Beaver up and head out to sea for a water launch to fly back to safety. He is wounded by a Howitzer blast and Robin helps him into the plane. They just barely make it over the pirate's fishing boat and in beep-beep Road Runner style a pirate unwittingly launches a shell straight up, which of course falls straight down and blows up the pirate's fishing boat.

Since Quinn is severely injured Robin is forced to fly the plane, relying on simple instructions she picked up from him earlier in flight. She manages a water landing right in the middle of a memorial service being held at the resort in memory of her and Quinn.

Robin consoles Quinn in a plantation-era hospital and they delicately discuss their opposites-attract love now they are away from all the action.

Frank confesses his indiscretion with Angelica and he and Robin head off for the airport to travel back to the U.S. Quinn who has decided to stop Robin from leaving, makes his way to the airport, but is a little too late. He is crestfallen as he watches her flight take off. Robin's surprise greeting snaps him out of it – she's not on the plane. On the tarmac Robin commits to loving Quinn, while he admits it's time for a big change in his life.

On the tarmac the couple are accompanied by gendarmes. One is played by Christian Marston, owner of Tahiti Nui restaurant and bar in Hanalei. Christian's late mother, Louise Marston, was a native of Tubuai, an outlier located hundreds of miles away from Papeete, just as Makatea is, in a chain known as the Austral Islands. Another Tahitian, and a close friend of Louise, the late Reri Tava Jobe, plays a flight attendant in the film. Reri had roles in

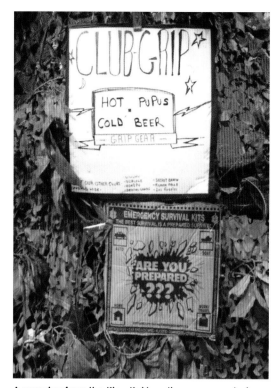

A gag sign from the Kipu Kai location camp posted during the filming of *Six Days Seven Nights*.

Six Days Seven Nights co-star Jacqueline Obradors as Latin bombshell Angelica with aerial stunt coordinator Steve Stafford on the set at Lihu'e Airpot.

Harrison Ford and Anne Heche are on the run from modern-day pirates in French Polynesia on the press kit cover for *Six Days Seven Nights*.

both the original *Hawai'i Five-O* and *Magnum P.I.* TV series. Reri was a noted dancer at the old Queen's Surf at Waikiki in what some call the Golden Age of Hawaiian entertainment in the late 1950s and 1960s.

Six Days Seven Nights was released by Touchstone in June 1998. A private screening was shown for local cast and crew members at the Kukui Grove Cinema in Lihu'e.

The popular romantic comedy lives on in the dreams of visitors planning a trip to Kaua'i.

Honolulu Star-Bulletin columnist Dave Donnelly wrote following the success of the film: "The Kaua'i Visitors Bureau continues to get calls from folks who've seen the Harrison Ford-Anne Heche film 'Six Days, Seven Nights' and want to know where the lovely, picturesque resort in the movie is located. It falls to KVB exec director Sue Kanoho to inform them it's a movie set in Hollywood. She does go on to let people know there are plenty of places on the Garden Island just as appealing…"

Pancho Graham

Pancho Graham performs at the Kilauea Theatre in 2011.

Hollywood directors cast Kaua'i singers, musicians, and dancers in their films to add authenticity to their productions. This began with the playing of the hap haole tune Kalua Lullaby in the 1934 film *White Heat*.

The film *The Descendants* features a carefully-selected list of Hawaiian tunes including Kilauea resident and long-time Kaua'i musician Pancho Graham's Kaua'i-inspired song "Pine Tree Slack Key."

Pancho appears in *Six Days Seven Nights* in the resort night club band. Pat Cockett, Carlos Andrade and Fred Lunt were joined by Pancho in the Kaua'i band Na Pali, recording Pacific Tunings in 1987. They met blues singer and former Kaua'i resident Taj Mahal at 'Anini Beach, and Taj later formed a band with Na Pali and recorded Taj Mahal and the Hula Blues Band. "One of our gigs was filming the bar scene playing 'The Calypsonians' in *Six Days Seven Nights*. Harrison Ford copped some moves from Taj for his 'drunk' scene where he falls off the stool," reports Pancho Graham.

The soundtrack for *The Descendants* was nominated in 2011 for a Grammy soundtrack award. *The Descendants* music is notable for presenting in a major feature film the authentic music of Hawai'i including tracks by the late Gabby Pahinui.

"Having my song chosen for the movie is a big honor, and I had the opportunity to play a concert with some of the other great players who have music in the film," Pancho says.

"The pine trees I was thinking of are at all my favorite beaches from Ha'ena to Anahola where we check surf," Pancho says of his song's inspiration. "From early morning surf checks to lunch breaks and sunset reveries, we find shelter at the beach in the comforting shade of the ironwoods. Fishing or shelling, spending time with family, friends and lovers, the pine trees are companions we share with the ocean, land and sky, and a place to go to find the inspiration that increases our appreciation of this island life."

Kaua'i Aloha

In the wake of the devastation of Hurricane 'Iniki, which swept across Kaua'i on September 11, 1992, Island leaders knew a message needed to go nationally that the beauty and aloha of the Garden Island was still alive and well. However all knew that in the first post-'Iniki weeks and months it was still too soon to again promote tourism to the Island as if nothing had happened.

In this sensitive time a vision came forth for a special song and a music video to promote the song. The song and music video would portray how the aloha of Kaua'i's people and the Island itself had survived the storm, a production that was called simply *Kaua'i Aloha.*

Getting behind *Kaua'i Aloha* – both financially and in spirit – were visitor industry leaders from Kaua'i's main resort destinations in Princeville, the Kapa'a-Wailua area, from Po'ipu and Kalapaki Beach, from the Kaua'i Visitors Bureau marketing committee, from the County of Kaua'i, and from hotel and economic development organizations.

With KONG Radio's Andy Melamed, who also chaired the KVB marketing committee, at the helm, about $250,000 was raised as production began under the able direction of music and film producer David Talisman of Honolulu.

Andy recalls: "...we all agreed that all (tourism) advertising needed to stop after 'Iniki, if we could communicate a stirring piece that captures the beauty of our island and its people, it was an opportunity that would work out quite well. Needless to say it was one of the most satisfying of projects that I created in my 42 years living on Kaua'i and creating events and promotions for individuals and organizations, and to this day the video still does bring tears to my eyes and heart, body and soul because of this sacred place where we are so fortunate to reside."

The concept for *Kaua'i Aloha* was Andy's.

"The idea behind this project came about due to some circumstances that all pointed me in one single direction. Nothing happened to my home in Hanalei. In fact the day after 'Iniki, we simply picked up some broken glass and neighbors' roofs in our yard, and we were fine. Because KONG Radio (where I was manager) was operating, however, we were not selling ads at that time. This left me with not much to do. The island needed generators, and I discussed such a need with some radio stations in Los Angeles who invited me to come to the Mainland for a possible fundraiser. After five days of getting no cooperation I decided to return home to Kaua'i. My wife and our kids were all getting ready to go to sleep when an ABC story about 'Iniki came on the Sunday news. We were seeing this while in Los Angeles and the story focused on a small church in Anahola where many without homes and shelter were staying at the church and they were joined in song, and most joyous. This was a remarkable piece that brought tears to my eyes, and I created the line that best represents the project from that piece: The beauty of an island instills a beauty in its people.

"And this is what rang true. I also came up with the line 'Where waterfalls have no ending,' which is a key phrase in the original song that Titus Kinimaka and I collaborated on one evening at my house upon my return. We then sent that song to David who forwarded it to Lester Gantan who composed the final version of the song." Gantan joined forces with David, Titus Kinimaka and Glenn Mederios on the final version of *Kaua'i Aloha*.

With the song written, now the companion video was needed. David Talisman went to work in Honolulu, recording the song in separate sessions with the Honolulu Boys Choir, Willie K, Kaua'i's own Glenn Medeiros, Graham Nash and Titus Kinimaka.

But something more was needed than musicians singing in a recording studio. Three weeks before Thanksgiving, about two months into the Island's recovery, David called Andy and said the video needed also to picture the local people of Kaua'i. Andy saw that a Thanksgiving feast at the Island's capital in Lihu'e, at Kukui Grove Park, would provide the setting the *Kaua'i Aloha* video needed. With an estimated price tag of $50,000 this wasn't going to be a holiday pot luck dinner, but where would the funds come from? Unexpectedly, and without prompting or request, a Kaua'i executive showed up at KONG's broadcast studio in downtown Lihu'e with a check for the total amount.

The event was on and a mini-Woodstock roster of rock stars committed to perform in person for the thousands of local residents who made it down to Lihu'e for the mid-day concert and feast. Performing were Nohelani Cypriano, David Crosby, Stephen Stills and Graham Nash, Jackson Browne, Jimmy Buffet and Bonnie Raitt.

Spectacular footage of Na Pali, waterfalls and more taken from a helicopter was added to the video montage. "I did a full day in the chopper to shoot aerials with a nose mount 16mm film camera for beauty shots," David recalls.

David added hurricane footage, scenes of relief workers aiding local folks, and Kaua'i Mayor JoAnn Yukimura with Gov. John Waihee striding in to help the Island. *Karate Kid* and *Happy Days* star Pat Morita flew to Kaua'i and stayed in the shuttered Westin Kaua'i to film the introduction to the video, wearing a purple lettered Kaua'i t-shirt for his scene filmed on the beach at Kalapaki.

Now David had the footage he needed for the final edit. "It was all put together at Pacific Focus in Honolulu with my editor buddy Jay Evans," David says. "We worked tirelessly to make it perfect."

Several weeks later the five-minute *Kaua'i Aloha* music video was released to much acclaim. A release party was held at the Kaua'i Hilton's Gilligan's night club with Kinimaka, Medeiros and others involved in the production attending.

Kaua'i Aloha went national, and was shown on CNN, Good Morning America and, of course, MTV. Locally the music video was aired all over the Honolulu television stations. David transferred the video to 35mm film at the request of Consolidated Theatres who screened it for six months as a trailer to their feature films in movie houses across Hawai'i. The project won a Pele award given to Andy for its conception and production against big odds in hurricane ravaged Kaua'i. Today you can type in *Kaua'i Aloha* at YouTube.com to watch the video, which is now a classic, arguably the most memorable memento of 'Iniki to many of those who survived the storm.

An amazing side-note to the *Kaua'i Aloha* story is the use of the song following the December 2004 tsunami that killed thousands in Southeast Asia. In Sri Lanka, the *Kaua'i Aloha* song "was used as the heart of a video by all of the most famous stars in Sri Lanka," David says, with the theme changed to "We Will Rebuild."

David's Sri Lanka connection came through a chance viewing of *Kaua'i Aloha* in a Honolulu theater by Killi Rajamahendran, a Sri Lankan who owns the the Maharajah Organization conglomerate in his home nation, a group that owns multiple companies including TV and radio stations. Rajamahendran wanted to use the *Kaua'i Aloha* theme for a music video that would tell the story of his company, which he led in rising from the ashes of a devastating fire in 1988, and David produced the video for him.

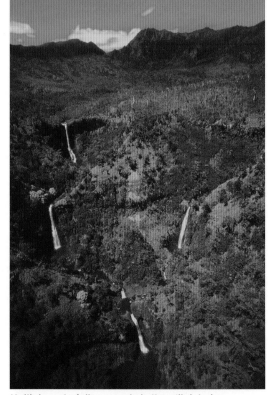

Multiple waterfalls cascade in Kaua'i's interior. Helicopter footage of similar scenes portrays the beauty of the Island in the promotional video *Kaua'i Aloha*.

The True Story of Kaluaikoʻolau

Ke Kula Niʻihau O Kekaha Learning Center students and staff joined forces in 2006 with filmmaker Koohan "Camera" Paik in creating *The True Story of Kaluaikoʻolau.*

The 30-minute video production aims at helping to perpetuate the Niʻihau dialect of the Hawaiian language, the first-language of the West Side indigenous school's community. The school is closely tied to Niʻihau, the island located about 15 miles west of Kauaʻi which is noted as the last remaining community of Hawaiian language speakers.

Paik introduced the concept for the film to the school, and provided her talent in filmmaking.

The plight of Kaluaikoʻolau is a famous Kauaʻi story that encompasses the plight of the Hawaiian people, their faith, their suffering from introduced diseases, and the changes that came with the overthrow of the Hawaiian Kingdom in the late 19th century. Koʻolau, a sharp-shooting Waimea-Kekaha paniolo, his wife Piʻilani, and their young son Kaleimanu fled in 1893 to a site deep within Kalalau Valley on Na Pali. Koʻolau suffered from leprosy and selected to be sent to the isolated leper colony located on the Kalaupapa Peninsula on the north shore of Molokaʻi. He refused to go without his "kokua" helper, his wife Piʻilani. Health authorities refused his request and the family fled to Kalalau. Koʻolau and his son died in the valley, but only after resisting attempts to remove the family. Piʻilani lived and made her way back to Waimea. In 1906 a Honoluu publisher recorded her story and released the book *The True Story of Kaluaikoolau,* written in the Hawaiian language.

In 2001 the Kauaʻi Historical Society published an English-language translation of the Piʻilani's book. Renowned Hawaiian language translator Frances Frazier of Kauaʻi provided the English language version. An interview with Frazier is included as an extra on the DVD produced by Ke Kula Niʻihau O Kekaha.

Some students at Ke Kula Niʻihau O Kekaha are related to Koʻolau and Piʻilani.

Principal Haunani Seward said students spent two years working on the film. Their dialogue is all spoken in the Niʻihau dialect, with English subtitles added. The dialect is soft and smooth compared to the more vowel-stressed, firmer dialect heard on windward Hawaiian islands.

Stars of *The True Story of Kaluaikoʻolau* are Oliwa Kanahele as Koʻolau, Kaehu Kanahele as Piʻilani, and Keoki Strickland as Kaleimanu.

In making the film, students learned about the botany of plants native to Kauaʻi that would have made up the diet of Koʻolau and his family, and served as medicine, during their years in Kalalau Valley. They also hiked in the highlands of Kokeʻe, following the supposed path the family took going up from the West Side to Kokeʻe and down into Kalalau Valley, and that Piʻilani took back home following the deaths of her son and husband. Students studied the overthrow of the Hawaiian Kingdom, which also happened in 1893, during the filmmaking; the issue is related to the story that troops

From left to right: Oliwa Kanahele, Kaehu Kanahele and Wehiwa Kelley, Ke Kula Niihau O Kekaha students at Kalalau. Oliwa played Kaluaikoolau and Kaehu played Piilani – they are first cousins and were seniors at the school when the film was made.

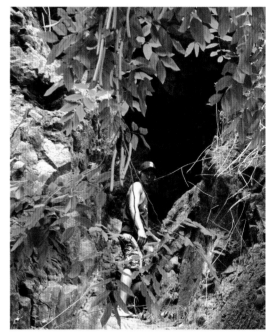

A unique location in Kauaʻi filmmaking, the Ke Kula Niihau O Kekaha filmmakers used this cave located on a cliffside in Waimea Valley to replicated Koʻolau and Piʻilani's hideout deep in Kalalau Valley.

The cover of the Kaua'i Historical Society's publication of Frances Frazier's English language translation of Pi'ilani's account features a vintage photo of Ko'olau, Pi'ilani and their son Keleimanu.

were sent by the provisional Hawaiian government set up after the overthrow to capture Ko'olau and his family, as well as a community of lepers who had also fled to Kalalau.

The film premiered at Kalaupapa, with students traveling to Moloka'i to present their film to the settlement of aging Hansen's Disease patients there, who were their first audience. Makia Malo from Kalaupapa visited the school and served as the connection between the students and his 'ohana on Moloka'i.

Frances Frazier attended the Kaua'i premiere of the film, screened at the Waimea Theatre.

The True Story of Kaluaiko'olau can be purchased from the Koke'e Museum's gift shop.

Ko'olau and his family sought refuge deep within Kalalau Valley, in the folds of this pali. This view is from the Kalalau Lookout at Ko'eke.

LIHUʻE / NAWILIWILI

Nawiliwili is a scenic harbor nestled beneath the jagged peaks of towering Mount Haʻupu and pictured as a South Pacific port town in *Pagan Love Song*. Flowing into the breakwater-protected, deep-water harbor is the Huleʻia Stream, where the seaplane rescuing Indiana Jones in *Raiders of the Lost Ark* took off just in time to escape the arrows and spears of headhunters. The romantic, winding waterway leads inland to the Menehune-built fishpond at Alekoko and to the isolated meadows where Steven Spielberg and George Lucas filmed the chase scene outside the South American cave in *Raiders*.

The white-sand beach at Kalapaki, just north of Nawiliwili, is today a resort strand fronting the Kauaʻi Marriott Resort and Beach Club. Director John Ford set up harbor shots here of John Wayne and Lee Marvin in *Donovan's Reef* and turned the balmy beach at Hanamaʻulu, the next major bay north of Kalapaki, into an idyllic South Sea coastline for the film.

Northeast of Nawiliwili is Lihuʻe Airport and its oceanfront runway, where Nicholas Cage plotted the return of his fiancée in *Honeymoon to Vegas*. Most of Kauaʻi's fleet of tour helicopters is based here, too, frequently taking up filmmakers and still photographers for various productions. The number of helicopters operating here is the largest in Hawaiʻi, offering a factual comment on the attraction of the spectacular beauty of Kauaʻi's locations to visitors and filmmakers alike.

Lihuʻe, the commercial center of the Island, sits on a plateau above Nawiliwili and is home to the government offices for the Island. South of Lihuʻe is picturesque Kipu Ranch and Kipukai, its oceanfront sister valley and beach. Charlton Heston starred in *The Hawaiians* as James Michener's Whip Hoxworth in the sugar fields near Kipu Ranch while a painstakingly recreated replica of Honolulu's Chinatown circa 1900 burned to the ground. Several years later, Heston had starred in *Diamond Head* as land baron Kong Howland, employing Lihuʻe and the Kipu Ranch homestead as his kingdom.

Just north of Lihuʻe, Highway 530 leads to the top of the twin falls of Wailua, the memorable establishing shot of TV's hit *Fantasy Island* series.

Nawiliwili Harbor and the Haʻupu Range.

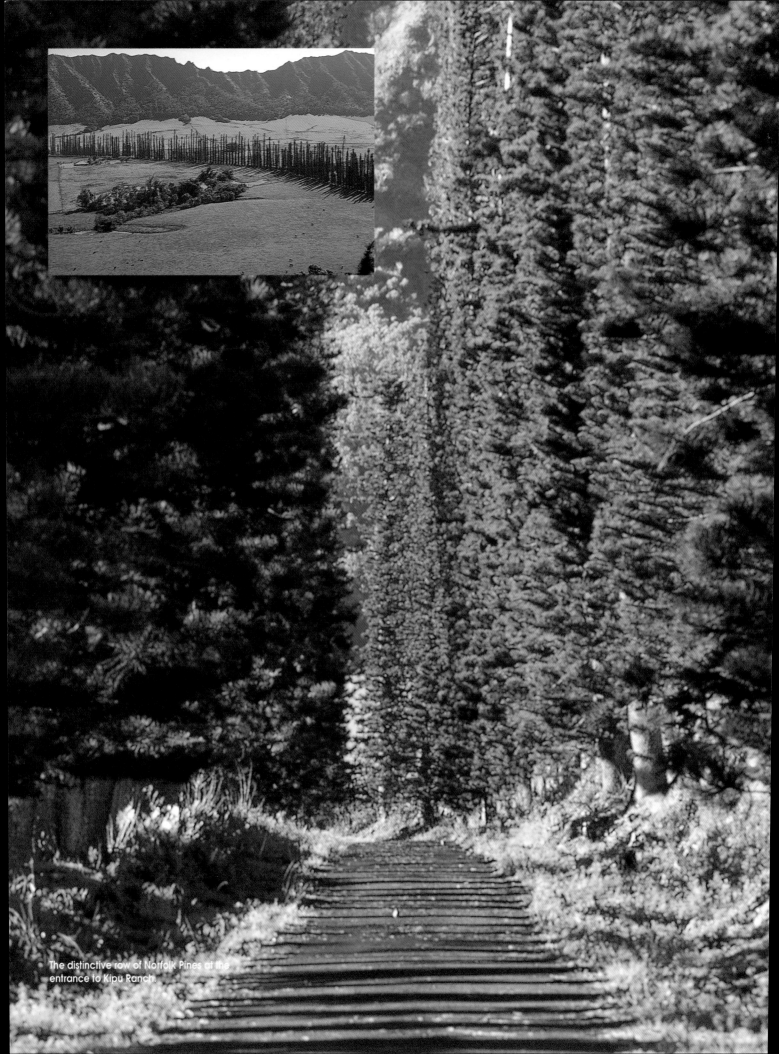

The distinctive row of Norfolk Pines at the entrance to Kipu Ranch.

KIPU RANCH

The Hawaiians

The spectacular burning of a painstakingly created Chinatown set, in a cattle pasture at Kipu Ranch, highlighted the filming of *The Hawaiians* on Kaua'i. Once titled *Master of the Islands*, *The Hawaiians* was the sequel to, and presented the third quarter of, James Michener's epic novel *Hawaii*.

While the film headlined Charlton Heston as land baron Whip Hoxworth, the true heart of the story was played by Tina Chen, an Asian actress. "(Tina) was a medical technician, stunningly beautiful, who had never acted before," Heston wrote in his book *In The Arena*. "(She provided) an almost flawless performance marked by her serene energy....The fine actor Mako played her husband; together, they put a spine in the film that my part didn't allow me to provide."

Directed by Tom Gries, *The Hawaiians* co-starred Geraldine Chaplin as Purity Hoxworth, Whip's deranged wife. The film was produced by Walter Mirisch.

For Kaua'i, the filming of *The Hawaiians* was a major event in 1969. Dozens of construction workers labored on the project to create a Hollywood-style Chinatown of building facades at Kipu and to restore the Isenberg estate in Lihu'e to become the Hoxworth home.

The film tells the story of a Chinese woman named Nyuk Tsin, her common-law husband Mun Kee, and her family, from their arrival in Hawai'i in 1882 to the disastrous Chinatown fire of Honolulu in 1900. A subplot is the fictionalized story of bringing pineapples to Hawai'i, which is based somewhat on the story of James Dole, nephew of Sanford B. Dole, who grew up in Koloa and became the President of the Republic of Hawai'i following the overthrow of the Hawaiian monarchy.

Filming and pre-production lasted from May through September 1969, a long time compared to most Kaua'i-based film production schedules.

Besides Kipu Ranch, the film's crew traveled for location shooting to Moloa'a; a ranch in Kapahi inland of Kapa'a; and the Wailua River.

The Chinatown set featured rickety staircases, mildewed awnings, a Chinese laundry, and a duplicate of historic Kaumakapili Church, which is located in downtown Honolulu.

A set replicating Honolulu's Chinatown, circa 1900, was erected and burnt to the ground at Kipu Ranch for the climax of the film *The Hawaiians,* the sequel to James Michener's *Hawaii*.

When director Gries staged a mob scene, where Hoxworth is surrounded by Chinese immigrants, he had to warn extras not to smile, or wear wristwatches, lest they ruin the scene. The set had walls with moveable backdrops, and the crew moved the buildings around to hide powerlines and block modern buildings out of the camera frame.

The burning of the Chinatown at Kipu replicated the torching of bubonic plague-ridden Chinatown in Honolulu in the early 1900s. Stagehands controlled the fire at Kipu, starting with small fires. The burning was highly organized, with sound and flames carefully sequenced. Hidden pipes squirted diesel fuel to flame the fire, and portable swimming pools were placed near the set as a safety feature. Horse-drawn fire wagons screaming through the exciting scene were driven by firemen from the Kaua'i Fire Department. By the wrap of filming the day of the fire, the entire set was burnt down to the ground.

Hook

Hook, the colorful 1991 remake of *Peter Pan* by Steven Spielberg's Amblin Entertainment, presents a quick, romanticized glimpse of a Kaua'i location.

In 1990, the special effects crew from director George Lucas' Industrial Light & Magic came from northern California to shoot footage for the special visual effects used to illustrate Never-Never Land. The ILM crew perched on an isolated mountain peak overlooking the coastal valley of Kipukai located between Nawiliwili and Po'ipu. The crew took large format images that were used as models for the dreamy island.

A careful look at the scene where Robin Williams, as Peter Banning/Peter Pan, returns to Never-Never Land provides a look at the fantasized version of Kipukai beach and valley and Mount Ha'upu, its looming backdrop.

A cameo role as a pirate is played by musician David Crosby, a frequent visitor to Kaua'i and son of Academy Award-winning cinematographer Floyd Crosby. The elder Crosby worked on several Kaua'i-made films.

A dirt road passes over the Ha'upu Range linking Kipu Ranch and Kipukai, which are both inaccessible to the public.

Wondrous Kipukai, the inspiration for Industrial Light and Magic's Never-Never Land aerial views in *Hook*, directed by Steven Spielberg.

LIHU'E

Diamond Head

James Darren, Yvette Mimieux, and Charlton Heston ride horses at Kipu Ranch in the 1962 film *Diamond Head.*

James Darren and Yvette Mimieux do a lively *hula* at the plantation manager's house used as a set in the film *Diamond Head.*

A royal palm-lined drive retains the past grandeur of an old plantation manager's house in Lihu'e. The once-stately mansion was the setting for a *luau* and party in *Diamond Head.*

Diamond Head is set in Hawai'i in the late 1950s and stars Charlton Heston as King Howland, a wealthy and ruthless land baron who runs for political office in the elections held just before statehood. The heart of the story is the romance between his kid sister Sloan, played by Yvette Mimieux, and James Darren, who with thick brown makeup plays Paul Kahana, a Hawaiian youth returning with Mimieux from college on the mainland. Howland strongly objects to the match, but the couple gets engaged anyway. However, Howland's ongoing romance with an Asian woman comes to light, proving him to be a hypocrite. But before Kahana and Sloan can be married, the handsome teen is accidently shot to death at a *luau* celebrating the couple's engagement. After this, Sloan falters psychologically, and the sins of Howland's life surface to haunt him.

Diamond Head is based on a 1959 novel, by one-time Honolulu newspaperman Peter Gilman, about the elections in Hawai'i . The novel ruffled feathers in Hawai'i among wealthy "Big Five" families, the descendants of missionary, Yankee, and British families who created financial empires in the Islands.

This film almost brought actor Clark Gable to Kaua'i. Unfortunately, Gable died while making the film *The Misfits* with Marilyn Monroe just months before location filming for *Diamond Head* was to begin. Charlton Heston writes in his autobiography *In The Arena,* "Columbia had developed it for Clark Gable, who'd given them a go on it just before he died."

Filming began in March 1962 and took about four weeks, using locations mostly in and around Lihu'e. Locations included the stables and pastures of Kipu Ranch, where Kipu cowboys Marmon Matsumura, Solomon Malina, and Hiram Matsumoto assisted the filmmakers.

A dream scene in which Sloan wears flesh-colored underwear riding a white stallion caused a stir among those watching the filming. John Midkiff of Hanalei, wearing a blonde wig, and horsewoman Tiny Fayé were stand-ins for Mimieux on horseback. Other scenes included an airplane landing at Lihu'e Airport, Howland's bashing by union heavies following a political speech filmed in Kaua'i Commercial Co.'s truck garage in Nawiliwili, and an indoor scene at the old Club Jetty, a nightclub which used to sit facing the docks at Nawiliwili Harbor.

The *lua'u* scenes employed dozens of local extras and were filmed at the former plantation manager's home, which still stands about a quarter mile towards Nawiliwili from the Kukui Grove Shopping Center. Kaua'i's ubiquitous toads caused a problem, croaking after "Quiet on the set!" was called, and a crewman was assigned to keep them quiet.

A supporting role in *Diamond Head* was played by France Nuyen, who spoke little English in 1957, when she first came to Kaua'i to play Liat in *South Pacific.* Nuyen became very popular with the local people on the Island and, during the *Diamond Head* filming, she was the center of attention due to her recent romance with actor Marlon Brando.

Raiders of the Lost Ark

R*aiders of the Lost Ark* again brought Kaua'i to the attention of the film world in 1981. The opening scenes feature the Kalalea Mountain range inland of Anahola, Hule'ia Stream, and a Kipu Ranch meadow upstream of the Alekoko or Menehune Fishpond.

The film is about Indiana Jones, (as played by Harrison Ford), an adventurous professor of archaeology in pursuit of the fabled Lost Ark of the Covenant of the Old Testament, and his on-again, off-again globetrotting girlfriend Marion Ravenwood, the daughter of a world-famous archaeologist. Marion is played by Karen Allen.

The Kaua'i scenes are a prelude to the hunt for the Ark of the Covenant and take place in the deep jungles of South America, where Indy is on the trail of Indian gold artifacts. He is attacked by headhunters led by a desperado archaeologist and flees for his life aboard a seaplane just steps ahead of death.

Filming on Kaua'i took place in September and October of 1980. Stills of director Steven Spielberg wearing a *Star Wars* hat while shooting along the Hule'ia Stream show him hard at work on the groundbreaking film. Although the Kaua'i scenes open the film, they were in reality the last to be shot, following an 85-day-long, high-intensity production schedule.

The high-stakes deal producer George Lucas and Spielberg made with Paramount for this movie was virtually unheard of in the film industry. It gave Lucas and Spielberg the largest profit margin ever agreed to by a Hollywood studio if the film was brought in under budget.

Doing advance work for Spielberg to ensure smooth filming was Robert Watts, his location scout. He came to Kaua'i in the fall of 1979 looking for a South American jungle scene location. "...(we) found everything we needed on the island of Kauai," Watts wrote in retelling the story of making *Raiders*. "We shot the Kaua'i sequences last in the schedule and had to move the crew, which was to join the Hawaiian technicians on Kaua'i, from Tunisia in North Africa, no simple task." Maile Semitekol of the Kaua'i Chapter of the Hawai'i Visitors Bureau served as a location scout for *Raiders of the Lost Ark*.

"The shooting went well and we found the local Hawaiian crew to be excellent and the cooperation on Kaua'i first rate....The Hovito Indians were played by local Kaua'ians who were persuaded to have their hair cut in an Indian pudding-basin style. The Waco biplane came from the U.S. mainland."

The plot and heroes of *Raiders* were based on the 15-minute-long serials popular at Saturday movie matinees in the 1930s and 1940s. Lucas gave Spielberg a specific formula—six dramatic situations involving a total of 60 scenes, each two pages long. "It's a serialesque movie," is how Lucas described the film.

Key to the film's success was a blockbuster opening scene, in the spirit of the Saturday afternoon cliffhangers. Kaua'i proved to be the perfect backdrop for the scene.

Reviewers raved about the film, and filmgoers filled theaters to see it.

Vincent Canby of the *New York Times* wrote, "(*Raiders*) is one of the most deliriously funny, ingenious and stylish American adventure movies ever made.

Director Steven Spielberg (in white hat) and producer George Lucas are briefly held hostage at Kipu Falls during the filming of *Raiders of the Lost Ark*.

"We shot scenes for two films on Kaua'i and both times had great support and cooperation from the people of the island and the Film Commission. The first was **Raiders of the Lost Ark** *and the second* **Jurassic Park**, *so Kaua'i rightfully played a role in two of the best filmmaking results we ever had."*
—Steven Spielberg

This pasture at Kipu Ranch is where headhunters pursued Indiana Jones. The picturesque field, inaccessible to the public but visible from tour helicopters, is now known as "Raiders Meadow."

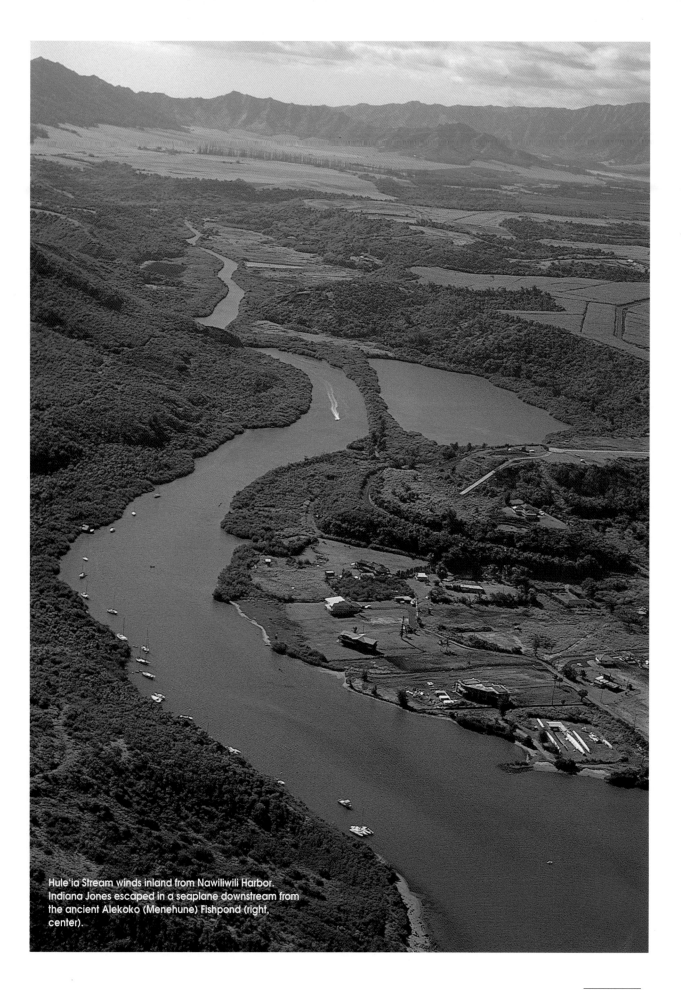

Huleʻia Stream winds inland from Nawiliwili Harbor. Indiana Jones escaped in a seaplane downstream from the ancient Alekoko (Menehune) Fishpond (right, center).

It is an homage to old-time movie serials and back-lot cheapies that transcends its inspirations to become, in effect, the movie we saw in our imaginations as we watched, say, Buster Crabbe in *Flash Gordon's Trip to Mars* or in Sam Katzman's *Jungle Jim* movies."

The headhunters were played by 28 Kaua'i men, cast for their "high cheek bones, almond eyes, dark skin, straight black hair, and a slender build," according to a *Garden Island* report of the filming. Popular Kaua'i stage actor and director Wil Welsh served as stand-in for Ford and appears with his back to the screen in the first 15 seconds of the film, a sequence filmed at Anahola. Local casting for *Raiders of the Lost Ark* was done by Kaua'i casting director Tom Summers.

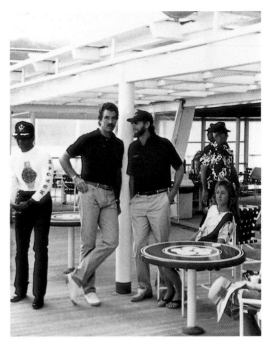

Tom Selleck and crew made one segment of *Magnum P.I.* on Kaua'i, sailing from Honolulu aboard an American Hawaii cruiseship. Here Selleck chats with local casting director Tom Summers, as Kaua'i surfer Nicki Bockwinkel waits for the action to begin.

Today Nawiliwili Harbor is a popular destination for cruise ships touring the Hawaiian Islands.

George Lucas (left) and Steven Spielberg with the Kaua'i men who played Hovito Indians in *Raiders of the Lost Ark.*

Steven Spielberg and Harrison Ford on a sound stage in Los Angeles that closely matched the film's locations on Kaua'i.

Harrison Ford as Indiana Jones sought a treasure cave near Kipu Falls in *Raiders of the Lost Ark.*

John Wayne as Guns Donovan (right) welcomes Elizabeth Allen, playing a South Pacific island doctor's daughter (left), in *Donovan's Reef.* The location is the center of Nawiliwili Harbor, and the white-hulled South Seas schooner is really director John Ford's 110-foot yacht, the *Araner.*

Honeymoon in Vegas

Kaua'i plays itself in *Honeymoon in Vegas,* a romantic comedy from Castle Rock Entertainment in association with Lobell/Bergman Productions. Nicholas Cage, James Caan, and Sarah Jessica Parker arrived in October 1991 to film location scenes. Director and writer Andrew Bergman, a veteran Hollywood director and screenwriter who began his movie career by co-writing *Blazing Saddles* with Mel Brooks, chose Kaua'i after a scouting trip based out of Princeville.

Honeymoon in Vegas tells the story of a love triangle involving neurotic New York private detective Jack, who flies to Las Vegas to marry Betsy, his girlfriend, counter to his mother's death-bed wish that he never marry. Cage is Jack and Parker is Betsy. In Las Vegas, hours before their planned quickie wedding-chapel marriage, Jack loses big time to professional gambler Tommy Corman, played by Caan. Corman, who sees a close resemblance between Betsy and his late wife, cuts a deal with Jack in exchange for forgiving Jack's gambling debt. He gets the girl for a long weekend at his vacation retreat on Kaua'i. Jack agrees, and his reluctant future wife is swept away to the Islands. Jack has second thoughts and in desperation flies to Lihu'e, where he tracks down Corman, who is wooing Betsy to marry him. In trying to get his fiancée back, Jack races around the Island with a Kaua'i taxi driver played by Pat Morita, seeking aid from characters like a New Age *kahuna* parodied by Peter Boyle.

Bergman chose to use a wide range of locations. His camerawork shows off Kaua'i's white-sand beaches, scenic highways, and world-class resorts. He adds a local flavor by filming at off-beat sites such as the Lihu'e Police Station and a rundown, but soulful, plantation shack at Waimea. The film's Kaua'i Club is the Inn on the Cliffs at Kaua'i Lagoons. A mock-up American Airlines counter is at Lihu'e Airport. Corman's vacation home is an elegant beachfront Anini home. Popular scenic spots Jack passes in his search include the Tree Tunnel leading to Koloa, Koloa Landing, and a beach at Hanalei with Bali Hai in the background.

More so than any filmmaker before, Bergman used Kaua'i-built sets to portray other locations. To keep the location filming moving on overcast days, Bergman and his crew created New York sets in the National Guard Armory at Kapa'a. Most film watchers are unaware that Jack's New York bedroom and the Brooklyn jail scene with snow falling were shot on Kaua'i. A Wilcox Hospital room doubles as a New York hospital in one of the first scenes in the film. Hundreds of local extras were used in the film, cast by local casting director Linda Antipala.

Check-in counters at Lihue Airport used for a Kaua'i scene featuring Nicolas Cage in *Honeymoon in Vegas.*

Popular Japanese-American character actor Pat Morita played a Kaua'i taxicab driver in *Honeymoon in Vegas.*

The New York hospital scene in *Honeymoon in Vegas* was filmed at Lihu'e's Wilcox Memorial Hospital.

KALAPAKI

Ray Walston (left) and Mitzi Gaynor entertained soldiers and sailors on Kaua'i for maneuvers in 1957. Their stage show was held on the beach at Kalapaki and filmed for *South Pacific.* Today the site of the stage is the beachfront of the Kaua'i Marriott Resort and Beach Club.

The Inn on the Cliffs restaurant above Kalapaki Beach was featured in *Honeymoon in Vegas.*

Nawiliwili Bay and Kalapaki Beach.

Rita Hayworth steps out of an old "sampan" car at Kalapaki Beach in *Miss Sadie Thompson.*

AHUKINI / HANAMAʻULU

Donovan's Reef

Academy Award-winning director John Ford and his long-time friend and leading man John Wayne arrived on Kauaʻi to film *Donovan's Reef* in the summer of 1962.

In setting Kauaʻi as a tropical South Sea island, Ford sought out palm tree-lined calm bays, a river with looming mountains for a backdrop, and a town to place Donovan's Reef, a South Sea bar founded by expatriate U.S. Navy men who stay behind after World War II was over.

At the time, Wayne was Hollywood's most popular male star and Ford was recognized as its leading director. However, this would be the last film the pair would do together, ending their 36-year partnership. "His last picture with Duke, *Donovan's Reef,* completed in 1963, had been a saddening experience for all the participants…a far cry from Duke's and Ford's glory days, an anticlimax to their long collaboration," recalls Pilar Wayne in her book *John Wayne—My Life With Duke.*

Earlier in the year Ford sailed across the Kauaʻi Channel in his prized 110-foot ketch, the *Araner,* to Nawiliwili from its berth in Honolulu. He surveyed Nawiliwili Harbor and Hanamaʻulu Bay for locations and chose Hanamaʻulu Beach and the nearby old Ahukini Pier as the main setting for the film. The South Pacific look of inter-island freighters docked at Nawiliwili and the palm tree-lined beach and calm surf at Hanamaʻulu were just what Ford was looking for.

The setting for *Donovan's Reef* is the imaginary South Pacific island of Haleokaloa. It's now the early sixties, over 15 years since Wayne as Michael Patrick "Guns" Donovan and two Navy buddies were shipwrecked there. Donovan owns a local bar named Donovan's Reef, and Jack Warden as "Doc" Dedham is a benevolent doctor whose Polynesian wife has passed away, leaving him with two children. Every year or so "Boats" Gilhooley, the third buddy, a South Pacific bum played by Lee Marvin, arrives in town to get drunk and fight with Donovan. The plot thickens when Dedham's daughter, played by Elizabeth Allen, arrives from Boston to once and for all write off her father and take charge of the family fortune back home. After experiencing island life firsthand, however, the daughter is won over to her father's take on life and, in the end, Wayne gets the girl and the daughter accepts her father for who he is.

The cast and crew moved frequently, filming additional scenes at the Allerton Estate at Lawai-Kai for the Coronation Ball sequence featuring 200 local extras costumed as Polynesian dancers. Trucks moved everyone to the old Koʻolau School site on windy Koʻolau Road near Moloaʻa, then up to Waimea Canyon, north to Smith's Boat Landing on the Wailua River, and to the Horner mansion, which was then located on the beach at Wailua just north of the Coco Palms Hotel. The shoot lasted about five weeks.

In the film, Ford and Wayne transfer the themes and roles of *Stagecoach* and other classic American westerns to the South Pacific. Fist fights, crusty jokes, and a Western point of view concerning indigenous people mark it as a John Ford film.

A tropical dawn at Hanamaʻulu Bay.

John Wayne took great pleasure in wearing his Kauaʻi Canoe & Racing Club T-shirt during the filming of *Donovan's Reef.*

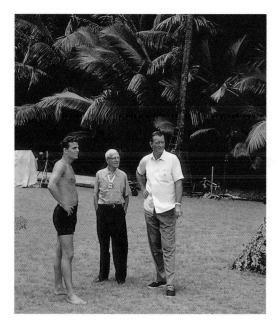

A casual John Wayne (right) relaxes during a break between scenes.

Ahukini Pier was set as Papeete, Tahiti, for *Pagan Love Song* in 1950. The pier was once an important shipping port for Kaua'i, but closed in the early 1950s.

John Ford (center) rarely showed his face to the camera. Here director Ford sets up a scene for *Donovan's Reef* at Hanama'ulu Bay, while star John Wayne waits for his cue.

Fantasy Island

Fantasy Island*'s weekly romantic dramas featured Kaua'i's twin Wailua Falls as its opening shot, making the picturesque waterfalls one of television's most famous images.

The host of Fantasy Island was the suave, mysterious Mr. Roarke (played by leading man Ricardo Montalban), who would lead the visitors into the fulfillment of their fantasies. As the series went on, Roarke gained magical powers, casting love spells and whipping up potions, calling up events from the past and future, and even doing battle with the devil.

The hit Saturday-evening telecast by ABC aired immediately following *Love Boat,* the television show it was based on. Viewers imagined that the setting for the show was an isolated island, something like Kaua'i. However, *Fantasy Island* was actually filmed at the Arboretum, a public park 25 miles from Los Angeles.

In 1979, the second year of the series, cast and crew traveled to Kaua'i to film a segment slated as the opening show of the fall ABC-TV network season. Writers concocted a fantasy marriage between Mr. Roarke and his fatally ill fiancée, played by red-headed Samantha Egger. Scenes were filmed in and around the Coco Palms Resort. Local touches included an appearance by singer Don Ho and his band.

Not counting the waterfall footage, this was the first location filming on Kaua'i for *Fantasy Island.* It also marked the first visit to the Island by Ricardo Montalban.

A second *Fantasy Island* special filmed on Kaua'i featured Roarke's sidekick Tattoo (played by Herve Villechaize) who has his fantasies come true in the segment. Surrounded by beautiful local girls, Tattoo was in his element, but the dream turned into a nightmare when he was placed in a cage and almost eaten by the unfriendly natives of the island.

The ongoing plot of the show was simple, but successful. Each week visitors would arrive aboard a seaplane to have lifetime dreams come true. The guests were played in cameo roles by a wide range of TV and film stars, including Peter Lawford, Dick Sargent, Carol Lynley, and others. The premise worked because it added glamour and excitement to the lives of ordinary people, something many TV watchers apparently enjoyed.

The most famous line in the show was 3-foot-11-inch-tall Tattoo's weekly exclamation of, "Da plane, da plane," as a new group of visitors arrived. Villechaize made his mark in the entertainment world through the series and went on to appear in films and television shows until his death in 1993.

A German television crew later came to Kaua'i to film *Dream Island,* a takeoff on *Fantasy Island* with a decidedly different twist. A Sigmund Freud-like character would analyze visitors, many suffering from mental problems deeper and darker than anything portrayed on the lighthearted *Fantasy Island* series. The problems were worked out, and the patients returned to Germany, healed.

The first run of *Fantasy Island* was telecast on January 28, 1978, and the show's last new segment aired on August 18, 1984. One of the most popular television series of all time, *Fantasy Island* continues to be aired in syndication worldwide.

Samantha Egger (left) and Ricardo Montalban romanced in the Coco Palms lagoon for a special *Fantasy Island* episode filmed on Kaua'i in 1977. The special launched ABC-TV's fall season. Notice the large pock marks on Egger's face; her character, fatally ill, married Montalban's Mr. Roarke in the episode, then died.

Herve Villechaize as Tattoo starred in another Kaua'i-made, season-opening episode of *Fantasy Island.*

The twin falls of Wailua added a glimpse of Kaua'i's scenic beauty during the establishing shots of each segment of ABC-TV's *Fantasy Island*.

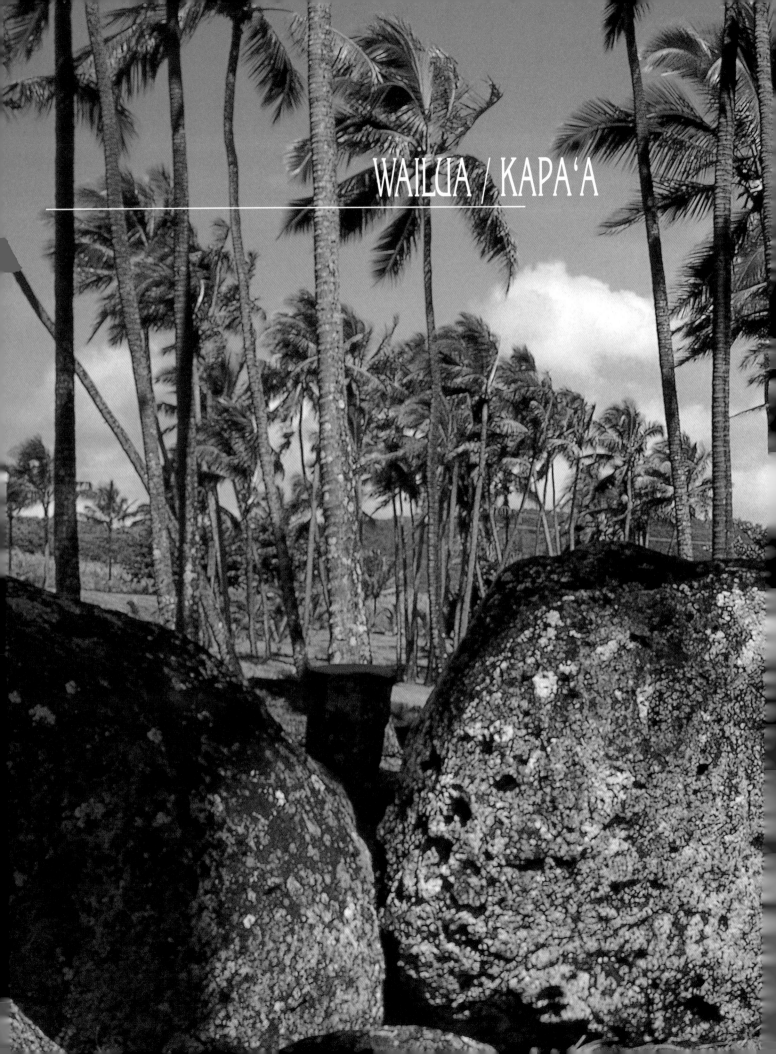

WAILUA / KAPA'A

Set between towering Mount Waiʻaleʻale and long, white-sand beaches, Wailua and Kapaʻa are areas rich in scenery. John Ford, Howard W. Koch, and other directors have been enthralled by the area's beauty.

Wailua is the former royal capital of Kauaʻi, and an ancient trail walked by Hawaiian priests once ran from the mouth of the Wailua River to the plateau atop Waiʻaleʻale. Wailua is traditionally an area famed for its visitor accomodations and attractions. Debora Kapule, Kauaʻi's last queen, greeted guests at her humble inn near where today's Coco Palms Resort stands. The Coco Palms opened in the early 1950s and was the main location for the Kauaʻi scenes of Elvis' *Blue Hawaii*. The cast and crew from *South Pacific* also enjoyed the Coco Palms, staying for two months at the Polynesian-themed hotel.

The Wailua River is the only navigable river in all of Hawaiʻi. It was used as a Cuban mangrove-lined river in *Islands in the Stream*, as an African river in *Outbreak*, a South Pacific landing in *Donovan's Reef*, and as a Solomon Island river in *Beachhead*.

Kapaʻa town retains its rural plantation flavor. Inland of Kapaʻa, picturesque roads snake past hills to the rain forest and meadows below Waiʻaleʻale. Here Steven Spielberg chose to film key scenes of *Jurassic Park*, and the *Flight of the Intruder* crew created North Vietnam for the plane crash combat scenes.

Just north of Kapaʻa, in the Kealia area once known as the Makee Plantation, stands Valley House. The former estate of sugar baron Col. Zepaniah Spalding, Valley House, still a private estate, is graced by two waterfalls and a lily pond and was the site of several *Jurassic Park* scenes. Horror filmmakers used Valley House as a backdrop for the killer baby-infested *Island of the Alive* in 1987 and Bros Karloff's *Voodoo Island* in 1957.

Hikina-a-ka-la Heiau near the mouth of the Wailua River, an area held sacred in the pre-western contact days on Kauaʻi.

Pagan Love Song

In the post-World War II years, location filming at exotic locales by Hollywood studios became a trend. With millions of G.I.'s now back home after tours in Europe, Africa, and the Pacific, telling tales of foreign lands and peoples, film audiences were hungry for a look at the world beyond Hollywood's sound stages and back lots.

Pagan Love Song, a Metro-Goldwyn-Mayer romance set in Tahiti, was a perfect vehicle to showcase Esther Williams and Howard Keel at a faraway location in 1950.

The film's director, Robert Alton, chose Kaua'i after a considerable search by location scout O. O. Dull and others. "We found the island to have exactly the Polynesian atmosphere we wanted—a beauty in its settings and a simple charm among its people that matched our story and our music." Alton commented in the September 1950 issue of *Paradise of the Pacific*.

Cinematographer Charles Rosher, who photographed a feature film in Tahiti in the thirties, raved about Kaua'i's locations, saying that on-screen they were more like Tahiti in appearance than Tahiti itself.

The South Seas genre film would be the first post-war Hollywood feature with a majority of its footage filmed on Kaua'i.

Williams, a champion swimmer noted for her on-screen water ballets and stunning beauty, plays a young Tahitian-American woman. Keel, who played on Broadway in *Carousel* and *Oklahoma!*, is cast as a young, but retired, Ohio schoolteacher who arrives on the tropical island to rebuild a run-down coconut plantation. While adapting to the slow pace of island life, the teacher falls in love with the island girl, only to find out she is really a sophisticated, well-bred and educated daughter of Tahiti's high society. The couple quarrel, reconcile, and live happily ever after.

In the spring of 1950, following a greeting by a sizable crowd at Lihu'e Airport, the cast and crew set in for their seven-week stay and quickly became part of the island community. They joined in at parties; Williams and unit manager Ed Woehler described the location filming live on local radio station KTOH; and she gave away a Pontiac at the Kaua'i County Fair. Williams was accompanied by her husband and baby, and Keel brought his wife for the unusually long location stay.

More than 1,000 Kaua'i residents, out of a population then numbering less than 30,000, became "Tahitians" in *Pagan Love Song*, setting off a holiday-like atmosphere on the Island for over a month, with updates appearing as front-page headlines in *The Garden Island*. The local actors pointed out to the Hollywood crew that their Hawaiian ancestors had come from Tahiti and proudly said that Captain Cook had chosen Kaua'i for his first "location" in Hawai'i. Philip Costa, a young Kapa'a boy, became an instant Kaua'i celebrity by being sent to Hollywood for indoor studio filming to complete a scene.

In *Pagan Love Song*, Alton fills the screen with spectacular South Pacific-looking sets. Williams and Keel romance each other at Kalapaki Beach, then known as Rice's Beach, and at Lydgate Park at Wailua; swim at the Valley House

A replica of Ernest Hemingway's fishing boat *Tortuga* cruises up the Wailua River in *Islands in the Stream*. In this scene, George C. Scott as Hemingway's Thomas Hudson eluded a Cuban shore patrol boat during World War II.

Wailua River is well known for its riverboat tours.

Star Esther Williams and Kaua'i extras wave aloha from a flower-and-palm laden outrigger canoe during the filming of *Pagan Love Song*.

Stanley Kaluahine spent most of his senior year at Kaua'i High School working on the film *Pagan Love Song*. Stanley trained for months as one of the Hawaiian swimmers who accompanied star Esther Williams in a tightly choreographed water ballet scene filmed at Ke'e Beach. He also held hands with *West Side Story* star Rita Moreno in a close-up.

pool; and ride bikes down the old pot hole-plagued road along the coast at Ha'ena. Keel's ramshackle coconut plantation home is set in a grove near the former home of Alfred Hills, on the grounds of what would soon become the Coco Palms Lodge. A party scene with many Kaua'i notables in attendance was set at the old Horner mansion along Wailua Beach.

Some 300 local extras appear in an Ahukini Pier scene, with the *Hawaiian Forester* freighter dockside, the only ship scheduled that month to arrive at the tiny port. A careful look shows Eric Knudsen, Kaua'i's famed "Teller of Tales," who at the time told spooky Hawaiian stories and myths on Sunday evenings over KTOH, at the helm of the ship. Extras earned $10 a day playing Tahitians rushing around on "boat day" at the Ahukini Pier, which was redone with a line of shop fronts decked with French language signs to replicate a Tahitian waterfront scene.

Esther Williams is joined by two dozen Hawaiian swimmers in what may be the first water ballet scene ever filmed in a natural setting for a Hollywood film. And at Ha'ena, Williams frightened the crew when an outrigger canoe she was paddling "hulied" (flipped) in the surf. She swam underwater for over 30 seconds to clear the wreckage, popping up and swimming casually, well away from the canoe.

The filming went well, with producer Arthur Freed and director Alton going home with excellent footage. "The heads of the location party here have expressed their pleasure over the kokua (help) which they have received from almost every islander who has been connected with the picture, either before or behind the cameras," *The Garden Island* said in its farewell story.

Outbreak

Kaua'i doubled for tropical Zaire in Central Africa for eight days in November 1994, when Warner Bros. filmed *Outbreak*, starring Dustin Hoffman as Colonel Sam Daniels, M.D., Rene Russo as Daniels' estranged wife Robby Keough, and veteran actor Morgan Freeman as General Billy Ford.

Producer Arnold Kopelson, whose productions include *Seven*, *Platoon*, and the film version of *The Fugitive*, and director Wolfgang Petersen, director of *In the Line of Fire* and the World War II submarine film *Das Boot*, came to Kaua'i to film at Kamokila Village on the banks of the Wailua River and at the Rice Family's Kipu Ranch. Kamokila was dressed as a Zaire village infected with an Ebola-like disease named Matoba. An African mercenary camp was staged at Kipu Ranch. The mercenary location was set in 1967. During the two months of set construction and pre-production work, great care was taken to make the set look as authentic as possible. Period props included a working field medical facility and authentic mercenary Foreign Legion uniforms for actors.

Sam Daniels, an epidemiologist with the U.S. Army Medical Research Institute for Infectious Diseases, is sent to Zaire, where a plague with a 100% mortality rate is sweeping through the rural village Kaua'i doubles for. His boss, Gen. Billy Ford, ignores his pleas to investigate the disease until a rain forest monkey with the virus is smuggled into the U.S. and ends up in a rural Northern California town. The disease is more deadly than the black plague, more contagious than the common cold, and spreads rapidly through the population. The town is quarantined as Daniels and his team search for the source of the disease. Based on its own agenda, the military wants to keep the disease under cover, thus dooming the entire town. As the tension mounts, Daniels and Keough, who works for the Center for Disease Control, rush to stop Matoba's deadly spread.

An environmentalist theme runs through the film—as man depletes the rain forest, forces are unleashed that attack man.

About 100 Kaua'i people were cast as extras playing African villagers and mercenary soldiers dying of the mysterious disease. Linda Antipala served as local casting director. To assure that the local "mercenaries" looked and acted the part, they went to a three-day mini boot camp run by Dale Dye, *Outbreak's* military consultant.

Dustin Hoffman impressed the Kaua'i people on the set, who saw him as "caring, witty and impressive."

Four Kauaians acted in important roles—Douglas Hebron of Princeville played the jujuman African medicine man; Larry Hine of Pacific Missile Range played the young Donald Sutherland; Nickolas Marshall played the young Morgan Freeman; and Eric Mungai Nguku of Poipu played a nurse in the mercenary camp.

Dustin Hoffman is dressed in a bio-containment suit at Kamokila Village for an African village scene in *Outbreak.*

A Belgian mercenary bunk house circa 1967 in Zaire was constructed at Kipu Ranch for *Outbreak.*

African-American residents of Kaua'i play dying African villagers in *Outbreak* on a set built at Kamokila Village in Wailua.

Former Kaua'i legislator Billy Fernandes' Kamokila Hawaiian Village, which became an African village in Zaire for *Outbreak*.

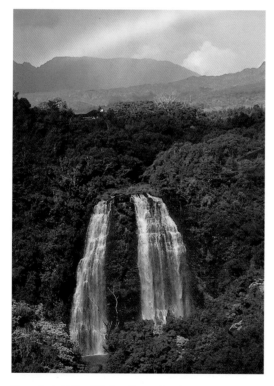

'Opaeka'a Falls at Wailua Homesteads was a backdrop for Ricky Nelson and Jack Lemmon in *Wackiest Ship in the Army*.

Director Wolfgang Petersen, Dustin Hoffman, and young Dontez Taylor of Kapa'a watch the video playback of a scene. Hoffman gave Dontez an autographed $20 bill after he cried on cue during the filming of *Outbreak*.

Beachhead

"The scenery, not the play, is the thing," a *New York Times* movie critic wrote, following the Manhattan opening of the Kaua'i-made World War II film *Beachhead* in April 1954. "Its punch stems straight from the ripe, Technicolor appraisal of the tangled, exotic Hawaiian terrain…indeed, this insidiously stunning background…supplies a perfect stage."

The film brought young rising star Tony Curtis, then married to Janet Leigh, to Kaua'i, along with veteran actor Frank Lovejoy and leading lady Mary Murphy, who later became the wife of actor Dale Robertson.

The United Artists-released drama follows the adventures of Marine reconnaissance scouts on an island in the Solomon chain. Four Marine scouts are ordered to find and deliver valuable information about Japanese mine placements vital in planning a massive landing at nearby Bougainville. They travel across Kaua'i, from swampy streams inland of Nawiliwili, to a boat on the Wailua River, through the Island's interior, and finally make their connection at Hanalei Bay. Cinematographer Gordon Avil chose to film Kaua'i as a dark and moody island.

Executive producer Aubrey Schenck focused on Kalapaki Beach at Nawiliwili, the flats on the south side of Wailua River *mauka* of the highway bridge, Keapana Stream *mauka* of Kuhio Highway at Kealia, a palm-thatched house at Coco Palms, Lydate Park, the pastures below 'Opaeka'a Falls at Wailua, and Black Pot Beach at Hanalei Pier. Unlike most films shot on location, the shooting schedule closely followed the script. The producers also reused ready-made sets built by Columbia for *Miss Sadie Thompson* at Ahukini Pier.

Curtis, who served in the Pacific aboard Navy ships during World War II, drew on his experiences during the filming of *Beachhead*. In *Tony Curtis—The Autobiography,* the handsome actor comments: "Making *Beachhead* was a very intense experience for me because it hit close to home and my own reality. It gave me my first long exposure to Hawaii, which I fell in love with…but I was relieved when the film was over."

Kaua'i filming started in early July, overseen by veteran producer Howard W. Koch. Koch vividly recalls his first sight of the Island and his first thoughts. "I was flying over Nawiliwili, in 1954, coming to film *Beachhead* when I said 'this would be a great place to film *South Pacific.*' Filming on Kauai was probably one of the best times of my life in filmmaking. The Island is so magic it just grabs you."

The crew, which frequented the Hanama'ulu Cafe for meals, spent 21 shooting days on Kaua'i, not taking much time off except for a charity softball game for Kaua'i's hospitals.

Koch and crew inadvertently ended up in a parade during the filming. "We tried to talk the Army on Oahu into loaning us a small cannon. It was essential for the film. They said 'we've got one on the hill, but you can't have it.' Finally a colonel said you can have it, but take it today and get it back to us in three days. We put it on a boat to Nawiliwili, and towing it to the set drove through a 4th of July parade, everyone thought we were part of it!"

Tony Curtis (far left) steers an outrigger canoe along the Wailua River in *Beachhead.* In the scene Curtis, a French planter, his beautiful daughter, and his compatriot Frank Lovejoy carry vital information across an island in the Solomons.

"Making Beachhead *was a very intense experience for me because it hit close to home and my own reality. It gave me my first long exposure to Hawaii, which I fell in love with…but I was relieved when the film was over."*—Tony Curtis

WAILUA

Miss Sadie Thompson

Sadie Thompson's wedding chapel still stands at Coco Palms.

Redheaded Rita Hayworth wows G.I.s with her dancing in *Miss Sadie Thompson*.

Columbia's *Miss Sadie Thompson* starring Rita Hayworth, a remake of W. Somerset Maugham's popular 1910s short story "Rain," began Kaua'i filming in May 1953. Kaua'i is set as the balmy, South Pacific island of Tusitala in American Samoa. Maugham's short story is updated to the late 1940s and loosely based on Hollywood productions of *Rain* made in 1928 and 1932.

Amazingly, the film was shot using a 3-D process. Kaua'i's skies provided the bright, clear sunshine needed for optimum 3-D effects. Stereophonic sound recording with three carefully spaced mikes provided another cutting-edge effect.

Over 100 local extras were selected by local casting director Walter Smith, Sr. of Wailua to play Samoan villagers. Honolulu TV and radio personality Robert "Lucky" Luck, who served in Samoa during World War II, was a technical advisor.

Jerry Wald, executive producer, and director Curtis Bernhardt, who worked with Fritz Lang in his native Germany in the post-World War I era, were visited during the filming by Harry Cohn, president of Columbia Pictures.

Redheaded Hayworth sings four songs, does two sultry dances, and carries the film. Jose Ferrer plays the missionary official Davidson, and Aldo Ray is Sadie's love interest—muscular, blond, American Marine Sergeant O'Hara.

The plot tells of a platoon of Marines sitting out the aftermath of World War II in American Samoa. They are smitten by Miss Sadie Thompson, a fugitive from the notorious Emerald Club of Honolulu who is stuck on their island for a week due to a ship quarantine. The "breezy dame," on the run to New Caledonia, sets the Marines afire as well as the self-righteous missionary leader Davidson, who suspects Sadie is a prostitute. Sadie is courted by brash, but kind, Aldo Ray as Sgt. Phil O'Hara, and preached at by Davidson, who tries to break up the romance. In the tragic climax of the film, Davidson, who had lusted after and attacked Sadie, kills himself. Downcast, the beautiful, but disillusioned redhead leaves the island from a set built at the Hanalei Pier.

The production required an authentic Samoan look with thatched roofs, dirt roads, groves of palm trees and South Pacific-looking waterfronts. Sets built for the film at Coco Palms included a Samoan village, a chapel and a tropical bar along a village street. The film's Horn's Hotel and a small home were constructed at Kalapaki, on the grounds of the former home of Charles Rice, now the site of the Kaua'i Marriott Resort, where the Kaua'i Fire Department provided "rain" on cue. Many of the east-side sets used eucalyptus lumber from Kipu Ranch.

Blue Hawaii

Elvis Presley made a big splash on Kaua'i during the filming of Paramount Pictures' *Blue Hawaii* in April 1961, his first film set in Hawai'i and commercially his most successful film ever. The film would set the pattern for all of Elvis' films made in the 1960s—plenty of pretty, but pure, girls; Elvis singing an album full of songs, including a Top 10 hit or two; and an exotic location. The "King" was in his prime in *Blue Hawaii*—young and fit; riding horses and paddling canoes with his girl and buddies.

Elvis arrived in mid-April at Lihu'e Airport and received a warm, *lei* greeting from Leimomi Buchanan, Miss Kaua'i of 1961. Location filming began on April 12. Elvis stayed with the production company at the Coco Palms Resort. Local teenage girls held a daily vigil outside the resort hotel. *The Garden Island* newspaper's former editor, Rita De Silva—then in high school—stuck it out with her friends long enough one day to be rewarded with a short visit by the "King."

In the film, Presley is cast as Chad Gates, an island boy who takes a job with a travel agency rather than go to work in the family plantation business.

Most of the Kaua'i location shooting took place on the long, white-sand beach at Wailua and at various sites on the South Pacific-like grounds of the Coco Palms. Other locations included Lydgate Park and the nearby Hauola Place of Refuge; along Kuamo'o Road near 'Opaeka'a Falls; and action driving scenes down Kaumuali'i Highway near Puhi and Kipu; plus scenes at Anahola Bay and Kealia Beach.

The highlight of the Kaua'i footage is the big wedding scene held in the Coco Palms lagoon, called by Grace Buscher Guslander "a traditional Hawaiian boat wedding." In the signature scene Elvis, in local-style white shirt and pants with a red sash draping down his side, floats across the lagoon atop a flower-covered platform set on two outrigger canoes.

Blue Hawaii had about a dozen pop and Hawaiian songs interlaced throughout the action. Tunes include Lili'uokalani's "Aloha Oe"; the film's namesake "Blue Hawaii," which was taken from Bing Crosby's early-1930s film *Waikiki Wedding;* the classic "Can't Help Falling in Love," and the all-around "Rock-a-Hula Blues." Elvis strums a tenor ukulele while singing the film's theme song, "Blue Hawaii."

Norman Taurog, who also directed Elvis in *G.I. Blues,* directed this picture, filming with wide-screen Technicolor stock.

Taurog arrived in late January 1961 to scout locations. The working script was titled *Waikiki Beach Boy.* The successful scouting trip to see Kaua'i locations may have resulted in the title change, as apparently more Kaua'i locations were used than originally planned.

On O'ahu, before coming to Kaua'i, Elvis played at a fundraising concert to help build a memorial over the rusting *Arizona* battleship off Ford Island in Pearl Harbor. The project was stalled at the time. Elvis and Colonel Parker donated $5,000, plus $52,000 in proceeds from the concert, to seed the construction of the white marble memorial that now floats above the sunken ship.

The grove of coconut trees at Coco Palms was planted by a German immigrant in the late 1800s.

The lagoons at Coco Palms were once the royal fishponds of Debora Kapule, Kaua'i's last queen.

Elvis' outrigger canoe wedding scene in *Blue Hawaii* is one of the most famous images in a Kaua'i-made movie.

COCO PALMS

John Kerr as Lt. Joseph Cable, Mitzi Gaynor as Nellie Forbush, and Rossano Brazzi as Emile DeBecque in *South Pacific*.

Mary Daubert holds a movie still of herself in *Blue Hawaii*. The Kaua'i native played a flower girl at Elvis' wedding in the early sixties movie.

The cast and crew lodged at the Coco Palms, a South Pacific-style resort hotel set across from the beach at Wailua in a grove of palm trees grown by a German coconut plantation planter in the late 1800s. The hotel was once an inn run by Kaua'i's last queen, Deborah Kapule.

Mitzi Gaynor enjoyed her stay there. "It was wonderful. When we arrived we'd never met such wonderfully warm and friendly people. Everybody was in muumuus. The stockings, bras and girdles, high heels, and matching gloves we had on went fast. We hit the store in Lihue (probably Lihue Store—ed.) and bought every muumuu. The Islands change you, you don't change the island. Where there was tension and nerves, they were washed away by listening to the Hawaiian music and surf. We had a couple of luaus at the Coco Palms and we stayed there for two months.

"Grace Guslander (the grand dame of the Coco Palms)—she said this came to her in a vision—saw she needed to build a house with large closets for Mrs. Brazzi and Miss Gaynor, so they could hang up their dresses from the mainland. In the house we kept hearing something little scampering around, but nothing would be there. One day there was a mouse looking at me. I said 'Aloha,' and it looked at me, and it came back with a friend. They reminded me of Tom and Jerry. Lydia (Rossano Brazzi's wife) saw them and brought them food.

"I think Kaua'i soothed a lot of our wrinkles out. You can feel it in the picture, there wasn't a lot of tension, but a lot of warm feelings. I think the particular location had a lot to do with it.

"One day we were driving home from location, and there were darling little girls standing on a fence along the highway with an attractive young woman. They lived by the Coco Palms and were there everyday. We stopped one day to talk to them and noticed they had been spectators at some of the location filming. I said 'Don't I know you?' and they became our friends. They were Dr. Fujii and his family, including Jocelyn, who became a writer. We've been friends all these years.

"We really took to Kaua'i, it became our home. Where else do you go on location and make friends you have for 30 years?"

Elvis led a group of adoring young women on a tour of Kaua'i in *Blue Hawaii*. Elvis showed off his riding skills on a trail ride up Kuamo'o Road towards Wailua Homesteads.

Flight of the Intruder

Full advantage was taken of the versatility of Kaua'i locations during the filming of Paramount Pictures' *Flight of the Intruder* in 1989. The Island doubled for the highland jungle of North Vietnam, a teeming port town in the Philippines, and a Navy base, providing executive producer Brian Frankish the perfect location for the wide ranging backdrops needed to bring to the screen the best-selling novel by Stephen Coonts.

Frankish knew Kaua'i well, having served as production manager for *King Kong,* which was filmed on location at the Honopu Arch and Kalalau Valley on the Na Pali Coast in 1976.

The film focuses on Navy fliers during the Vietnam War. One flier, frustrated by the death of his bombardier and by meaningless bombing missions, takes things into his own hands. He guides his A-6 Intruder into North Vietnam and without orders bombs a downtown Hanoi missile depot, getting himself into big trouble.

Flight of the Intruders stars Danny Glover as a strong-willed squadron leader, William Dafoe as an ace bombardier, Brad Johnson as a top-gun pilot, and Rosanna Arquette as his love interest. The director was John Milius, who has a long list of directing, producing and screenwriting credits. His work includes directing *Conan the Barbarian,* producing Steven Spielberg's film *1941,* and *Uncommon Valor* (also shot on Kaua'i). Mace Neufeld, the film's producer, started out with *The Omen* in 1976 and produced the Tom Clancy techo-war films *Hunt for Red October* in 1990 and *Clear and Present Danger* in 1994.

The Department of Defense and the U.S. Navy at the Pacific Missile Range Facility cooperated with the filmmakers by providing uniformed sailors and other personnel for the filming, and shooting locations such as the officers' beach facility and a runway used in the rescue scene.

Kaua'i filming began on October 16, 1989 at the Pacific Missile Range Facility at Barking Sands, where an A-6, low-level attack bomber sat on the beachfront runway. Three nights of dusk-to-dawn shooting followed along the main street of old Hanapepe town, with 10 days of jungle scenes in the Island's interior near the base of Wai'ale'ale Crater.

Hanapepe was converted into the bustling and colorful Philippine village of Olangapo, a town which in the early seventies was teeming with brothels and bars outside of the former Navy at Subic Bay, north of Manila.

Location manager Robert Lemer complimented the local community in *The Garden Island:* "The cooperation of the Hanapepe community the last three nights has been tremendous. Everything has gone extremely well. We couldn't have done this in Los Angeles or in any other big city, and if we did, we'd have to use cattle prods and call in riot police."

The bombing scenes just miles above Wailua Homesteads, a populated residential area, took careful logistical planning. The moving of an A-6 fuselage, daytime bombing runs, and detonation of explosives on cleared, state-owned land provided cast and crew with a challenge. The scenes came off well and the forset land was replanted following the filming.

Stars Willem Dafoe and Danny Glover took cover behind their crashed Intruder fighter jet near an area known to local residents as "Blue Hole."

This fiery crash scene in the island's interior made for great footage in *Flight of the Intruder.*

Initially the producers were torn between Mexico, the Philippines, and Puerto Rico for locations. But Kaua'i had it all. "The set is there, that's why we've come," Frankish told Kaua'i's news media.

The *Flight of the Intruder's* film crew prepares for close-ups of the A-6 cockpit.

A-6 Intruder aircraft flies a raid over mauka Wailua for *Flight of the Intruder.*

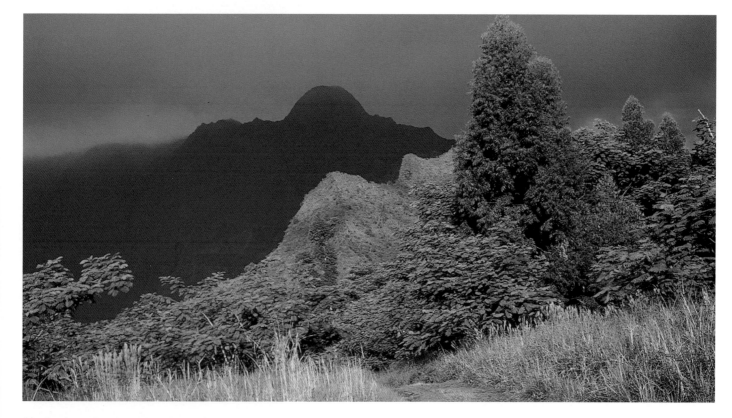

Grasslands and forests mauka (inland) of Wailua provided the perfect scenery for *Flight of the Intruder,* a wartime film set in North Vietnam. Trees are rapidly growing back at the location, covering the once-cleared field where a fighter jet crash scene was filmed.

Jurassic Park

In choosing to film *Jurassic Park,* director Steven Spielberg started with a good story, thanks to novelist Michael Crichton. But it was Spielberg's decision to use cutting edge special effects and Kaua'i as a backdrop that made *Jurassic Park* convincing on screen. Crichton, renowned for his intriguing, and believable, scientific hypotheses as central themes for his fiction, reportedly wrote parts of *Jurassic Park* during a sojourn on Kaua'i.

Jurassic Park is a story about a group of scientists trapped in a real live dinosaur theme park on the fictional Isla Nublar, a tropical island supposedly set off the coast of Costa Rica.

To shoot *Jurassic Park,* Spielberg's cast and crew arrived on Kaua'i in late August 1992 for three weeks of location filming. On August 24, the 140-member team gathered at Olokele Canyon, deep in the dirt-red and emerald-green interior wilderness of the Island's west side. With over two years of pre-production work behind him, Spielberg was ready to go.

The gates to Jurassic Park were built along a plantation road deep in the island's interior near the base of Mt. Wai'ale'ale.

Cinematographer Dean Cundey captured Kaua'i's beauty on film, inspired by Spielberg's vision for the look of *Jurassic Park*. His challenge was to blend sound stage footage to be filmed in Los Angeles with footage of Kaua'i's majestic vistas, and to shoot scenes that would perfectly merge with the digital and mechanical dinosaurs concurrently being created in Northern California by George Lucas' special effects wizards at Industrial Light and Magic and by Stan Winston's team of model makers in Los Angeles.

In *The Making of Jurassic Park,* Cundey comments, "Most of the storyboards illustrated a film that was pretty confined in its images...You can only see so far beyond the trees in a jungle. So one of the reasons for going to Kauai was to reveal this island where the story takes place. We wanted to get larger background behind some of the action—in the daytime, particularly—and Kauai had wonderful locations to show off." Lead actors Sam Neill, Richard Attenborough, Laura Dern, and Jeff Goldblum joined Spielberg and producers Kathleen Kennedy and Gerald R. Molen on location. The actors had been chosen only weeks before location filming began.

Looming ahead of Spielberg and his troupe was a tightly scheduled string of key location shoots. The list included the daytime arrival of scientists sent to check out the dinosaur park; the dangerous raptor pen; the electrical shed where Ellie tries to reboot the park's power system; the towering trees where the scientists first see the reborn dinosaurs; the plain where a herd of gallimimus hurdle over logs; the ailing triceratops and pile of dino dung; the finely crafted visitor center; a heliport at the foot of a cascading waterfall; and an oceanfront Costa Rican café.

Work on sets began on Kaua'i in June under the direction of production designer Rick Carter. The main task for Carter's crew was to construct buildings and structures within Jurassic Park. Foremost was the almost 200-foot-long visitor center facade, erected within the grounds of Valley House, a tropical estate in Kealia Valley on windward Kaua'i. Another challenge was the long lengths of 24-foot-tall high voltage electrical fences that served to isolate the most ferocious of Jurassic Park's dinosaurs. By design the sets were spread across

These gates on a plantation road inland of Wailua Homestead stand near where the gates of *Jurassic Park* once stood.

the Island, including extremely remote locations with only four-wheel drive access. Some of the roughest roads were improved by the film company at a cost of over $100,000.

Carter was very favorably moved by the Kaua'i locales as he noted in *The Making of Jurassic Park* book: "There is a sense you get in some movies that you've really traveled somewhere and *Jurassic Park* has that, largely because of Kauai and the power of its imagery and diversity. There is a very romantic quality about the island, but it is not all benign. There are areas which are some of the most beautiful pasture land in the world; other areas are more mountainous, with rougher terrain. For *Jurassic Park*, we took everything Kaua'i had to offer and jam-packed it into our own little island."

Spielberg and his staff relied on Kaua'i's residents in making *Jurassic Park* a spectacularly successful film. Extras cast on the island played Costa Ricans, dino-hands around the raptor cage, park workers, and other roles. However, the movie was so set-intensive that the real stars included the carpenters, the myriad of suppliers, road pavers, helicopter pilots and even the crew of linemen expert at stretching high power lines in Kaua'i's interior. They, among dozens of other skilled workers, provided vital support services.

On September 10 Spielberg was on schedule to complete the three-week location filming. But the elements, true to *Jurassic Park*'s theme of nature overtaking the best laid plans of mere mortals, brought filming to an abrupt halt. The only scene remaining was to be set in a pasture in Kilauea with Neill, Dern and the children running from invisible gallimimus. The hurdling dinosaurs would be added to the footage later inside a Silicon Graphics computer. However, all day long humid equatorial air enveloped Kaua'i, a portent of the arrival of a hurricane. The morning of September 11, the last scheduled day of filming, found Spielberg with his cast and crew seeking shelter inside their Kaua'i home, the beachfront Westin Kaua'i, currently the Kaua'i Marriott Resort. By mid-day Hurricane Iniki was pummeling Kaua'i with sustained winds near 175 m.p.h. A quick glimpse of the fury is visible in *Jurassic Park* when Hammond and his workers, looking at the computer monitor, see huge waves splashing over a breakwater, stirred up by the tropical storm off Costa Rica that knocks out the park's power. The breakwater is actually located at the entrance to Nawiliwili Harbor.

The day after Iniki, Kathleen Kennedy managed to fly to Honolulu aboard a military helicopter and, amazingly, was aided once she arrived in Honolulu by the pilot Spielberg employed to rescue Indiana Jones in *Raiders of the Lost Ark*, filmed on Kaua'i over a decade earlier. Once all hands were safely back in California preparing to work in the controlled world of a sound stage, a second unit company returned to film the gallimimus scene at Kualoa Ranch near Chinaman's Hat on windward O'ahu. Interestingly, while *Jurassic Park* has brought Kaua'i international exposure, the film's Central American setting was so well replicated by carefully weaving the story with the Island's scenery that Kaua'i has retained its singular beauty and hasn't become stereotyped in the least by its connection to Hollywood's biggest blockbuster of all time.

KAPA'A TOWN

Jurassic Park, Throw Momma from the Train

In *Jurassic Park*, the rambling, old wooden-walled Otsuka warehouse along the beachfront north of Kapa'a town provided a perfect location for Ramona's Costa Rican coastal café. Pre-production work drew curious glances for days prior to filming, especially after Kaua'i artist Carol Bennett painted the landmark Ramona's sign on a back wall of the building. Buxom, white blouse-garbed Ramona looked like she came straight off the label of a salsa jar. The café scene, perhaps more than any other in the film, captures the flavor of Central America, with its thatch-roofed tables and Latino extras. It is here that traitorous Dennis Nedry (Wayne Knight), the fat nerd computer programmer, holds a clandestine meeting and secures a deal to smuggle dinosaur embryos out of Jurassic Park in false-bottomed shaving cream cans. A Filipino jeepney, imported to Kaua'i in the early 1980s from the Philippines, served well as a wildly decorated Costa Rican taxi; today the vehicle is on view at Nawiliwili at a parrot shop adjacent to the Kaua'i Marriott Resort. The Otsuka warehouse, part of an appliance and home furnishing establishment that dates back several generations on Kaua'i, made its swan song in *Jurassic Park*. Along with dozens of other historic structures, the dark-green, plantation-style building collapsed under the force of high winds during Hurricane Iniki just days after its starring role before Steven Spielberg's movie cameras. Today a modern, pastel-colored concrete building is Otsuka's new home.

Ramona's open-air café was set up along the side wall of Otsuka's old warehouse in Kapa'a, which is no longer there. Here Nedry (below) makes a deal to sell dinosaur embryos to a competitor of Jurassic Park.

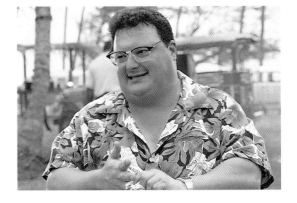

Dennis Nedry plots to steal dinosaur embroys on location at Kapa'a.

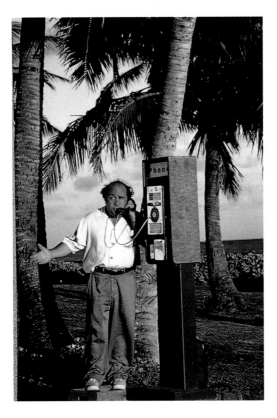

Moviemakers like to place unique telephone booths in Kaua'i-made movies. Here, along the coast near Wailua, Danny De Vito, perched on a soda box, tried to set up a murder in *Throw Momma From the Train.* Waimea was the actual location of the phone booth where Nicolas Cage spurted out "Kapa...a...ah...ah...a" in *Honeymoon in Vegas.*

Frank Sinatra sits in a director's chair at the beach where he almost drowned at Wailua in 1965. Notice the airbrushed halo around his head made by Honolulu Star-Bulletin artists to highlight the star's face.

Frank Sinatra (left), Nancy Sinatra (third from left) and her husband Tommy Sands arrive at Lihu'e Airport for filming of *None But the Brave*. They are greeted by Laola Ohai, Bernadette Bettencourt, Ku'ulei Punua and Esther Fong.

Singer and actor Frank Sinatra saw his life turn around, and almost lost his life, during two Kaua'i visits. The first one, in the early 1950s, saw him filled with the *aloha* of Kaua'i's people, which enabled him to overcome a low point in his life. The second visit, in 1964, almost ended in tragedy when Sinatra came within moments of drowning on an unusually rough day of surf at Wailua Beach.

Frank Sinatra marked a major turning point in his career on Kaua'i, according to the late Honolulu journalist Buck Buchwach, during a series of concerts in 1952. Buchwach was a personal friend of Sinatra's. At the time, the singer's marriage to Ava Gardner was falling apart and his singing career was at a standstill. Sinatra flew to Kaua'i to perform at the Kaua'i County Fair, feeling low. The warm *aloha* of the Kaua'i audience inspired Sinatra, Buchwach said, pulling him out of the doldrums and giving him the spark he needed to get his career on the upswing.

Sinatra was on Kaua'i in 1964 to direct and star in the film *None But the Brave*. With him was long-time pal Jilly, producer Howard W. Koch and his wife Ruth Koch, and some of the cast. They were relaxing on a Sunday afternoon in the singer's beach house across Kuhio Highway from the Coco Palms Hotel. Ruth Koch, failing to heed her husband's warning not to go in the high surf, announced that she wanted to go for a swim. Sinatra, a good swimmer, joined her, to protect her from the undertow. The two were in shallow water when a big, tradewind-generated swell swept Ruth offshore about 75 yards, and Sinatra went out after her. A second wave drove her back close to shore, but pulled Sinatra out about 200 yards. Ruth yelled to the people inside the house for help and actor Brad Dexter swam out to help. He went to Ruth first who said, "I'm holding my own. Go to Frank. He's drowning."

Sinatra was in the water for about 20 minutes. "In another five minutes he would have been gone," said Fire Lieutenant George Keawe, who took part in the rescue. "His face was starting to turn blue.'"

A neighbor, A. O. Giles, paddled out on a surfboard, and county supervisor Louis Gonsalves and Harold Jim, an assistant manager at the Coco Palms, rushed from the Coco Palms and swam out to Sinatra from Wailua Beach. Meanwhile, an ambulance from Wilcox Hospital and the Kapa'a Fire Station rescue team rushed to the scene. Gonsalves slid Sinatra on Giles' surfboard, and a fireman rescued Mrs. Koch. With Sinatra on the board, high surf kept Giles and Gonsalves from getting him to shore. Keawe threw a rope to the rescuers, who made it to about 50 feet from shore, and finally got Sinatra on the beach. He was placed on a stretcher and carried to the house. A doctor checked him over and said he was exhausted but otherwise okay. After the ordeal, his daughter Nancy made him eggs and peppers and the two watched TV until he fell asleep. Meanwhile, producer Koch and his party worked off the stress of the situation by drinking "until we didn't know where we were." Koch took over directing duties the next day, while Sinatra rested, and on Tuesday Sinatra was on the set at Pila'a back to full strength.

VALLEY HOUSE

Jurassic Park, Voodoo Island, Island of the Alive

Action central for *Jurassic Park* location filming was the 125-year-old Valley House plantation estate, inland a few miles from the coast at Kealia. Built by late 1800s sugar baron Colonel Zephaniah Spalding, Valley House is worthy of its own movie. Planted with aromatic camphor trees from China and rough-skinned lychee trees, the estate has been a race horse stable, a resort, military headquarters during World War II, a speakeasy, a dance hall, and brothel.

Boris Karloff cavorted with vampires here in the late fifties in *Voodoo Island,* and killer babies attacked their hunters in *Island of the Alive* in the 1980s.

Today, the estate has been restored to its past grandeur and is managed by Bill Budd and his dog Boo, one of the few real critters in *Jurassic Park.* Spielberg's set designers stated that the entire location filming could have been done at Valley House and its grounds, if the director so wished.

Their statement wasn't an exaggeration. With waterfalls, a stately home, acres of grounds, the backdrop of Wai'ale'ale and easy access to the Island's main road, the set was a welcome site for crew members who had earlier blazed their own trails into the Kaua'i wilderness. The massive visitor center facade, over 60 feet high and 200 feet long, with 10,000 square feet of floor space, was one of the largest set pieces ever constructed outside of Los Angeles. The construction crew worked for three months to create it. All exterior footage at the visitor center was filmed at Valley House, while interior scenes were set on sound stages in Los Angeles.

Production designers chose a field at Valley House for the scene featuring the sick triceratops, the only dinosaur model actually brought to Kaua'i for location filming. To further mask crossing over into the digital world for most of his dinosaurs, director Spielberg wisely decided to film one scene with a realistic-looking, handmade model shot in full daylight. The model was brought to Kaua'i to help make the illusion of the film's many computerized dinosaurs more believable. The big, rubbery model was animated like a huge puppet, controlled by technicians hidden underneath the dinosaur model in a 12-foot-deep pit. For the curious, the pile of dinosaur dung that archaeologists-turned-biologists Ellie and Grant go through was made from a rotten-smelling mixture of alfalfa and molasses. In yet another amazing transformation of the Valley House location, the crew built the South American mine set for the scene where the Jurassic-era, amber-encased insects are extracted from the ground.

A highly detailed, working model of a triceratops was the only dinosaur figure brought from California for *Jurassic Park* location filming. Steven Spielberg and Laura Dern discuss the live-action figure.

One of Valley House's waterfalls served as a backdrop for former Tarzan Lex Barker's 1950s film *Jungle Heat.*

The visitor center was the key set on Kaua'i for Steven Spielberg's dinosaur park film *Jurassic Park* and one of the largest sets ever built for a Hollywood film outside of Los Angeles.

Royal palms frame the location where the huge visitor center set was built at historic Valley House for *Jurassic Park*.

The Costa Rican mine where insects embedded in amber were collected to create modern-day dinosaurs in *Jurassic Park* was filmed at this waterfall at Valley House.

ANAHOLA / PAPA'A

Raiders of the Lost Ark, North

Paramount's mountain-top logo dissolves into Anahola's Kalalea Mountains for the opening image in *Raiders of the Lost Ark*. Some call the distinctive, King Kong-looking peak Amu, a place name perhaps associated with Kaua'i's ancient links to the Marquesas Islands of the South Pacific. The legendary "hole-in-the-mountain" can be seen to the right of the peak; the hole partially collapsed in the 1980s.

Two views of isolated Papa'a Bay, location for Hawaiian scenes in director Rob Reiner's film *North*.

A detailed Hawaiian Governor's mansion was erected at Papa'a Bay for *North*. The main character of the movie arrived at the bay aboard a double-hulled canoe.

Rob Reiner, shown here directing a scene at Papa'a Bay, is the son of comedy writer and comedian Carl Reiner. He first made his mark as a director with the heavy metal rock parody film *This Is Spinal Tap*.

NORTH SHORE

Traditionally known as Halelea, the "House of Rainbows," the North Shore begins at the former sugar plantation town of Kilauea and literally ends at Keʻe Beach in Haʻena. Between the two points lie beautiful valleys planted in taro (the staff of life for ancient Hawaiians), picturesque white-sand beaches, dramatic seascapes and landscapes, towering waterfalls, and ever-changing mountains capped by mysterious clouds. Hawaiian roots run deep in the valleys in and around Hanalei, Lumahaʻi, and Wainiha.

Princeville, a 12,000-acre resort on a plateau above Hanalei, was created in the 1860s by Scotsman Robert Crichton Wyllie, then the Foreign Minister of the Hawaiian Kingdom, Wyllie named his estate after young Prince Albert, the son of Kamehameha IV and Queen Emma.

Director Joshua Logan and his *South Pacific* colleagues from Broadway had an easy decision in choosing the North Shore as the main location for the film version of the play. The area was ideal, with Haʻena's Mount Makana serving as a double for *South Pacific* author James Michener's Bali Hai. The Birkmyre Estate at Princeville, that once overlooked the mouth of the Hanalei River, served as the French planter's home. The house and the low-rise hotel that replaced it in the early 1960s are now gone, and the site lies overgrown and abandoned.

The verdant taro fields of Hanalei Valley, the largest taro patch in all Hawaiʻi, became Vietnamese ride paddies in *Uncommon Valor*, starring Gene Hackman. Nearby Lumahai Valley became a Laotian P.O.W. campsite along the valley's river for Hackman and crew. Danny DeVito soaked his feet in the shallows of Keʻe Beach in *Throw Momma From the Train*, just a spear throw away from where the wild boys of *Lord of the Flies* gathered around a fire.

Steven Spielberg chose misty Limahuli Valley for the dinosaur cage scene in *Jurassic Park*, and Kathleen Turner, the murderess in *Body Heat*, appears in the film's last scene sunning herself at Makua Beach near Haʻena Beach Park.

Elegant country homes dot the North Shore, providing excellent interior settings to accompany the action filmed outdoors. An Anini Beach home is featured in *Honeymoon in Vegas* as the gambler Tommy Corman's resort home, and the Wilcox home near Hanalei Pier appears in *Miss Sadie Thompson* as an island mansion.

Historic Hanalei Pier at Hanalei Pier.

Gilligan's Island

Larsen's Beach near Moloa‘a.

B ob Denver, Gilligan of *Gilligan's Island,* reminisces in his 1993 autobiography *Gilligan, Maynard & Me* over the Kaua‘i location filming for *Gilligan's Travels,* the pilot film that sold the popular mid-sixties TV series to CBS. Denver and his family stayed at Lyle Guslander's Hanalei Plantation Hotel, which then overlooked the Hanalei River, in November 1963. The hotel was built on the site of the Birkmyre Estate, the Princeville home featured in *South Pacific,* and was designed by *South Pacific*'s art directors.

Denver recalls staying at the Coco Palms, then driving out to Moloa‘a Bay the next morning. Quickly, he says, he fell in love with Kaua‘i. He wrote, "That might sound weird, but I felt I'd come home. We wound our way down a single-lane road through a jungle. The warm trade winds were blowing, hundreds of birds were singing in the trees, and then we were at the bay. Huge breakers were pounding the beach. We all stood there for a while, just absorbing the scene; then some of us took off our clothes and went in the ocean. As I floated around, looking at the shoreline, I thought, this really can't be happening. I am one lucky dude."

In a 30-minute pilot film, seven castaways land on a tropical island, with the action focused on their struggles with each other and the elements.

Cast and crew spent two weeks filming at a remote Moloa‘a beach, with Denver traveling from Hanalei each day. The Kaua‘i Fire Department supplied rain from their pumpers and the right man for a key stunt. County fireman Damien Victorino doubled as Gilligan for a coconut tree-climbing scene, but his arms were getting cut from his slipping and sliding down the tree wearing Denver's white Top Siders. To solve the problem the crew painted Damien's feet white.

Denver brought his family along, and they were soon all embraced by local people. His four-year-old son Patrick was invited to a local *lua'u* by Hawaiians who worked at the hotel. Denver wrote: "I was just getting to know the Hawaiian people and knew I could trust them. When my son came back, he wasn't even a little sunburned."

The Kaua‘i location work, from which most of the pilot's footage was taken, ran through the third week of November 1963, the same week as the assassination of President Kennedy. In a way, Denver and the production team were really on *Gilligan's Island* that week. Without television in then-remote Hanalei, news of the tragedy reached them slowly, and the cast longed to be back in Los Angeles during that mournful time.

The famous *S. S. Minnow* charter boat of *Gilligan's Island* was bought at a boatyard in Honolulu. The film crew smashed a hole in its hull and shipped the boat to Moloa‘a. After filming wrapped on Kaua‘i, the *Minnow* was loaded aboard a cargo ship and sent to the mainland, to be trailered out to a back lot in Los Angeles for reuse in the *Gilligan's Island* series.

After filming opening scenes for the pilot in Honolulu, Denver flew back to Kaua‘i for a two-week vacation. In the early 1980s rumors spread that Denver was living in a home in Wainiha; some say he was spotted in disguise during shopping trips to Hanalei.

"Kauai was dark when we arrived. The air smelled so good. We stayed that night at the Coco Palms.... The next day we drove for about thirty minutes to the location, and I fell in love with the island. That might sound weird, but I felt I'd come home."
—**Bob Denver**

Gilligan, the Skipper and crew wake up at a beach on Moloaʻa Bay that mimicked a deserted island, after being blown off course in a storm during a day trip out of a harbor in Honolulu.

Moloaʻa Bay, the location of the pilot for *Gilligan's Island,* filmed in 1963.

The Castaway Cowboy

A mixture of *paniolo* (Hawaiian cowboy) fact and fancy colors the Walt Disney Studios' production *The Castaway Cowboy*, a G-rated, mid-seventies Disney film about a shanghaied Texas cowhand who washes ashore unconscious in the 1860s on a rural Kaua'i beach.

Originally titled *Paniolo, The Castaway Cowboy* stars James Garner, who played western marshal Maverick on TV, as Costain and veteran actress Vera Miles as Henrietta MacAvoy. Feature roles were played by Samoan actor Manu Tupou as Kimo and singer Nephi Hannemann as Malakoma.

Costain is rescued by a widowed potato farmer and her son. To help the family survive, he trains local farmhands to be cowboys and foils the efforts of villain Robert Culp, who wants to marry the widow and take her land.

The family's ranch house and barn were built down a private dirt road on a red-soil bluff at remote Pila'a, about five miles north of Anahola. The land-owners of the site agreed to allow the filming if the buildings were left intact following the shooting; they had hopes of creating a visitor attraction there, but nothing apparently came of the plan.

A beachfront set at Mahaulepu shows how, in the pre-dock days of the 1800s, cattle were shipped off-island by swimming them out, or floating them on wood rafts, to steamers. A huge, white Brahma bull is featured in the film as one of the animals transported offshore.

Maile Semitekol, then Executive Director of the Hawaii Visitors Bureau-Kaua'i Chapter, handled many of the arrangements for the filming. She and United Church of Christ minister William Ka'ina joined Garner at a blessing of the Pila'a set.

Sarah Myles and castaway cowboy James Garner, discuss ranch business on a bluff at Pila'a.

In *The Castaway Cowboy,* Disney Studios attempted to re-create the *paniolo* (cowboy) era of Kaua'i in the mid to late 1800s. Here, above Pila'a Beach, a *paniolo* tries to break a horse.

A cove at Pila'a used as a backdrop for James Garner's *Castaway Cowboy* in 1974.

PILA'A

None But the Brave

Pila'a Beach, the remote location of Frank Sinatra's *None But the Brave*.

None But the Brave is an anti-war story that deals with a group of Americans and a group of Japanese stranded together on a Pacific island during the war. I have tried to show that when men do not have to fight there is a community of interests."
—Frank Sinatra

Olympic athlete-turned actor Rafer Johnson attempts to cut free a boat to escape from a Japanese-held island in *None But the Brave*.

Frank Sinatra, a man of many talents, returned to Kaua'i in April 1964 to direct and act in *None But the Brave,* an anti-war film set on an uncharted island near Bougainville in the Solomons in 1943. Sinatra performed at the Kaua'i County Fair in the early fifties and this time received a royal welcome from his hosts at the Coco Palms resort hotel.

Howard W. Koch, who had filmed Tony Curtis in *Beachhead* in 1953, returned to work with Sinatra as the film's producer. Koch and Sinatra traveled to Japan together to secure Toho Studios' financial and acting support for the film. Koch said he and Sinatra were somewhat befuddled in negotiating with the Japanese studio, but all worked out well. The Japanese studio promised to send actors to Kaua'i, while Koch and Sinatra offered support from Hollywood in enhancing the film studio in Japan.

Sinatra describes the theme behind *None But the Brave* in his daughter Nancy's book, *Sinatra—My Father*: "*None But the Brave* is an anti-war story that deals with a group of Americans and a group of Japanese stranded together on a Pacific island during the war. I have tried to show that when men do not have to fight there is a community of interests."

The plot of the film revolves around a plane-load of American Marine fliers and Navy men who crash-land on an isolated island held by Japanese soldiers. Both the Americans and Japanese are stranded on this tiny Pacific island and are forced to make a temporary truce and cooperate to survive. The story is told through the eyes of the American and Japanese unit commanders, who are faced with quarrels within their own ranks, as well as battles with their enemy. The Japanese and Americans begin trading food and medical services and become friends, until an American radioman fixes his transmitter and begins sending out calls for help. This sends both sides into an all-out bloodbath, wiping away the simple peace.

None But the Brave, made two decades after the end of World War II, is the first American war film sympathetic to Japanese servicemen. The marooned Japanese soldiers speak their native language throughout the film, with English subtitles displayed during their scenes.

The filming marked Sinatra's debut as a film director. Artanis (Sinatra spelled backwards), Sinatra's production company, filmed the movie in Technicolor and Panavision. The film was released by Warner Bros. Japan's Toho Studios co-financed the picture. The screenplay was a Japanese-American collaboration written by John Twist and Katsuya Susaki.

The popular singer told *Honolulu Star-Bulletin* reporter Joe Arakaki that he chose Kaua'i to film *None But the Brave* because of the Island's broad stretch of beaches. "Just what we were looking for," Sinatra commented, "it's a very lovely island."

For the main set of the film, Koch and Sinatra decided upon a beach at Pila'a then known as Huddy's Beach. Sinatra, who commuted daily to the set from Coco Palms, was flown by Jack Harter of Kaua'i Helicopters. Harter's company is now known as Jack Harter Helicopters.

A surplus C-47-B plane was bought in Honolulu for $17,500 to be used as the wrecked plane that crash-lands on the beach at Pila'a. The plane was shipped on a barge to Nawiliwili and trucked with plantation equipment to remote Pila'a. There, the plane was sawed up to simulate a crash scene, and thick vegetation was planted around it. The Federal Aviation Administration at Lihu'e Airport assisted Sinatra and crew by advising pilots flying over Kaua'i that the plane crash wasn't a real one.

A cast and crew of about 100 stayed in 61 rooms at the Coco Palms, with Sinatra and entourage staying at a spacious home on Wailua Beach, just north of the beach fronting the Coco Palms. Lyle and Grace Guslander, operators of the Coco Palms, had the home painted a shade of orange, Sinatra's favorite color, and the vacation retreat was known as the "Sinatra House."

David Penhallow, the drama teacher at Kaua'i High School in 1965, brought his students to the set at Pila'a and was rewarded with funds from Sinatra for a drama prize to be awarded to star students.

Sinatra plays Chief Pharmacist Mate Francis Maloney; Clint Walker is Capt. Dennis Bourke, pilot of the crashed plane; and Olympian Rafer Johnson is a Marine private.

Wave-smoothed basalt boulders line Pila'a Beach.

Basalt boulders served as the backdrop for Clint Walker, Frank Sinatra and Tommy Sands in *None But the Brave.*

Idyllic Pila'a Beach.

KILAUEA

Jurassic Park, South Pacfic

Because Hurricane Iniki cut short shooting of *Jurassic Park* by one day, a still photograph of this reservoir located on the Mary Lucas Estate *mauka* of Kilauea town was transformed through computer graphics into a lake with rippling water where Brontosaurus came to drink. At this location, Laura Dern and Sam Neill (left) caught their first sight of a modern-day dinosaur at Jurassic Park. They spotted the towering leaf-eating dinosaur through this row of eucalyptus trees (below) that somewhat resemble dinosaur legs.

The mountainous backdrops and wide grassy plains of the *mauka* (towards the mountains) ranges bordering Kilauea, a former plantation town along Kuhio Highway on the way to Hanalei, offer prehistoric-looking backdrops ideal for daytime scenes in *Jurassic Park*.

The row of trees where the towering dinosaurs nibble on the topmost branches and first amaze Grant, Malcolm, Ellie, and developer Hammond's other guests, is located inland of Kilauea on the Mary Lucas Estate, which is inaccessible to the public.

The movement of the treetops as the dinosaurs munch on them was rigged with ropes to create actual movement to compliment the computer-rendered dinosaur images. The reflecting pond that glimmers in the sunlight in *Jurassic Park* is here, too, or at least its image is here. In the movie, the pond is actually a still frame digitally enhanced because the scene was to be shot the day Hurricane Iniki struck Kaua'i.

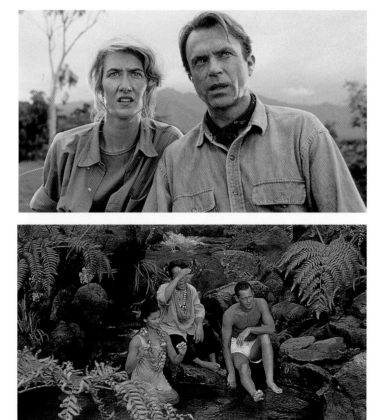

Bloody Mary talked with Liat and Lt. Cable at this man-made "slippery slide" on the Kilauea River in *South Pacific*. The slide, still there, is on private property and inaccessible today.

KALIHIWAI / ANINI BEACH

Throw Momma from the Train

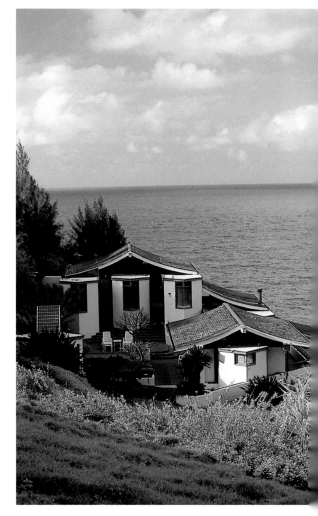

The Falling Waters estate at Kalihiwai, used in *Throw Momma from the Train*.

Comedians Danny DeVito and Billy Crystal tour Kauaʻi in Orion Pictures' 1987 production of *Throw Momma from the Train*. The location filming site, originally slated for Oʻahu, was changed to Kauaʻi by DeVito upon the advice of Hawaiʻi-based location coordinator Stephanie Spangler. Spangler told DeVito that Kauaʻi's lush beauty was the perfect location for the tropical Hawaiian getaway called for in the script.

DeVito is Owen Lift, a would-be mystery writer from Los Angeles who is dominated by his very mean mother. Larry Donner (Billy Crystal), his writing teacher, is a college instructor and writer who had his most recent unpublished novel ripped off by his estranged wife. His stolen words have become a best-seller. Larry advises dimwitted Owen to study Hitchcock films to better his mystery writing. Owen assumes Larry wants him to kill the estranged wife in exchange for doing away with his mother.

The plot moves the characters from Los Angeles to Kauaʻi, as Owen tracks Larry's wife to murder her on remote Kauaʻi, and the chase is on.

Rookie director DeVito takes the action to Keʻe Beach, the Falling Waters estate at Kalihiwai, where DeVito spies Larry's wife embracing a gardener, and to the docks at Nawiliwili Harbor, plus a number of stops for DeVito to make phone calls at a variety of odd-ball phone booths. Producer Larry Brezner said he found the 15 Kauaʻi locations used "perfect" for the film in an interview with *The Garden Island*.

A key scene in the film features DeVito standing knee-deep in the crystal-clear waters at Keʻe Beach; he's garbed in a bathrobe with a majestic backdrop of Na Pali. Meanwhile, Crystal mugs it up on a beach chair, doing a Kathleen Turner *Body Heat* parody.

During the filming, DeVito, his wife TV comedian Rita Perlman, and the couple's family stayed at the Haʻena beach house of Danny Serafin, the former drummer for the band Chicago.

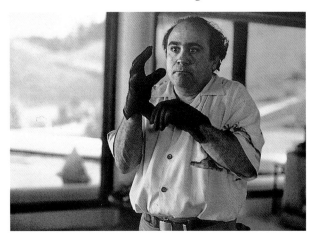

Danny DeVito gets ready to murder Billy Crystal's wife in *Throw Momma from the Train*.

KALIHIWAI / ANINI BEACH

Honeymoon in Vegas

James Caan as Tommy and Sarah Jessica Parker as Betsy embrace along the beachfront at Anini in *Honeymoon in Vegas*.

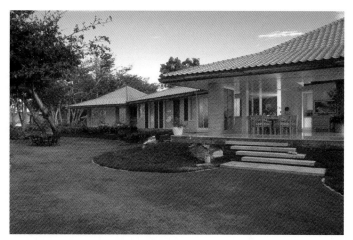

This gorgeous home at Anini Beach was featured as gambler Tommy Corman's Kaua'i vacation house in *Honeymoon in Vegas*.

An iwa bird view of Anini Beach.

South Pacific

Word that Kaua'i was to be the main location for the hit musical *South Pacific* arrived as a short item on the front page of *The Garden Island* in early 1957. It read: "Oscar Hammerstein II said in Honolulu Monday that he especially liked Kauai as the locale for the film version of the James Michener story."

The choice of Kaua'i as the principal location was soon secured, and 20th Century Fox, the Hollywood studio that purchased the rights to the Pulitzer Prize-winning stage play, named Buddy Alder as producer and Joshua Logan as director. Logan was co-author, co-producer and director of the stage musical; he is also known for his film versions of the musicals *Camelot, Picnic,* and *Bus Stop*.

Logan, then wrapping up a film version of Michener's book *Sayonara*, was looking ahead to the hurdles of capturing *South Pacific* on film. He told reporters: "Our main problem is to find an island with twin volcano peaks to portray Bali Hai. I'm not sure whether one exists or whether Michener made it up."

Logan scouted Kaua'i and returned enthralled. "Kauai is a place that will enchant movie audiences, giving reality instead of a stage illusion," he later commented in *Parade* magazine.

Considered a sure box-office blockbuster, the film musical was based on the Rodgers and Hammerstein adaptation of Michener's popular late-1940s book *Tales of the South Pacific*. On Broadway, the stage version of *South Pacific,* starring Mary Martin and Ezio Pinza, played 1,925 performances at the Majestic Theater from 1949 through 1954. Over 20 million people had already seen the stage show, with 32 companies touring in Europe alone.

The importance of the film to 20th Century Fox was underscored by the studio's unheard of $5 million budget for a musical, plus a $1 million budget for publicity.

The location company heading for Kaua'i from Hollywood numbered 185, the largest company ever brought to Hawai'i and probably, at the time, the largest ever sent out by a Hollywood studio.

The weight of the film's success rested on the shoulders of cheery Mitzi Gaynor. As was standard in the 1940s and 1950s, lead actors in Broadway plays adapted for the screen were replaced for the film versions.

In the months prior to casting of the film earlier in 1957, it was assumed that Mary Martin would play Nellie Forbush, the lead female role. But Martin backed out, saying she felt uneasy in front of cameras.

This left casting for the part wide open. "Every actress you can think of," said director Logan in an interview in *Parade* magazine, "and many you can't, campaigned strenuously for the part." But, explained Logan, "Mitzi has that inner quality of goodness, that inexplicable magic of making the audience fall in love with her...she is completely without malice or cunning or female wiles."

Gaynor was the only actress screen-tested for the role. During the filming the Michigan-born actress commented, "In my whole life I've never wanted anything so bad as I've wanted this part..."

Lei-shaped Hanalei Bay. Lumaha'i Beach is in the far left foreground, and Princeville Resort sits on the plateau in the background.

Mitzi Gaynor in a *South Pacific* sailor's costume during a *Life* magazine photo shoot.

Producer Howard W. Koch, a young Steven Ching, and actor Tony Curtis taking it easy at Hanalei's Ching Young Store circa 1953. Koch and Curtis were on Kaua'i to film *Beachhead.*

Sweeping vistas of Hanalei Bay in the movie *South Pacific* were filmed from a plateau at Princeville overlooking the mouth of the Hanalei River.

The ruins of a failed condominium project peek through the jungle at the former Hanalei Plantation Hotel site used as the French planter's home in *South Pacific*.

Gaynor was first approached about playing Nellie at a gathering held at Logan's East Side apartment in Manhattan. She then sang for Rodgers and Hammerstein and took one of the most expensive and secretive screen tests in Hollywood's history. The screen test cost $135,000 and was shot in color and Cinemascope, with live background music provided by a 40-piece orchestra led by Alfred Newman. She would be their only candidate.

Mitzi Gaynor was joined by the romantic Italian film star Rossano Brazzi as Emile DeBecque, the wealthy French planter and male lead in *South Pacific*. Brazzi made his mark in Hollywood in *Summertime* with Katherine Hepburn and *Three Coins in the Fountain*. He would return to Kaua'i in the mid-eighties to recall his days filming the musical for a commercial production shot at the *South Pacific* location at Princeville, to sell planned condominiums, but never completed.

The cast and crew met in Hollywood in mid-June to record music and rehearse. Logan decided to prerecord the film's music then and play it through loudspeakers on the location sets for the actors to lip-sync to—another location first. Many of *South Pacific*'s songs are American classics, including "Some Enchanted Evening" and "Wash That Man Right Out of My Hair."

Problems foreshadowed the arrival of the film crew, most importantly a tsunami that struck in March 1957 and swept away the old bridge on the coast at Kalihiwai, the only link for trucking heavy filming equipment to key sets at Hanalei and Ha'ena.

Filming began in August 1957. Four oversized Todd AO cameras weighing 200 pounds each were shipped to Kaua'i. The cast and crew would spend eight weeks filming, followed by about seven weeks on Hollywood sound stages.

Additional location footage for *South Pacific* was filmed in Fiji, most noticeably the aerial footage of islands shot out of the windows of the Navy patrol planes in the film.

The plot of the film involves Ensign Nellie Forbush, as played by Mitzi Gaynor, who falls for wealthy French planter Emile DeBecque, Rossano Brazzi's role, on a South Pacific island in French New Caledonia during World War II. When Nellie discovers that DeBecque has two half-Polynesian children by his late wife, she breaks off the love affair. DeBecque departs on a heroic mission, spotting a Japanese invasion fleet on a remote island. When he returns, Nellie finally accepts him for who he is. A parallel love story tells of the love of young Liat (France Nuyen), the Tonkinese daughter of stout Bloody Mary (Juanita Hall) and Lt. Joseph Cable (John Kerr). Cable tells Bloody Mary that he can't marry Liat because he has a girl at home in the States. On the mission with DeBecque, Cable reconsiders and decides to marry Liat, but is killed before he can get back to her. Adding comic relief is veteran actor Ray Walston as wheeling-and-dealing sailor Luther Billis.

The promotion of the film was substantial. During the filming, a series of radio and television sequences telling how the film was made on location were produced. Five TV featurettes running five minutes and one 20-minute TV subject featuring points of interest on Kaua'i, plus radio interviews with the picture's principle actors, were distributed.

A full-time "familiarization" press tour of Kaua'i was ongoing during the filming, too. Top *LIFE* magazine photographers did a special series of color photographs, shot at the Coco Palms and built along lines from songs in *South Pacific*, to coincide with the release of the film. Free six-day location trips were accepted by some 50 nationally known press people, including Louella Parsons and Hedda Hopper, then leading rival Hollywood columnists.

When first released in 1958, the film was shown only on the road, outside of major metropolitan areas, with seats going for $2, a high price for the late 1950's. The story, the backdrop of Kaua'i's spectacular scenery captured on Todd AO big screen color process, and the enhancement of six-track soundtrack combined to fulfill all expectations, with the film grossing over $30 million during its first run. Choreographer and second unit director LeRoy Prinz told the Kauai Chamber of Commerce, "*South Pacific* will, we feel…open Hollywood's eyes to the artistic advantages of making pictures…on Kauai."

South Pacific continues to boost Kaua'i's reputation as a film location and still differentiates the Island within the Hawaiian chain for many visitors. Rita De Silva, editor of today's *The Garden Island* newspaper and a child actor in *South Pacific*, sees the film as helping both Hollywood and Kaua'i: "Kauai may have been perfect for *South Pacific*, but the movie was also perfect for Kauai."

Hanalei Pier was first constructed in the 1910s. Scenes for *Wackiest Ship in the Army, Miss Sadie Thompson, South Pacific, Pagan Love Song, Beachhead*, and other movies were shot here. Today a modern replica of the pier stands in for the older pier, which was demolished and rebuilt in the late 1980s and early 1990s.

An MGM technician takes a Technicolor reading at Hanalei Pier for *South Pacific*. Notice the traditional crab-claw outrigger sailing canoes built especially for the film.

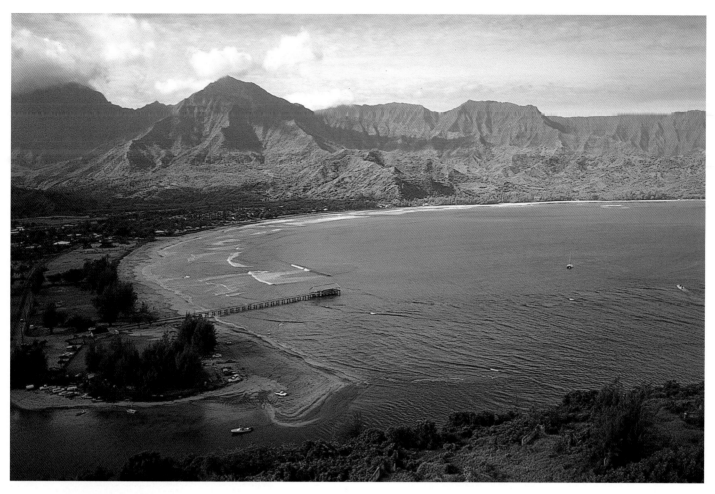

Hanalei Bay from the bluff at Princeville used as the French planter's home in *South Pacific*.

Actor Ray Walston as entrepreneuring sailor Luther Billis leads his men on a moneymaking venture in *South Pacific*.

As it sailed off Hanalei Bay, the Polynesian Voyaging Society's sailing canoe *Hokule'a* provided an authentic setting for MacGillivray-Freeman Films' IMAX production *Behold Hawaii*.

Scenes in *Bird of Paradise* were filmed at Hanalei Bay.

HANALEI BAY

The Wackiest Ship in the Army

The lush green mountains and white-sand beaches of Kaua'i stand out in the somewhat overlooked World War II comedy *The Wackiest Ship in the Army.* In the Columbia Pictures film, made in 1961, Kaua'i is set as Port Moresby, on a New Guinea-looking coastline.

Jack Lemmon plays Lt. Rip Crandall, a peacetime yachtie, now a Navy officer, who is assigned to sail a former South Pacific copra boat manned by a crew of misfit sailors into Japanese-held waters. With more than a touch of Ensign Pulver, the role Lemmon had played in the Academy Award-winning film *Mister Roberts,* Lemmon is the center of the action in the film. The twist in the plot is Crandall's being hoodwinked into taking command of the salt-encrusted, rusting island schooner that's everything but a spick-and-span U.S. Navy ship. The late Ricky Nelson, then a teen idol thanks to his hit records and starring role in the popular *Ozzie and Harriet* network television show, plays a handsome young Navy man who acts as Lemmon's go-between with the crew. In spite of Lemmon's griping, the ship casts off on a top secret mission to work with native shore watchers on the alert for patrols by the Japanese fleet.

Director Richard Murphy jumped the gun on filming, choosing to roll the cameras on overcast, showery days in early May. Soon, the sunny skies of late spring prevailed, forcing the director to make rain to match the inital footage.

The Island is evenly displayed in the film, with Hanalei the site of an Allied base, and Nawiliwili Pier as home to the Japanese invaders. Waimea Canyon provided a backdrop for scenes featuring isolated coast watchers on the lookout for Japanese ships. Allied soldiers and Japanese soldiers were played by National Guardsmen, who drove vintage Army transports out to Hanalei to be used as props.

Off-camera, Lemmon and Nelson hammed it up with the local children. The stars were delayed in arriving on Kaua'i by over a month due to a strike in Hollywood. The strike also forced the cancellation of hotel reservations, and Al Ezell, of Niumalu, had his hands full putting up a cast and crew of 70 that arrived weeks late during a peak tourism season with hotels sold out. But, Ezell worked it out with help from the local Chamber of Commerce and other local groups, putting the group up at digs stretching from Anini on the north shore to Kukui'ula near Poipu. The filming was overseen from a command center set up in the old Kauai Inn.

A mishap during filming at Hanalei, when the filming barge twice broke loose, resulted in damage to the concrete-and-wood-frame covering at the ocean end of the historic pier. Repairs were paid for by the barge company and the film studio.

"The Wackiest Ship" is actually Martin Vitousek's 70-foot schooner *Fiesta.* An authentic South Pacific tramp schooner, the yacht was used to carry cargo between islands prior to being brought to Hawai'i.

The Garden Island newspaper saw the film as part of a trend and reported: "…tourists should definitely include the Garden Island in their Hawaiian vacation. Perhaps they might find themselves chosen for a part in some future production."

Ricky Nelson and Jack Lemmon aim their machine gun towards Japanese soldiers in *The Wackiest Ship in the Army.* Hanalei Bay was set as WWII New Guinea in this early 1960s film.

Rita Hayworth in *Miss Sadie Thompson* arrives to catch a boat out of "Samoa."

A lobby card used to publicize *Beachhead.* Tony Curtis fights his way through a wall of flames at Hanalei Pier in the lower center photograph.

HANALEI VALLEY

The ancient taro fields of Hanalei Valley are watered by an irrigation system hundreds of years old.

Gene Hackman (center) and the men of *Uncommon Valor* in Hanalei Valley.

Viet Cong troops pursue American soldiers in Hanalei Valley during location filming for *Uncommon Valor*.

Hanalei surfer Bill Hamilton and heavy weight boxer-actor Tex Cobb. Hamilton played a wounded soldier tossed into a helicopter from a rice paddy by Cobb in Hanalei Valley in *Uncommon Valor*.

Kaua'i played Southeast Asia for Paramount's 1983 production of *Uncommon Valor,* doubling for Vietnam, Laos, and Thailand. Location filming offered spectacular live action scenes of exploding Army helicopters and gunfights in rice paddies easily visible from Kuhio Highway in Hanalei Valley; night scenes in a smoky Bangkok bar in a ramshackle plantation village in now-razed Wahiawa Camp; the destruction of an authentic Laotion P.O.W. camp along the Lumahai River; and Thai riverboats cruising along the Hule'ia Stream.

In all, 12 sets were created on Kaua'i. In the final edit Kaua'i scenes make up about 70 percent of the film. Production ran from mid-July through mid-August.

By far the most expensive scene was the rescue of G.I.'s from the Viet Cong, which took place in Hanalei Valley with two Vietnam-era Huey helicopters. Due to the controversial theme of the film—rescuing MIAs left behind in Southeast Asia by the U.S. government—using federally-owned choppers was out of the question. Instead, the two helicopters were rented on the mainland and shipped to Kaua'i, at a total cost of $1 million, according to the filmmakers.

Scenes filmed at the old plantation buildings at the now-demolished Wahiawa sugar camp, which was turned into a Bangkok bar, offer indentifiable glimpses of a few dozen local actors. In the scene, Colonel Rhodes (Gene Hackman) meets a gun dealer/bar owner in the La Liberte Café, which Kaua'i dancers work out, sixties style, on a stage.

Kaua'i's cosmopolitan population provided the almost 200 extras needed by local casting agent Tom Summers. Kaua'i residents were costumed to appear as U.S. G.I.'s in Vietnam and as Thais, Vietnamese, and Laotian.

Paramount's location scouts toured Florida, the Caribbean, and Mexico during pre-production, but chose Kaua'i for its Southeast Asia-looking scenery and its proximity to Los Angeles. Co-producer John Milius, a long-time surfer who took time off during the production to surf Kaua'i's waves, may have had a hand in selecting Kaua'i.

Uncommon Valor's storyline revolves around Rhodes, a Vietnam vet whose G.I. son is missing in action following the Vietnam War. Armed with recent photos of his son in a bamboo-and-thatch Laotian prison camp, Rhodes rounds up a motley crew of his son's battle comrades to go back in to rescue him. They arm themselves with bottom-of-the-barrel weapons, join forces with tribal hill people and cross over into Laos to pull off the mission.

Outgoing, oversized boxer Randall "Tex" Cobb, who plays a spacey gung-ho vet in the film, had a good time while shooting the rescue scenes in Hanalei Valley.

Uncommon Valor stars enjoyed themselves on Kaua'i. Handsome Patrick Swayze water-skied, went scuba diving and hiking, plus hit the local discos at night; Cobb worked out with the Kapa'a Boxing Club; and Hackman sat back and painted, enjoying Kaua'i's relaxed atmosphere during his free time.

The cast and crew stayed in Kapa'a at the Sheraton Coconut Beach Hotel, now known as the Courtyard by Marriott Kaua'i at Coconut Beach Hotel.

Uncommon Valor

Pristine Lumaha‘i Stream winds its way through placid Lumaha‘i Valley.

A Laotian prisoner of war camp was constructed and blown up in Lumaha‘i Valley during the filming of *Uncommon Valor.*

LUMAHA'I BEACH

South Pacific, Behold Hawaii, North

Lumahai Beach

Mitzi Gaynor and Rossano Brazzi embrace following the famous "Wash That Man Right Out Of My Hair" scene in *South Pacific*.

A Wainiha Valley taro shack served as the modern-day home for the young Hawaiian boy who goes back to the past in *Behold Hawai'i*.

One of Hawai'i's most scenic beaches fronts Lumaha'i Valley, a dreamy-looking area just west of Hanalei Valley. Once peopled by taro and rice growers, it is now uninhabited. Here, director Logan chose to film the first location scenes featuring principal actors. The crew spent three days filming Mitzi Gaynor's "Wash That Man Right Out of My Hair" song at the eastern section of the beach, an area native Hawaiians call Kahalahala in reference to the many stands of native *lau hala* trees on the edge of the beach.

A major problem arose for Mitzi Gaynor during the filming. She recalls: "In Lihue there was a little store that saved my life. We drove out to the location for 'Wash That Man Right Out of My Hair' and the property man gave me shampoo. It was a gorgeous Kauai day, and after I squirted the shampoo on my hair the soap got in my eyes. Josh is having a stroke, yelling 'The girl is going blind!' On Broadway, Mary Martin used egg whites, avoiding the problem. So the production man had to go into Lihue to the little store and buy what was then a new shampoo, Johnson and Johnson's baby shampoo. The little store saved the day."

Anna Fayé Thiele, daughter of Lindsay Fayé of Kekaha, the first Kaua'i resident to be cast in the film, appeared as one of Nellie Forbush's fellow nurses. She was joined by Deborah Wilcox, who later became the wife of Kaua'i's David Pratt. Cinematographer Leon Shamroy brought in powerful arc lamps powered by generators to keep the light even during the light rain and passing clouds that crossed over the set. The scene had to be filmed twice due to mechanical problems in the camera, which were not discovered until rushes were sent to Hollywood for processing.

South Pacific

"The village of Bali Hai came to life yesterday before the cameras at Ha'ena…More than 300 people, many of them children, turned out for the first scenes at the $40,000 set erected as a New Caledonian village," *The Garden Island* headlined in mid-August.

The Bali Hai beach arrival scene was a mammoth production, featuring dozens of extras, painstakingly created costumes made by the best costumers in Hollywood, and intricate scenes with activity coming from many directions. All created an illusion of an island turning out to welcome a new visitor.

The main Bali Hai village location was on the beach fronting the John Allerton and William Chandler properties, near the Ha'ena Beach Park and Manini-Holo Dry Cave. The pier in the scene was along Makua Beach, near where boats heading for Na Pali load passengers today.

The filmmakers chose the Ha'ena location because of the twin towering peaks inland of the beach. Makana, one of the peaks, became commonly known as Bali Hai due to this scene. The Bali Hai seen in the film from Hanalei Pier is actually a hand-painted Hollywood matte.

To duplicate a New Caledonian village, Fox researchers studied Bishop Museum documents and ordered tapa cloth from Samoa to cover the thatched buildings. To add authenticity to the village, 2,000 eucalyptus poles were cut from trees at the Rice family's Kipu Ranch to be used in place of two-by-fours during construction.

The set featured a village on land, and reef-top thatched houses placed on a 400-foot pier laid atop steel pilings put in place with an antique pile driver and a crane provided by the County of Kaua'i. Work on driving the pilings could go on only at low tide, forcing crews to sometimes work in the middle of the night.

Rita De Silva, the current editor of *The Garden Island* newspaper, played an 8-year-old French schoolgirl in the Bali Hai sequence filmed at Ha'ena. "Every morning at the crack of dawn, we boarded a bus that took us to the North Shore. It was like going to a fantasyland because the beaches looked entirely different as movie sets. One of the first things we had to do was check in with wardrobe. I was supposed to be one of several little French schoolgirls herded from place to place by nuns. Everyday I put on a black-and-white pinafore costume topped by an ugly, round straw hat and finished off by black-and-white Oxford shoes. My brothers would have rolled on the floor in laughter if they could have seen me."

Nuns in the scene included an appearance by Duke Kahanamoku's wife, Nadine. School children brought to the north shore for the scene included 100 from Lihu'e, 74 from Hanalei, 25 from Kilauea and Anahola, and 50 from Kapa'a.

De Silva also recalls lovely France Nuyen, a Southeast Asian actress discovered in the South of France: "She was as beautiful off-screen as on. She spoke very little English but as Bloody Mary's Tonkinese daughter all she had to do was look innocently alluring. We introduced her to salty seeds, the Chinese delicacy that makes your mouth pucker up just thinking about it."

John Kerr as Lieutenant Cable and Juanita Hall as Bloody Mary talk about his romance with her daughter, Liat, on Bali Hai.

Makua Beach looking east towards Hanalei.

John Kerr as Lt. Cable entertains a host of local extras at Makua Beach during filming for *South Pacific*.

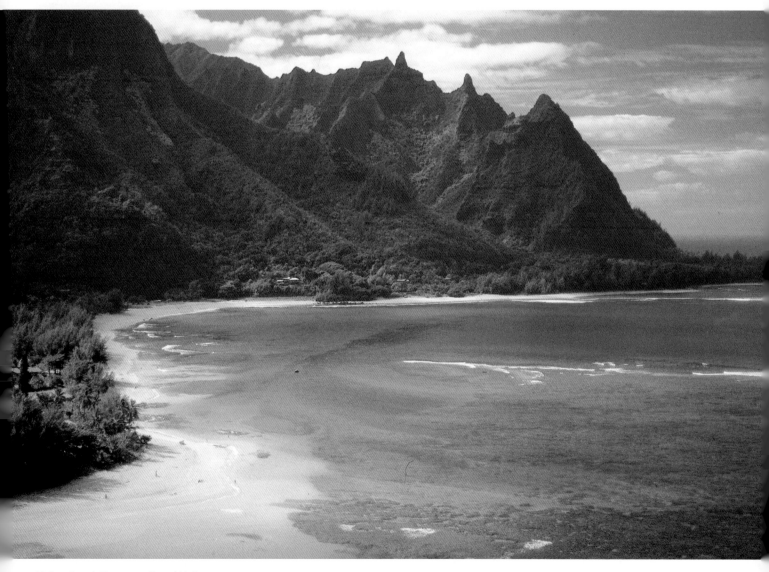

Makua Beach (foreground) and Makana mountain, better known throughout the world as the landmarks of the mystical island of Bali Hai in *South Pacific*.

Roger Corman

N aked Paradise, an 80-minute-long Roger Corman low-budget movie classic, was shot in tandem with *She Gods of Shark Reef* in September and October of 1956. In true Corman style, location shooting for both films lasted a total of four weeks. Cinematographer Floyd Crosby, after completing filming for Hemingway's *Old Man and the Sea* on the Big Island, joined the crew on location for the summer filming. Crosby won the Pulitzer Prize earlier for his photographic work in Gary Cooper's *High Noon.*

In *Naked Paradise,* the plot involves three hoods, led by Corman regular Jonathan Haze, cruising in Hawaiian waters as modern-day pirates, robbing the safes of rich plantation owners. They hire square-jawed actor Richard Denning's yacht as a getaway vessel for a plantation robbery, which they cover by setting a cane fire. A storm moves in and destroys their getaway boat, and Denning pursues them. The thieves become involved with local women, and end up murdering and running amuck. The murder scenes are highlighted by a Cormanesque touch when one of the hoods' faces is pushed into a moving boat propeller. Denning is well known to *Hawaii Five-0* fans as the Governor.

"Filming this movie and *She Gods of Shark Reef* was one of the most pleasurable experiences I've ever had," Corman says in Ed Naha's compendium of the director's films. "We shot the films back to back on location on Kauai. Visually, these two movies are probably the most beautiful I've ever shot. Although many of the locations we used were practically inaccessible by road and we would end up dragging our equipment all over the island, the friendliness and cooperation of the Hawaiian people made filming a sheer joy."

Corman and crew stayed at the Coco Palms, where they worked out a deal to trade movie theater exposure for room nights. The crew also roughed it at Camp Naue on the north shore during location shooting there.

The Garden Island reported packed houses at the Pono Theater and the Kaua'i Theater in August 1957 for the opening of *Naked Paradise.* In the audience was Jerry Nakau, who is shot dead in the film. Louie Victorino had a speaking part, yelling "Fire! Fire!" to launch a key cane fire sequence Corman coordinated with a Lihu'e Plantation routine burning of a mature sugar cane field.

In *She Gods of Shark Reef,* two brothers on the lam from Hawai'i in an outrigger canoe wash up on a tropical island populated by only beautiful women who dive for pearls in shark-infested waters and worship a stone shark god. One of the brothers clad in *malo* (traditional Hawaiian working and swimming garment, similar to a bathing suit), with a large dive knife around his waist, turns on the other, attempts to flee the island with stolen pearls, and is devoured by the sharks in front of the stone god, while the other falls for an island beauty. *Variety* lauded the location shooting and rich color of the film and the underwater photography of cinematographer Crosby, but panned the 63-minute-long story while praising director Corman for pulling it off. The film was paired with *Night of the Blood Beast* as a drive-in and Saturday matinee horror double feature.

Richard Denning (center) would later play the Governor in *Hawaii 5-0.* Here he kibitzes at Hanalei Bay with two Bronx hoods who are robbing sugar plantations in director Roger Corman's *Naked Paradise.*

"We shot the films back to back on location on Kauai. Visually, these two movies are probably the most beautiful I've ever shot. Although many of the locations we used were practically inaccessible by road and we would end up dragging our equipment all over the island, the friendliness and cooperation of the Hawaiian people made filming a sheer joy."
—Roger Corman

Limahuli Valley.

LIMAHULI

Jurassic Park's raptor loading pen was erected in Limahuli Valley.

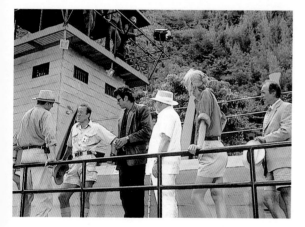

The floor of Limahuli, a lush tropical valley bordered by awe-inspiring pinnacles, remains lined with ancient taro terraces and rare native Hawaiian plants that flourish in Limahuli Garden.

Within this lush, mysterious valley at Haʻena on the north shore, Steven Spielberg chose to film what is perhaps *Jurassic Park*'s eeriest scene–the deadly raptor cage where unseen beasts devour live cattle and a human worker who accidently gets too close to the captive raptors.

Following the filming, months later at the Kauaʻi County Farm Fair the prize cow, painted black for filming and lowered into the steel-cased cage, was put on display. There, the bovine's proud owner hung a prominent sign around the cow's neck, stating "I was eaten in Jurassic Park."

The ancient taro terraces and fantastically sculpted pinnacles surround the new visitors center for National Tropical Botanical Garden at Limahuli Valley, near the valley's entrance.

KE'E BEACH

The Thorn Birds, Behold, Hawaii

The paved road ends on Kaua'i's north shore at Ke'e Beach, where the narrow hiking trail along the Na Pali Coast to Kalalau Valley begins.

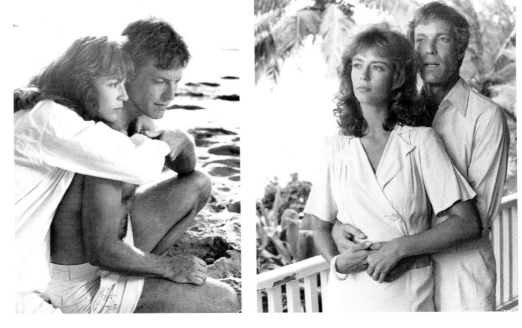

The former Allerton Home at Ha'ena's Ke'e Beach was set as the romantic hideaway of Richard Chamberlain as the Catholic priest Ralph de Bricassart and Rachel Ward as Maggie Cleary in *The Thorn Birds.*

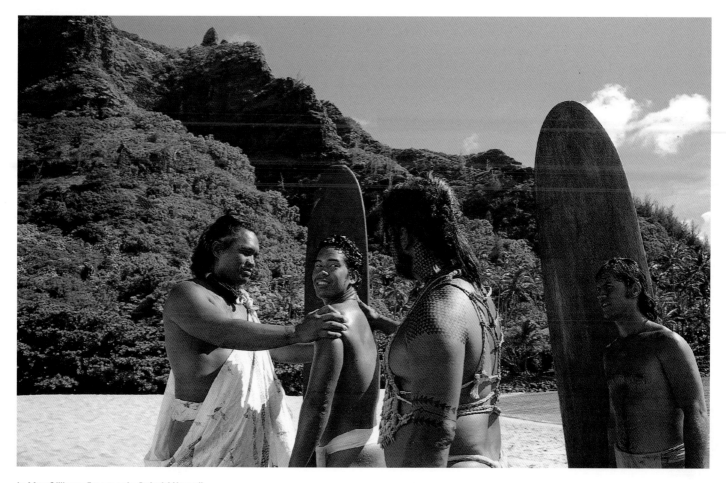

In MacGillivray Freeman's *Behold Hawaii* authentically garbed native Hawaiian surfers at Keʻe beach are filmed with reproductions of ancient Hawaiian surfboards. The former Allerton home at Keʻe, which burned down in the early 1990s, is carefully blocked out by the surfboard in the foreground.

Rocky point off Keʻe Beach.

KOLOA / PO'IPU

The sunny beaches and rolling hills of Koloa, Po'ipu, Kalaheo and Lawa'i lie in the shadow of Mount Ha'upu, an ancient volcanic peak. Here, the first commercial sugar cane plantation was founded in 1835 at Koloa, and whalers called in at nearby Koloa Landing for much-needed supplies.

Maha'ulepu, the easternmost part of this area, is a geological wonderland of headlands, laced with the remains of Kaua'i's last lava flows. The home of George C. Scott, who played the Hemingway character Thomas Hudson in *Islands in the Stream*, was built on the sand dunes here, near where the cattle-loading scene in Disney's *Castaway Cowboys* was set for James Garner.

The resort area at Po'ipu is lined with white-sand coves, coral reefs, and crystal-clear water and is known for its sunny days. To the west of Po'ipu is Kukui'ula Harbor, which was set as a port in World War II Bimini for *Islands in the Stream*.

Further west, past the Spouting Horn blow hole, is the valley of Lawa'i, home to the headquarters of the National Tropical Botanical Garden and oceanfront Lawa'i-Kai, the site of the Allerton Garden estate. The fertile valley is a favorite location for filmmakers on Kaua'i. Among others, the children in *Jurassic Park* found a dinosaur egg here, amidst snake-like tree roots. John Wayne was entertained by a company of Hawaiian dancers and singers in *Donovan's Reef*, and Liat and Lieutenant Cable romanced among its rare plants in *South Pacific*.

Above Lawa'i is Kalaheo, a town favored by the Island's Portuguese immigrants who arrived in the late 1800s. Set on hillsides facing into the balmy trade winds, Kalaheo retains a rural atmosphere that would not be out of place on the island of Madeira in the Atlantic, the homeland for many of Kaua'i's Portuguese settlers.

Maha'ulepu was set as Bimini in the Bahamas for Hemingway's *Islands in the Stream*. The undeveloped coastal dunes—a haven for native plants and seabirds—is located just east of the Grand Hyatt Kaua'i Resort & Spa.

MAHA'ULEPU

Islands in the Stream, The Castaway Cowboy

Kaua'i became the main island of Bimini in the Bahamas, an Atlantic island 50 miles east of Miami, in the early 1940s for Paramount Picture's 1975 filming of Ernest Hemingway's posthumously published novel *Islands in the Stream*. Paramount chose Kaua'i for its tropical rivers and variety of beaches for the film, which starred George C. Scott as a character similar to Hemingway.

The filming marked a change in the attitude of filmmakers towards Kaua'i location filming, as the sets were closed during most of the production, opened only on occasion for local people to see what was going on. However, at a community party thrown for director Franklin Schaffner and his cast and crew, even the Kaua'i Red Raider marching band showed up to kick off a major celebration reminiscent of earlier major Kaua'i studio productions. Between pre-production and production, the crew for *Islands in the Stream* was on Kaua'i for about one year.

Hemingway's story tells of New York artist-turned-sculptor Thomas Hudson, who has isolated himself far away from family and career. He, with his boating buddies, played by Gilbert Roland and David Hemmings, fish, drink and stir up trouble whenever he's not sculpting. The world outside catches up with him as World War II begins drawing the U.S. into the conflict, and his adolescent sons visit from New York. Against his wishes, his eldest son enlists. Months later, his ex-wife, played by Claire Bloom, visits him with news of the death of their son, killed flying in the air battle over Europe. Hudson becomes introspective and his entire life comes to a climax as he helps to smuggle European Jews into Cuba during a detour on a fishing boat ride back to the mainland U.S.

A detailed dock and port town, looking like the main port of Bimini, were created by a Paramount crew at Kukui'ula Harbor over two months of pre-production construction. Buildings included a bar, fish market, and stores, with authentic props throughout, including circa 1940 goods on store shelves. A seaplane and the cars of Kaua'i antique auto collector Augie Souza added to the transformation of the south shore port to a dock in Atlantic waters. Hudson's house and studio were set at Maha'ulepu, which provided a credible double for the lonely white-sand beaches of the Bahamas. The climactic scenes take place along the upper reaches of the Wailua River. There, the Cuban navy chases Hudson's fishing boat through hau tree thickets, in imitation of the mangroves along Cuba's coastline.

A highlight for the 200-plus Kauaians working on the film was a Sunday evening *lua'u* held in honor of Mary Hemingway, Hemingway's widow, who helped edit the text of *Islands in the Stream* after the author's death. *The Garden Island* newspaper reported, "Production paused Sunday evening to welcome his widow, 'Miss Mary,' a sparkling, vibrant lady who put her stamp of approval on the sets as expressing the atmosphere Hemingway created." Chris Chang catered the event, held in the Ponce De Leon bar set. At the party Cuban songs played in the background, recalling the Hemingways' 17 years in Cuba. "The set on Kauai is perfect and I think the film will be good," Mary Hemingway said at the party. The next day, she carried on a Hemingway tradition by going big-game fishing aboard the boat of John Duarte.

Kaweikoa Point separates Maha'ulepu and Kipukai.

Sculptor Thomas Hudson's home built at Maha'ulepu for *Islands in the Stream* was a painstakingly detailed reproduction of a Bimini island retreat.

On location at Maha'ulepu, George C. Scott as Thomas Hudson and Claire Bloom as Audrey, his former wife, recall old times in *Islands In the Stream*.

The landmark Ha'upu Range looms behind the beach at Maha'ulepu.

Cattle, and film crew, floated offshore at Maha'ulepu for *Castaway Cowboy*. In the 1800s Kaua'i steers commonly swam to waiting ships for transport to markets in Honolulu.

Islands in the Stream

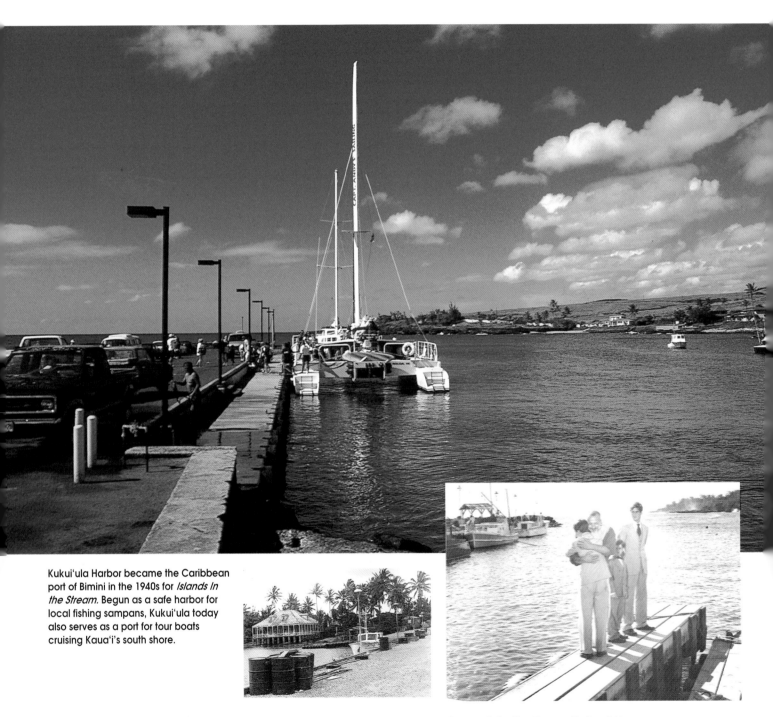

Kukui'ula Harbor became the Caribbean port of Bimini in the 1940s for *Islands In the Stream*. Begun as a safe harbor for local fishing sampans, Kukui'ula today also serves as a port for tour boats cruising Kaua'i's south shore.

George C. Scott as Thomas Hudson bids farewell to his sons in *Islands in the Stream*.

KOLOA / PO'IPU

Lt. Robin Crusoe, The Thorn Birds

Ever sunny Po'ipu Beach.

On location at Po'ipu Beach near the Waiohai Hotel, Dick Van Dyke plays a downed Navy flier washed ashore on a mythical isle near New Guinea for Disney's *Lt. Robin Crusoe.*

McBryde Sugar Mill near Koloa town became a tropical Queensland sugar mill in *The Thorn Birds.*

Location filming for *Lt. Robin Crusoe, U.S.N.* lured Walt Disney and his film crew to Kaua'i. Disney took a summer working vacation, frequently visiting the set at Lydgate Park, Po'ipu Beach and Lawa'i-Kai in August 1966 with his grandson, Walter Disney Miller. Disney, then 62 years old, "chatted amiably with both tourists and local people," *The Garden Island* newspaper reported.

The story credit for the mid-sixties light comedy reads "Retlaw Yensid," or Walt Disney spelled backwards. He may have been hoping for a second *Mary Poppins,* as many of the cast and crew had worked on the widely popular film made two years earlier.

Disney told *The Garden Island:* "I hope this will be a funny movie. Dick Van Dyke, Nancy Kwan, and Akim Tamiroff are all very capable. I've wanted to do Robinson Crusoe for a long time. Your weather has also been very cooperative."

"Incidentally," Disney added, "we've had two Kaua'i boys working for Disney Studios. Vittorio Bodrero is still with us, and his brother Jimmy was 20 years ago. They are grandsons of Colonel Spalding of Makee Sugar Co. at Kealia. I used to play polo against their uncle, Jimmy Spalding."

Disney was mistaken about Jimmy Bodrero, who was actually Spalding's son-in-law and the screenplay writer and location scout in 1933 for steamy *White Heat,* the first Hollywood feature made on Kaua'i.

An island-wide casting call went out over radio station KTOH for 24 young local women and 20 young local men to act as natives of Crusoe's island. The radio broadcast asked that the girls appear in either bathing suits or shorts, and be 18 or older. After a number of underage candidates were shooed away, Disney's director Byron Paul selected Peggy Bukoski, Vida Kilauano, Phyllis Texeira, Leilani and Noelani Kanoho, Ellie Lloyd, Cheryl Iida, Veralyn Rego and other local girls.

In this parody of Robinson Crusoe, Van Dyke plays the title role of a young Navy flier based on an aircraft carrier who is forced to ditch his plane near a mythical island in the South Pacific. After a series of mishaps while floating at sea waiting to be rescued, Robin beaches on an apparently desolate island. Unknowingly, he has landed on a savage island ruled by Tanamashu (Akim Tamiroff). After some Mary Poppins-ish adventures he is saved by Tanamashu's daughter Wednesday (Nancy Kwan), who falls for him. A bevy of Kaua'i girls costumed as South Pacific sirens assist Wednesday. Teaming up with Robin is Floyd, a chimp shot into space in an early NASA flight who re-entered near the island. Van Dyke leaves the island girl behind as a rescue helicopter arrives to take him back to civilization.

Van Dyke, then at the peak of his TV career, enjoyed his Kaua'i visit. "Now that I've seen how delightful Kauai is, the last thing I want to do is work. My wife and four children came with me, and my two sons have already learned to surf."

LAWA'I-KAI

Donovan's Reef, Islands in the Stream

The lush tropical gardens of Lawa'i-Kai, the former home of Robert Allerton, and the adjoining Lawa'i Valley, the setting of the National Tropical Botanical Garden, lure filmmakers searching for an accessible, yet exotic, filming location.

In *Jurassic Park*, dinosaur eggs are discovered here by paleontologist Grant and the children; Liat and Lieutenant Cable romance in *South Pacific* amidst the tropical plants; and John Wayne as Guns Donovan in *Donovan's Reef* is entertained by Kaua'i hula dancers and musicians on a South Sea island. The main scenes for Disney's *Last Flight of Noah's Ark* with Eliot Gould, featuring a crashed World War II bomber, were filmed along the coast here, plus scenes from *Honeymoon in Vegas, Islands in the Stream, South Pacific,* and *Lt. Robin Crusoe.*

Lawa'i-Kai is located at the end of Lawa'i Road, just beyond Spouting Horn, and is a 100-acre estate of peace and beauty. It was bought by Robert Allerton from the Alexander McBryde Estate in 1937, and the Allerton name remains associated with Lawa'i-Kai today. However, the history of the valley goes back to Emma, the Hawaiian queen of the 1860s who spent time here after the death of her husband, Kamehameha IV. Emma's uncle, James Young Kanehoa, then owned the entire *ahupua'a* of Lawa'i, from the mountains to the sea.

In 1886, following Emma's death, the estate was bought by the McBryde family for $50,000 and their oldest son, Alexander, planted Lawa'i-Kai with royal palms, varieties of coconut trees, many shades of bougainvillea, and a garden of ferns.

Allerton continued and enhanced McBryde's labors in making Lawa'i-Kai a paradise. Robert and his adopted son John Gregg Allerton built a beautiful home near the beach and landscaped the grounds, using fountains and classical statues to add a sophisticated touch to the magnificent setting. They also brought plants from Australia, Ceylon, Fiji, the Philippines, and Puerto Rico, and set about preserving Queen Emma's cottage.

Near the end of his life, Robert saw one of his dreams fulfilled—the establishment of a tropical botanical garden in the United States. He was one of the founding trustees of the Pacific Tropical Botanical Garden, which became the National Tropical Botanical Garden, but, unfortunately, he passed away shortly after Congress established the Garden's charter.

Lawa'i-Kai's blue water and white sand beach is at the mouth of lush Lawa'i Valley.

The half-moon bay at Lawa'i-Kai marks the coastal border of the National Tropical Botanical Garden at Lawa'i. Queen Emma's home was lowered down in the 1930s from the upper valley and is now located to the right and just inland of the white-sand beach.

John Wayne as Guns Donovan joined director John Ford at Lawa'i-Kai to film the coronation scene of *Donovan's Reef* in 1962. Dozens of Kaua'i hula dancers, musicians and costumed extras appeared in the scene.

A Disney executive hams it up with Kaua'i beauties at Lawa'i-Kai during location filming for *Lt. Robin Crusoe U.S.N.*

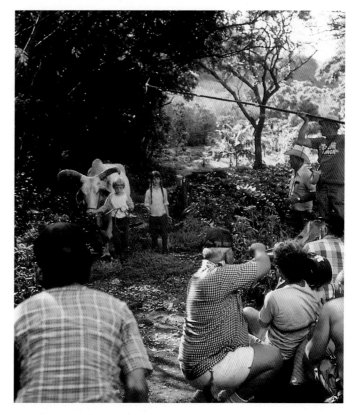

Young Ricky Schroder walks a Brahma bull up a path at Lawa'i-Kai for Disney's *Last Flight of Noah's Ark.*

The fuselage of an Air Force bomber, a Brahma bull, and other exotic props were brought to Lawa'i-Kai for *Last Flight of Noah's Ark.*

LAWA'I-KAI

Honeymoon in Vegas, Jurassic Park

In *Honeymoon In Vegas*, James Caan as Tommy and Sarah Jessica Parker as Betsy took a romantic outrigger canoe ride in the stream at Lawa'i-Kai.

In *Jurassic Park*, a dinosaur egg and dinosaur bones were found nestled in the distinctive roots of a Morton Bay Fig tree on the grounds of the National Tropical Botanical Garden at Lawa'i. The find drew the rapt attention of Sam Neill, Joseph Mazzello, and Ariana Richards.

WEST SIDE

Dramatic, yet subtle, Kaua'i's West Side is an arid, desert-like land located in the lee of Wai'ale'ale. The pastel reds and greens of 2,000-foot-high cliff faces within Waimea Canyon are geological wonder as marvelous as Arizona's Grand Canyon.

The rural plantation towns of the West Side retain a pre-World War II atmosphere. The producers of *The Thorn Birds*, the popular TV mini-series, found Hanapepe Town a perfect location for a 1930s Australian outback sugar town. And location shooting for Kaua'i's first major feature film took place at Waimea, when Lois Weber, Hollywood's first woman director, directed *White Heat,* filmed at the Waimea Plantation.

To the north of the sunny plantation town of Kekaha, alongside the Island's first airstrip, is the Navy's Pacific Missle Range Facility. The base is a high-tech military training range which is uniquely capable of supporting research, development, test, and evaluation programs and provides filmmakers with a military backdrop when needed. The beaches in and around the base are known as Barking Sands for the distinctive yelp made with one slides down a sand dune along the miles-long white-sand beach. Here, Joshua Logan timed filming for *South Pacific* to coincide with the landing of thousands of Marines during official maneuvers. The Officers Club at PMRF was set as a Vietnam-era "O" Club in *Flight of the Intruder.*

Above Waimea and Kekaha lies the highland forest of Koke'e. Some of the world's rarest birds live here, many nesting in native *ohia lehua* trees. The climate at Koke'e distinctively chilly for Kaua'i residents, who drive up Waimea Canyon Road for a taste of weather more akin to the U.S. mainland.

Though sparsely used in feature films, Koke'e is a popular site for documentary filmmakers from across the globe, drawn to Kaua'i to film the Island's rare native birds and plants.

A tranquil sunset at Polihale Beach.

HANAPEPE TOWN

The Thorn Birds, Flight of the Intruder

Kaua'i locations from Ke'e Beach, at the end of the road on the north shore, to sleepy Hanapepe Town are featured in *The Thorn Birds,* a 10-hour, made-for-television mini-series. The series, which ranks behind only *Roots* in audience ratings for a TV mini-series, was produced by David L. Wolper-Stan Margulies Productions, Edward Lewis Productions, and Warner Bros. Margulies also produced *Roots.*

Most scenes for the $21 million mini-series were filmed in California, rather than going on location to Australia. For tropical sugar cane plantation scenes, the producers chose Kaua'i. Kaua'i's beaches, cane fields, and plantation-era towns are set as sugar-growing districts of tropical Queensland Australia, serving as backdrops for the romance of stars Richard Chamberlain and Rachel Ward.

Chamberlain plays handsome and popular Roman Catholic priest Ralph de Bricassart, who is torn between his career as a priest and his love for Meggie Cleary, an Australian woman played by actress Rachel Ward in her American TV debut. Bryan Brown co-stars as Luke O'Neill, and Barbara Stanwyck, coming out of retirement in a rare late-career performance, is Meggie's overbearing grandmother.

This dramatization of Colleen McCullough's romantic novel first aired in March 1983 and follows the fortunes of an Australian family from the 1920s through the early 1960s.

Kaua'i locations included the Allerton home at Ha'ena's Ke'e Beach, which burnt down in the early 1990s, and the nearby beach for a romantic interlude between Chamberlain and Ward; the old main street of Hanapepe town, which was transformed into a tropical Queensland sugar town; the McBryde sugar mill at Koloa, which had an Australian sugar company sign painted on its walls; the National Tropical Botanical Garden at Lawa'i; and sugar cane fields at Koloa.

Burly Kaua'i locals, including Bubba Prince and Scott Furgeson, played sugar cane cutters in the film. Other local residents were dressed very much out of character in period suits, with ties and hats, for the Hanapepe street scenes.

Many of the period cars in the filming belong to retired dairy farmer August Souza of Wailua Homesteads. The 1930s Queensland bus in the film was used in the 1940s as a prop in Humphrey Bogart's film *Treasure of the Sierra Madre* and brought in from Hollywood for the filming.

Historic Hanapepe town was set as a tropical Queensland sugar cane town in *The Thorn Birds.*

Actors sit in a passenger bus brought specially from Hollywood for *The Thorn Birds.* The bus was also used in Bogart's *Treasure of the Sierra Madre.*

In *Flight of the Intruder,* the old mom & pop store, Seto Market, and other distinctive plantation-era buildings at Hanapepe town became Olongapo, a popular Philippine bar and brothel strip during the Vietnam War. The building used in the brawl scene was one of many historic Kaua'i buildings damaged by Hurricane Iniki in 1992. Today many of the buildings have been restored.

"The cooperation of the Hanapepe community the last three nights has been tremendous. Everything has gone extremely well. We couldn't have done this in Los Angeles or in any other big city, and if we did we'd have to use cattle prods and call in riot police."— Robert Lemer, location manager

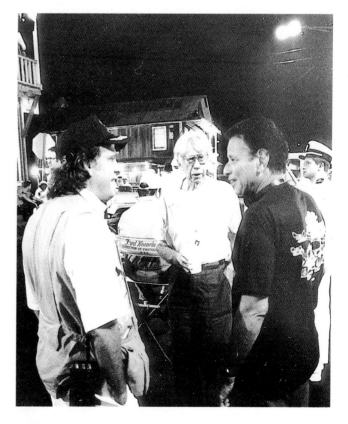

Direction of *Flight of the Intruder* scenes in Hanapepe went on late into the night as Executive Producer Brian Frankish and Producer Mace Neufeld confer.

MANAWAIOPUNA FALLS

Jurassic Park

Seen mostly from the windows of touring helicopters, the idyllic falls of Manawaiopuna feed the winding Hanapepe River deep within the folds of the ancient valleys on Kaua'i's west side.

Here the *Jurassic Park* crews created Isla Nublar's helicopter landing pad. It took four attempts due to heavy interior rains washing out the concrete pad three times. The steep 200-foot falls are featured in the beginning of the film, when the helicopter lands at their base to unload the visitors to the island. Dave Nikimoto of Ni'ihau Helicopter flew the helicopter, which was specially painted for the film. Workers from Ni'ihau Ranch and other operations of the Robinson family, who own Ni'ihau and ranchlands along the west side, helped construct the set, which was accessible only along a four-wheel drive trail or by helicopter.

OLOKELE

Jurassic Park

Laura Dern, Sam Neill, and Joseph Mazzello discuss a *Jurassic Park* scene with director Steven Spielberg above Olokele Canyon.

Special effects supervisor Michael Lantieri was delegated the tough task of erecting 24-foot-high electrical fences at very isolated locations on Kaua'i. At Olokele Valley, overlooking the southeast reaches of Waimea Valley—Kaua'i's Grand Canyon—Lantieri's crew, assisted by locally-based linemen, set up a steel cabled fence upon which young Tim is electrocuted as he struggles to climb over. Deceivingly simple-looking, the fences were ordered to be built twice as high as the highest guard fences, to hint at the enormous size of the dinosaurs they contain. In *The Making of Jurassic Park*, Lantieri tells of erecting the fence at Olokele: "One of our locations in Hawaii was a canyon that was a forty-five-minute, four-wheel drive to get into. So we had to haul all of this steel up there, drill holes like you would for telephone poles, pour concrete, and then pull all of the cables, which were three-quarter-inch aluminum with steel in the middle. We used more than six-miles of that cable—it was like running power from the Hoover Dam to Los Angeles."

Cane Fire / White Heat

White Heat is the first Hollywood film to feature Kaua'i locations. Originally titled *Cane Fire*, the Seven Seas Film Corporation melodrama takes place at a 1930s-era sugar cane plantation set at Waimea, and was one of the first talking pictures filmed in Hawai'i.

Interestingly, *White Heat*'s director Lois Weber was Hollywood's first woman director, and her films were considered controversial in the early days of Hollywood. For the location filming, she sailed to Honolulu with movie mogul Cecil B. DeMille aboard the Matson Line steamship *SS Malolo* in August 1933, along with her 28-member cast and crew. DeMille was scouting locations for a Claudette Colbert and Leo Carillo film to be set on O'ahu.

Unlike most Kaua'i films, *White Heat* was written by someone with ties to the Island. Screenwriter Jimmy Brodrero had gone to Hollywood after marrying into the family of Colonel Zephaniah Spalding, the builder of the first Valley House. His ties to the Island may have influenced Weber in choosing Kaua'i as the film's location.

The film company stayed at the turn-of-the-century Sea View Hotel at Waimea near the mouth of the Waimea River, where star David Newell enjoyed swimming in the surf. The hotel, operated and owned by C.W. Spitz, Kaua'i's first hotel general manager, no longer exists.

The real-life characters making the film were worthy candidates for inclusion in a W. Somerset Maugham Pacific island story. Director Weber was a veteran filmmaker, directing her first talkie, and near the end of a tumultuous career and life. Weber, who started out as a Salvation Army evangelist on the streets of Pennsylvania, was associated with DeMille in the early 1920s, making thousands of dollars a picture. She is remembered for her controversial "situation" films of the 1910s, such as the banned *Where Are My Children*, which touched on the topic of abortion. Weber brought to Kaua'i her second husband, Capt. Harry Grantz. Her first husband, Phillips Smalley, had produced, written, and directed a number of films in collaboration with her for film companies in the East and in Hollywood, including spinoffs from Thomas Edison's first film studio. The content of her films touched on love themes much deeper than the lightweight Hollywood fare of the day, and the interracial love story behind *White Heat* was a continuation of her career's focus.

White Heat was filmed as a three-act stage play, with Kaua'i's west side as the backdrop. The plot, according to a contemporary *New York Times* review, tells of "an account of the amorous difficulties of a young sugar planter." The film opens with William Hawks, a Kaua'i sugar planter (David Newell), leaving Leilani (Mona Maris), his local girlfriend, for Lucille (Virginia Cherrill), the daughter of a sugar cane baron from San Francisco, whom he marries. This all takes place at the now-gone Knudsen home at the family's compound at Kekaha, at the home of Lindsey Fayé at Waimea, and at the Waimea Sugar Mill, with many Kaua'i residents playing bit parts.

Time moves on and the combination of steamy weather and long absences by her husband causes Lucille to long for an outside romance. She

Actress Mona Maris plays Leilani, the local girl involved in a love triangle with plantation manger William Hawks, played by David Newell in *White Heat*. Here she rides a handsome Arabian. Note the distinctive Kaua'i-made saddles.

The production crew takes a break near the Waimea Sugar Plantation. Made in the early days of the "talkies," *White Heat* required trunk loads of sound and film equipment that were shipped from Hollywood via the Matson Line.

Plantation manager Hawks dukes it out with an Hawaiian actor in a cane field just outside of Waimea town during the filming of *White Heat*.

A fire alarm goes off at the Waimea Sugar Plantation, setting off *White Heat's* most dramatic scene. An open-air shed at the plantation provides the set for the scene.

The Waimea Plantation Cottages are owned by the Kikiaola Land Company, which provided the movie stills from *White Heat*. The photographs come from the scrap books of the Fayé family. It is uncertain who took the photographs. Lihu'e photographer W. Senda was also at the Waimea location taking pictures for the Honolulu newspapers, and stills to promote the film.

The Waimea Foreign Church was built of native stone in 1853. The historic church is a landmark in Waimea town and appears as a backdrop in *White Heat*.

The Waimea Foreign Church serves as a backdrop for this cane field scene in *White Heat*. Truckloads of Kaua'i sugar workers were used as extras in the film.

This steamy ad for *White Heat* appeared in the movie section of Honolulu's newspapers during the film's mysteriously short run.

infatuates a local youth, then drops him for Chandler (Hardie Albright), a former beau from San Francisco who is visiting the Islands. Rejected, her husband returns to Leilani.

The loyalty and unselfishness of Leilani is contrasted to the shallowness of the weak-willed wife and her villainous mainland lover. The climax of *White Heat* has Lucille setting fire to a cane field supposedly near the mill, but, probably for the sake of safety, actually set in a cane field at remote Wahiawa just east of Hanapepe. Lucille plans to end her problems by doing away with her husband, Hawks, who is intent on beating up her visiting lover. Leilani heroically pulls the unconscious Hawks from the flames.

The New York film critics panned the film, but loved the location: "The film is technically inferior to the studio product, but it compensates for this by the reality and beauty of its Hawaiian setting."

Reports of the filming said additional location filming was done at Na Pali's Kalalau Valley and Miloli'i Beach and Olokele Canyon inland of Waimea; however, it isn't certain these locations were used. The last known screening of *White Heat* was a 1960 television broadcast in Honolulu, according to Hawai'i film chronicler Robert C. Schmitt. If and where a print of the film exists remains a mystery.

Local Hawaiian singers and hula dancers also performed in front of *White Heat*'s cameras to add an island flavor to the film. Receiving a good acting review was Korean immigrant son and professional Kaua'i-born actor Peter Hyun.

A technician waters down a wrecked train loaded with cut cane for *Cane Fire*.

The clopp-clopp of David Newell's mount was recorded as a cane train loaded with plantation workers pulled out.

Actress Virginia Cherrill dressed up for her role in White Heat. The identity of the man is uncertain; he may be Capt. Harry Grantz, the husband of director Lois Weber, or Jimmy Bodrero, the son-in-law of Valley House's builder Colonel Spaulding, and the screenplay writer for the film.

WAIMEA CANYON

Donovan's Reef, Wackiest Ship in the Army, Honeymoon in Vegas

At lookouts above Waimea Canyon, Kaua'i's "Grand Canyon," John Wayne visited a monument to the WWII heroics of his crew in *Donovan's Reef,* and in *Wackiest Ship in the Army,* Ricky Nelson and a scouting patrol crossed a mountain range set in New Guinea.

PMRF/BARKING SANDS

Flight of the Intruder

The Mana Plain, Barking Sands Beach, and the Pacific Missile Range Facility from a red-dirt overlook below Koke'e.

The Pacific Missile Range Facility's Officers Club served as the set for an officers' party in *Flight of the Intruder*.

Sun-lit whitewater washes ashore at Barking Sands.

Sailors from the Navy's Pacific Missile Range Facility played Vietnam War-era servicemen on leave in the Philippines for *Flight of the Intruder*. Young women from Kaua'i played the bar girls who served the sailors.

POLIHALE

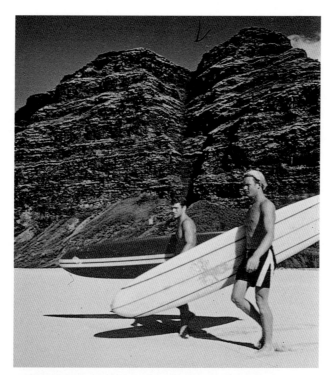

Mark Martinson (left) and Bill Hamilton traveled to Kaua'i in 1966 with filmmakers Greg MacGillivray and Jim Freeman to film Hawai'i's waves for the surfing movie *Free & Easy*. Here the two young California surfers with their mid-60s longboards head for the waves at Polihale.

The shoreline at Polihale, one of the longest white-sand beaches in Hawai'i.

NA PALI

Na Pali, which translates into English as "The Cliffs," is arguably the most spectacular wilderness area in all the Hawaiian Islands. Here, towering pinnacles and deep valleys hold the geological and archaeological secrets of the Island. Hawaiians once populated the 15-mile-long string of valleys, but all left by 1920 to live in the modern ways.

Access to Na Pali is available only aboard charter boats in times of low waves, by hiking the narrow Kalalau Trail, which begins near Ke'e Beach, or by helicopter. No roads cut through the valleys, which are home to rare native plants and archaelogical sites that date back over 1,000 years to the days of the first Polynesians settlers on Kaua'i.

Dino De Laurentiis selected Honopu Valley as the landing site for the explorers of Kong's Island and Kalalau Valley as King Kong's home. Rumors of daring fly-throughs of the landmark arch at Honopu persist, but no film proof of the feat is readily available. The red-dirt trail cutting down into Kalalau Valley is featured as an end-of-the-world site in *Millennium*. Visitors to the Smithsonian Institution's Air and Space Museum will recognize Na Pali as the wonderous backdrop for a hang-gilder pilot navigating through the otherworldly cliffs in the film *To Fly*.

The valleys of Na Pali looking northeast towards Ke'e Beach and Haena.

King Kong

In March 1976 Paramount Pictures and Dino De Laurentiis re-created the Valley of Kong at Kalalau and Honopu on the isolated Na Pali Coast. The uninhabited, towering pinnacles and jungle-covered landscape of Na Pali and its relatively close proximity to civilization made the location ideal.

To film the Na Pali sequences of the $15 million remake of the classic 1933 film *King Kong*, actors and filmmakers flew in daily from Princeville aboard chartered helicopters. Noticeable by his absence was King Kong, who remained on a back lot in Hollywood during the filming except for a huge paw print dug out of a sea cliff just east of Kalalau Valley. Two tons of filming equipment were shipped to Kaua'i, including a small boat sent from Hollywood to match studio shots with Na Pali scenes.

The Kaua'i footage simulates the arrival of an exploratory crew who row in from an oil company research vessel to the white-sand shores of a cloud-covered, mysterious island somewhere off the north coast of Java. There, at Kalalau Valley, they discover a towering, carved wooden wall that protects islanders from the wrath of a huge beast. Jessica Lange, in her screen debut re-creating Fay Wray's famous heroine role from the first Kong film, has been rescued at sea by the research vessel, only to be captured by island natives and offered as a sacrifice to Kong. The oil company crew strikes into the hidden valley to rescue Lange. A night-time chase scene for the film was shot in the albezia wood forest just off Kuhio Highway between Kilauea and Kalihiwai. When he sees Kong, a villainous oil company executive, played by Charles Grodin, decides there is a fortune to be made back in civilization from the huge ape and he has his men capture Kong. The hero, and environmental conscience of the film, is Jeff Bridges, who plays a stowaway Princeton anthropologist seeking to explore the isolated island.

Some of the Paramount location crew for *King Kong* was familiar with Kaua'i, having filmed *Islands in the Stream* on Kaua'i just months before. Cast and crew stayed at the now-demolished Hanalei Racquet Club at Princeville. The hotel, formerly the Hanalei Plantation Hotel, was built on a plateau where the manager's house in *South Pacific* once looked out over Hanalei Bay. Remote communications for the location filming in this pre-cellular phone era were handled by using a radio transmitter set up at the hotel.

The producers were on a tight schedule, with a Christmas opening in 1,000 U.S. theaters already promised. De Laurentiis sent his 21-year-old son Fredrico to be the Kaua'i location producer. Filming at the remote Na Pali locations provided the biggest challenge. Every day actors and crew members, food, and filming gear had to be flown out to the valleys by helicopter. During the boat-landing scene, larger-than-normal surf caused problems. Kaua'i actor Wil Welsh, done up with fake sideburns, doubled on camera for actor Grodin in long shots of the landing scene.

Special effects on-site were minimal, limited to technicians creating a morning fog with aerosol canisters near the Honopu arch. Footage taken within Kalalau Valley is overlaid with the studio-created Kong's valley wall in the finished film.

Honopu and the valleys of Na Pali beyond Kalalau in profile.

King Kong destroys the huge gate to his valley, supposedly located at Kalalau Valley on Na Pali.

Honopu Valley is around the corner from Kalalau Beach (foreground). Adjacent beaches at Honopu are connected by an arch.

An animal trainer leads a pack mule in Kalalau Valley for a *Raiders of the Lost Ark* scene never used in the film.

Jessica Lange takes a nap under Honopu Arch.

Landing through the surf at Honopu Beach added excitement to location filming for *King Kong*.

"It's been a classic for 43 years. And there's good reason for that. People think of it as a picture where an ape climbs the Empire State Building. But metaphysically, it's a rape of the environment. You take some great treasure of the environment and destroy it."—
Charles Grodin

Behold Hawaii, To Fly

o Fly, the film that pioneered the 70 mm IMAX format, daily presents a soaring five-story-high hang glider's view of Na Pali's pinnacles and valleys along with other bird's-eye-view flying scenes to audiences at the Smithsonian Institution's Air and Space Museum, the most well-attended space museum in the world.

"In *To Fly* we developed special camera mounts and set-ups that enabled us to create an 'experience' of flying in IMAX that had never been accomplished before," recalls director and producer Greg MacGillivray of MacGillivray Freeman Films of Laguna Beach, California.

IMAX is the largest screened film format in the history of the cinema. The 70 mm film frame used in IMAX films is ten times the size of the 35mm frame usually used for Hollywood feature films, and can be projected up to nine stories high and 120 feet wide. A highly sensory experience, IMAX films are accompanied by a six-channel, surround sound system.

To Fly had a Bicentennial world premiere at the Washington, D.C. museum in 1976. To date, over 180 million viewers have seen the Kalalau sequence in theaters, schools, and on television in various film formats.

In 1995, the National Film Registry of the Library of Congress added *To Fly* to its select collection of 175 American-made films.

Bob Wills hang-glides Kalalau Valley for MacGillivray-Freeman's *To Fly*.

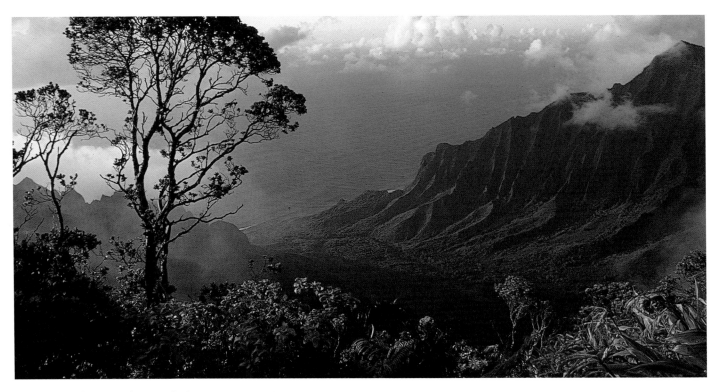

Kalalau Valley from one of two overlooks in Koke'e State Park.

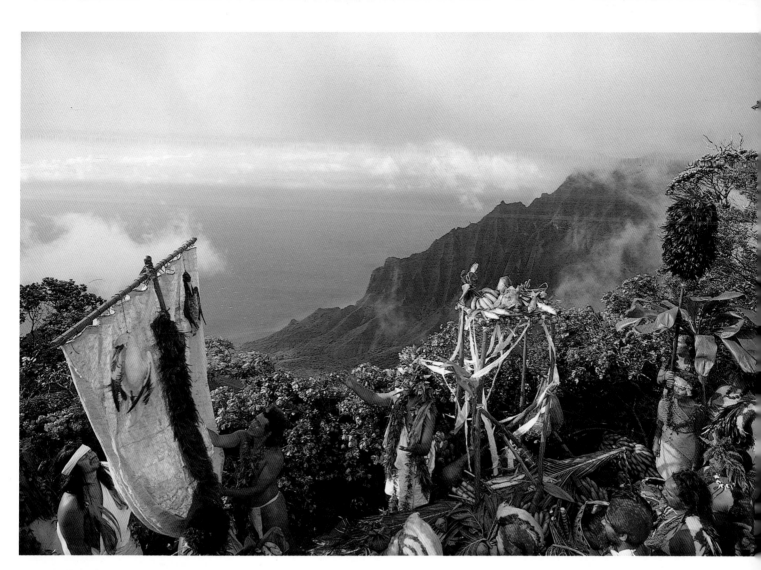

In *Behold Hawaii,* aliʻi in red and yellow feathered capes stand beneath the distinctive cross and cloth symbol of the Hawaiian harvest god Lono at Kalalau lookout.

Kalalau Beach is majestic with its backdrop of pinnacles and knife-edged ridges taller than big city skyscrapers.

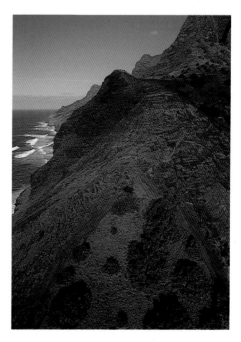

Red Hill at Kalalau Valley. The closing scene of the late 1980s end-of-the-world film *Millennium* features Red Hill as the way into a survivors' haven.

SURFING FILMS

Titus Kinimaka is Kaua'i's premiere big wave surfer. His Hawaiian School of Surfing offers lessons at Hanalei Bay.

Kaua'i is considered a hidden gem of a location in the world of surfing movies—that is, real surfing movies, not to be confused with Gidget and the beach blanket films of the sixties. In this genre of films made by surfers for surfers, Kaua'i is considered a rural, laid back outlier of the fast-paced surfing world found on O'ahu's North Shore.

In the surf films Kaua'i is infrequently shown, and rarely named. This is due in part to the unwritten laws of surfing traditionally laid down by local surfers who are very protective of Kaua'i's surfing breaks. Visiting surfing photographers and filmmakers, here to capture the premiere surf spots on film and publicize them worldwide, are highly advised to work cooperatively with the Island's leading surfers. Often they are asked to give fake names to the breaks they film. Bold, uncooperative filmmakers have more than once been asked to leave the Island.

The perfect pre-arrival message to visiting filmmakers and photographers would be: Catching good days of Kaua'i surf on film is much more difficult than on O'ahu or Maui due to the long distances the waves break offshore; the Island weather is more fickle, and at times deadly; and because of an increase over the past decade of tiger sharks around the surf breaks. Surfers paddling over offshore reefs are sometimes mistaken for green Hawaiian sea turtles, a favorite meal of the predators.

The first known film footage of surfing on Kaua'i comes from big wave rider Greg Noll's archives. In 1957 Noll, Dewey Weber (whose distinctive logo and name became famous in George Lucas' *American Graffiti)* and a handful of other surfers came to Kaua'i on a surfing safari. The surf explorers rode one-speed bikes pulling surfboards, bedrolls, and filming equipment propped on small trailers from Lihu'e to Hanalei along the old winding road that once hugged the coast. In Noll's recently released *Search for Surf—Da Bull* video, an edited version of his 1950s and early-1960s surf films, the crew camps out under the open-air shelter at the end of Hanalei Pier. The then-young surfers ride longboards at Hanalei Bay to a background of unbuilt Princeville.

In the 1960s famed Kaua'i surfer and waterman Percy Kinimaka acted in, and assisted in filming, a number of films on Kaua'i, including *Donovan's Reef.* Kinimaka brought some of the first modern, custom-shaped fiberglass surfboards to Kaua'i. Percy's family is still renowned for producing top surfers such as Titus Kinimaka and Alekai Kinimaka. Titus is featured in a number of Kaua'i surfing films and is a top-rated big wave rider. Interestingly, the graceful Hawaiian surfer travels to Tahiti to surf and has re-established ties with one of the ancient homelands of Kaua'i's native Hawaiian people. Titus sees being protective of Kaua'i's surfing breaks as part of the traditional Hawaiian ways of Kaua'i. "Respect for our lifestyle is what we are asking."

Bruce Brown, the filmmaker of *Endless Summer,* came over a few years later to film his 1961 film *Barefoot Adventure,* but struck out, riding sloppy east side waves, and failing to hit Hanalei in the proper season.

Another pioneering film was *Gone with the Wave*, with Kaua'i scenes filmed in 1963 by Honolulu's Phil Wilson. Kaua'i-born Carlos Andrade has been riding

This late sixties-early seventies psychedelic-colored surfboard made by Vinney Bryan belonged to Bunker Spreckles, the stepson of actor Clark Gable. Spreckles was a descendent of late-1800s Hawai'i sugar baron Claus Spreckles. Bunker's controversial surfing style, persona, and life-style made him a standout surfer during his days as a teenager riding waves on Kaua'i. Holding the board is Charlie Cowden of Hanalei Surf Company. Cowden features a mini-museum of prize surfboards within his surf shop in Hanalei town.

Veteran Kaua'i surfer Tex Wilson was a staff photographer for S*urfing Magazine* in the spring of 1970 when he captured Brian Kennelly of Kaua'i in the tube at Pipeline on a fiberglass, pre-Boogie Board kneeboard for this poster. Kennelly also made his mark in the hollow waves of Kaua'i's north shore.

Kaua'i surfer Alekai Kinimaka played a South American Indian in *Raiders of the Lost Ark*.

Dressed like a riverboat captain in Disney's *The Castaway Cowboy* is the late Mike Diffenderfer, one of the most influential surfers and surfboard shapers to come out of California in the modern era of surfing. Diffenderfer lived on Kaua'i during the 1970s and was known locally for his skill as a golfer. He's joined by a young Tom Summers (right).

Mike Wellman of Kalaheo is the son of famed Hollywood director William Wellman. Mike rides a thick-lipped wave off a Kekaha Beach in *Bali High*. A long-time surfer and noted surfboard manufacturer on Kaua'i, he follows in a tradition started by his father, who was filmed surfing the rollers at Waikiki.

SURFING FILMS

Kaua'i's waves on surfboards and other water vehicles for over 40 years, and rode Pakala on the west side in Wilson's surf flick. Andrade recently celebrated his 50th birthday by traveling with his son Makali'i to surf in East Java. He recalls: "There were some shots of Kealia beach and a segment on Pakala. We asked that the place not be named. By the time the sixties came around we were telling all photographers that we didn't want our surfing spots to get advertised due to the advent of crowds. It didn't stop the crowding, but might have kept the less hard core voyeurs from coming over."

Andrade, who serves as a counselor for Hawaiian students at the University of Hawai'i at Manoa provides a Kaua'i-based perspective on surfing films shot here:

"The surfing genre projects its own fantasies on our islands just like the Hawaii Visitors Bureau does in another context. For surfers, the usual image of Kaua'i is one of exotic landscapes, heroic Caucasian surfers 'discovering' pristine surfing grounds, and beautiful women waiting in the wings for après surf service. In the case of Greg Noll's film, it was the adventurous Jack Kerouac offbeat adventure to a primitive place. Roughing it! In Bali High, I think it was, 'we've got a secret spot (the land of Kong), can you guess where it is?'

"Surfers (coming to Kaua'i to ride waves) are an extension of the colonialism that started with Captain Cook and continues to this day. Surfers rename the places and consider the surf spots their own now that they have arrived. In the process, they displace native people and practices born of the culture that nurtured surfing for thousands of years."

Greg MacGillivray and Jim Freeman, founders of MacGillivray Freeman Films from California, captured in 1966 what is arguably the most beautiful surfing footage ever taken of Kaua'i while filming *Free and Easy*. The filmmakers from Laguna Beach introduced Bill Hamilton and Mark Martinson to Kaua'i and caught perfect waves on the West Side and North Shore months before the shortboard era began.

World of Waves was filmed in 1968-69 by Hanalei Elementary School principal Nick Beck, a native of Kaua'i and pioneer surfer of the modern era on Kaua'i, with Kaua'i *kama'aina* and Editions Limited publisher Gaylord Wilcox during a round-the-world surf film trip. Beck and Wilcox took their families along on the trip, including David and Hobey Beck, both noted watermen today on Kaua'i. After surfing on Mauritius in the Indian Ocean, Noosa Heads in Queensland, Australia, and along the wild coast of Portugal plus other exotic spots, Beck and Wilcox found some of the best waves at Ha'ena on Kaua'i for their epic surf film. There, sometime Kaua'i resident Joey Cabell ripped hollow Pipeline-like waves on one of his thick, turned-up nosed late sixties semi-gun surfboards.

Somewhat forgotten surf films of the early 1970s include Aussie Paul Witzig's *The Islands*, which featured Hanalei's Brian Kennelly ripping on his pre-Boogie Board-days fiberglass knee board.

In the mid-1970s, MacGillivray and Freeman returned to film a hang-gliding segment for *Five Summer Stories*, a recently re-released surfing film

SURFING FILMS

Life-long friends Nick Beck & Gaylord Wilcox at Hanalei Pier.

considered by many to be the best of the shortboard era. In the Kaua'i segment, then-world champion Bob Wills soars off a ledge at Koke'e and flies down a Na Pali valley, literally touching the tips of 3,000-foot-high pinnacles. The filmmakers employed similar footage in their classic IMAX format film *To Fly*. MacGillivray returned to Kaua'i, following the accidental death of Freeman while shooting aerial footage in California in the early-seventies, to film *Behold Hawaii*, the first IMAX film with characters and a dramatic story; the film features reproductions of ancient Hawaiian surfboards made on Kaua'i.

Stephen Spaulding, a Carmel, California-based cinematographer swam out in the early 1980s to film local big wave rider Terry Chung riding the hollow tubes offshore of Ha'ena in his film *Bali High*. Playing upon a backdrop of Mount Makana—Bali Hai of the film musical *South Pacific*—Spaulding compared the waves to the tubes of Indonesia's Bali. He failed to disclose the location of the surfing, teasing viewers that it was "The Island of Kong," in reference to King Kong.

Carlos Andrade today.

Spaulding commented: "After numerous screenings of raw footage and assurances that only pseudonyms would be used for the names of surfing spots, the boys agreed to the release of *Bali High*. Another reason I think I was able to balance getting good footage with the bad vibes from the locals was because I was a surfer as well, and everyone could see my ties to the island were deeper than your ordinary off-island cameraman."

The number of surfing films now produced each year, mostly released on videotape, has increased. Most are quickly shot, heavy on flashy surfing and hard rock music made to the beat of today's young surfers, offering a new take on Kaua'i's waves, and presenting quite a contrast to the soulful style of the earlier surf films.

Brian Kennelly (center), his son Gavin and daughter Keala. Keala is now a ASP Women's champion and premiere big wave rider.

Terry Chung and his taro trademark logo.

Character actor and surfer Scott "Lunchmeat" Furgeson has appeared in a number of feature films. Today, he is following in the paint drops of artist Jackson Pollack.

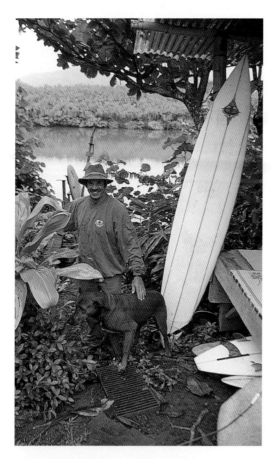

Bill Hamilton at home in Hanalei with his son Laird's dog Ridge.

SURFING FILMS

Free and Easy

Bill Hamilton is today one of Kauai's leading surfboard makers, and a veteran of both surfing and Hollywood films. He traveled to Kaua'i for the first time in 1966 as a featured surfer in MacGillivray Freeman's Free and Easy.

In 1966 surfing was pretty much central to O'ahu. Traveling to the outer islands on a "surf safari" was a rare adventure and not a common occurrence as it is now. In those days Maui was the destination for traveling surfers. Kaua'i was pretty much an unknown place with very few rumors circulating about its vast potential as a surfing location. This is a reality that continues today to a certain degree. When we arrived at the postage stamp-sized airport of Lihu'e in November of that year to film a segment of the surfing movie *Free and Easy* we were entering a world that seemed to be removed from time itself.

Our destination, Hanalei Bay, was a long, solitary drive over a bumpy patchwork of asphalt and pot holes. I remember the only thing that seemed to be open for business was the old Dairy Queen in Kapa'a, a virtual ghost town from beginning to end. Princeville was one big cow pasture. Our first stop was the old Plantation property, a beautifully landscaped entry that meandered past a white-columned building with a green copper roof and opulent gold trim. The road ran down a steep descent bordered by neatly kept white bungalows which overlooked the most beautiful place I had ever seen, Hanalei Bay. It was raining that day, and continued to do so for the entire two-and-a-half weeks we were there. We explored Kaua'i from one end to the other in search for surf. One day we tried to explore the PMRF range in Mana but were denied access. So we drove back towards Kekaha a mile or so, parked the car on the side of the road and walked the long thorn-filled walk through the kiawe-tree forest to the ocean. The effort was rewarded with the best surf we found on Kaua'i, and what would be a special segment to the film. We named this place Whispering Sands, a distant cousin of Barking Sands. Today this spot is called Rifle Range.

We surfed Hanalei on a beautiful Saturday afternoon with no one out. In fact, we didn't see another surfer the entire time we were here. Greg and Jim found the Hanalei Bay location very hard to film. Even after making the perilous climb to the peak of the roof on top of the pier, camera, tripod and all.

For a traveling surfer in the 1990s, I think Kaua'i is still a very special experience. It is a place that is filled with secret spots, little off-the-road nooks and crannies that take hours to explore and find. This can be an intimidating prospect, however; some of these places have strong feelings of privacy, of Kapu, and a sense of local ownership.

In this respect, Kaua'i has become a special place to visit, film, and document. The local surfers here are notoriously territorial and large motorized camera equipment on or near the beach is internationally rumored to be strictly tabu.

—Bill Hamilton

JAPANESE FILMS

Sadaharu Oh, Japan's Babe Ruth and all-time home run king, plays baseball at a ballfield in Kilauea for a Japanese television Christmas special featuring Japanese all-star ballplayers from today and yesterday. Oh played for Tokyo's Yomiuri Giants.

Japanese moviegoers and television viewers know Kaua'i well through both western-made films and Japanese productions filmed on Kaua'i.

The generation that came of age in the 1950s remembers Elvis' *Blue Hawaii* at the Coco Palms. Fan clubs from Japan have held Elvis conventions at the hotel, and special tour packages were created just to see the locations at Wailua.

The younger generation, aware of environmental problems around the world, knows Kaua'i as an untouched natural world they hope to protect. They know Kaua'i as the island where the tropical rain forests of *Jurassic Park* were filmed.

Millions of avid baseball fans in Tokyo, Osaka, and other big cities see Kaua'i as a spring training ground and golfing vacation spot for their heroes of the baseball diamond.

The first known Japanese feature film with Kaua'i scenes is the comedy *Hawaii Chindochu*, or *Sunny Travels in Hawaii*, a 1954 production of the International Theatrical Company.

This was followed by *Sanga Ari, (There are Mountains and Rivers)*, a 1962 peace movement film, starring Hideko Takamine, Japan's first lady of the screen. The film tells the story of Japanese immigrant sugar cane workers who came to Hawai'i in the early days of plantation immigration, and of their sons and daughters. The plot involves the family sorrow over the deaths of Japanese American soldiers during World War II while fighting in Italy and the Pacific.

Yoake No Futari, (Rainbow Over the Pacific), was filmed in 1968 with locations on Kaua'i. The rambling travelogue/musical was part of the Meiji Centennial, honoring the first Japanese immigrants to work in Hawai'i's sugar fields.

Yumi San and David Boynton join the crew of *River Watching* for a photo opportunity on location at Kawaikoi Stream in Koke'e. The segment was the first one of the popular series filmed outside of Japan.

Japanese-speaking Art Umezu, the film commissioner for Kaua'i during the administration of Mayor Tony Kunimura, offers an interesting perspective on Japanese filmmaking on Kaua'i. His production company assists visiting film crews from Japan, and Umezu is a friend of the famous Japanese actor Toshiro Mifune, who used to be a frequent Kaua'i visitor.

Umezu said the image of Kaua'i presented to the Japanese people is changing.

"Kaua'i became a mecca for Japan Air Lines, Shiseido cosmetics, and other large corporations during the Bubble Economy of the 1980s from the early eighties to '87," Umezu said. "They liked the clean air and tropics, and found something beyond the typical *Blue Hawaii* locations. Once they get over here they personally take an interest and focus on the fact we are preserving nature and beauty; they like having more access to wildlife. Now, instead of the grandeur of *Blue Hawaii*, they film the rain forest. Colors in the films are more subdued, in general they are more concerned about preserving things."

Much of what is filmed on Kaua'i for Japanese audiences is never shown here, though the location filming by Japanese crews often provides interesting anecdotes. Umezu recalls a recent Kaua'i production that made headlines in Japan.

Actors from Japan's Toho Studios acted in Frank Sinatra's 1964 production of *None But the Brave*. Here at Pila'a Beach an American soldier sneaks up on a Japanese Army guard.

Taro farmer Rodney Haraguchi and his mother Janet were featured in the 1995 Japanese television documentary *River Watching.*

Yukio Hashi, Walter Omori, and other stars from the 1968 Japanese production of *Yoake No Futari* (*Rainbow Over the Pacific*) were sent to Kaua'i by the Shochiku film company. The movie tells the story of a young Japanese photographer who falls for an island sensei woman.

Toshiro Mifune, Japan's most famous actor, and Art Umezu take a break during a film festival held on Kaua'i.

JAPANESE FILMS

"One TV movie filmed here in 1989 starred one of Japan's top television actors, Makoto Fujita, and the actress Mitsuko Baisho. The storyline was about a middle-aged husband in the financial market, and his wife who was starting to lose it because of stress. He's the company president and they take a vacation where they took their honeymoon 25 years before, on Kaua'i. Meanwhile, back in Japan, the banking company is negotiating with another bank to merge. The president does not know that because he is in Hawai'i. The Bubble Economy is bursting in the show, but fiction became a reality because before the show aired, the economy did burst. Because of this the producers were asked not to release the show because it was too true. Finally it aired three weeks later. They filmed mostly at Coco Palms and Fern Grotto, but also shot at Princeville Hotel two weeks before Mirage began gutting the hotel.

"We restarted the Kaua'i segment of the Hawai'i International Film Festival in 1985, and to make it special we invited Toshiro Mifune at Mayor Kunimura's behest. Mr. Mifune decided to bypass Honolulu and come to Kaua'i. This started the whole thing. It had lot to do with Mayor Kunimura's friendship with him.

"Mr. Mifune is a stickler for consistency, and continued to come for the film festivals. The fourth year he came he personally made sure his movie, *Sen No Rikyu—The Grand Tea Master,* from Toho films in Kyoto, which won an award at the Venice Film Festival—would be premiered on Kaua'i. An overflowing crowd filled the theater, with lines stretching outside. He told the crowd to enjoy the movie and apologized that so many people had to wait to come in."

A Japanese TV movie filmed in 1987 on Kaua'i, featuring actress Keiko Takeshita, was about a famous writer of a cartoon character named Sazae San, one of Japan's top manga (oversized comic book) magazines. *Tabiaruki* (globe trotting travels of) *Sazae San* presented a Blondie-like character, based on a story by writer Machiko Hasagawa from Japan. The story told of a lost dog, and of Sazae San's search on tropical Kaua'i for the dog. Locations included the Fern Grotto; helicopter shots of the Island's interior: Lihue; the former Kaua'i Hilton, now the Outrigger Kaua'i; and other sites. As a tie-in, the story of going up the Fern Grotto appeared in the Sazae San manga cartoon book.

The actor Makoto Fujita and the actress Mitsuko Baisho played a business executive and his wife trying to find peace on Kaua'i for a Japanese television drama.

DOCUMENTARIES

Along the Na Pali Coast, a New Zealand Television film crew focuses in on *'o'opu nakea*, a native goby fish that climbs waterfalls.

David Boynton is a leading nature and landscape photographer in Hawai'i. Born and raised in Hawai'i, Boynton has been active in conservation efforts and as an educator on Kaua'i for over 20 years. His work has appeared in dozens of books and magazines.

Documentary films tell factual stories and aim to educate viewers. Award-winning documentaries filmed on Kaua'i tell of the history of Kaua'i's Native Hawaiian musicians and the struggle to preserve rare native birds and plants, and have been shown on public television stations throughout the world.

While the documentaries don't reach as wide an audience as feature films, they perhaps paint a truer picture of Kaua'i's natural, unadorned beauty, focusing on the location, rather than the superimposed action.

The most popular subject of documentaries made on Kaua'i is the Island's wide diversity of native ecosystems with numerous plants, birds, and insects found nowhere else on earth. The native flora and fauna is, for the most part, quite easily accessible. Add the Island's spectacular scenery for a backdrop and you have a world-class setting that attracts documentary filmmakers from around the world.

Nu'aolo 'Aina valley was one of numerous Kaua'i locations featured in the National Geographic special *Strangers in Paradise*, a documentary that won two Emmys.

The British Broadcasting Corporation (BBC) has sponsored several documentaries filmed on Kaua'i, going back to the 1950s, when they recorded a segment on the mysterious deaths of single men among the Filipino immigrants working on the Island's sugar cane plantations. In 1980 BBC producer Roger Jones filmed several segments of a university-level educational film about evolution for Great Britain's Open University. Kaua'i footage included native birds, scenes of a rare "vining" cousin of the Maui silversword, and another silversword relative, the *iliau*, that grows along the rim of Waimea Canyon. The series was later adapted into the television documentary *Crucible of Life, Island of the Fire Goddess*. BBC producer Keenan Smart also sent a crew to Kaua'i in the late 1980s during filming of a documentary entitled *Islands of the Fire Goddess*, an Emmy award-winner.

While traveling throughout Polynesia for the documentary *Splendid Isolation: Islands, Television*, New Zealand television producer Rod Morris brought a crew to Kaua'i in 1989. In addition to filming native birds and plants here, the Kiwi crew flew into Nu'alolo 'Aina on the Na Pali coast to get scenes of the o'opu, a freshwater goby fish that can climb waterfalls.

The award-winning husband-and-wife team of Grace and Paul Atkins ventured into Kaua'i's remote interior searching for the *'o'o'a'a*, an endangered forest bird that was last seen in the mid 1980s for *Strangers in Paradise*.

Japanese film crews have come to Kauai on several occasions, including a recent trip for *River Watching*, a Nippon Television news feature. Kaua'i was the first location outside Japan for the series, which previously had shown over 50 Japanese locations. Television commentator Yumi-san enjoyed sunrise at the petroglyph boulders near the mouth of Wailua River, went crabbing from a canoe on Hanalei River, talked story with the Haraguchi family in a Hanalei taro field, and walked along Kawaikoi Stream with me, and filmed at Valley House.

Waterfalls flowing down from the summit of Mt. Wai'ale'ale were filmed by Paul Atkins, who waited for a day with heavy rains to capture the essence of one of the world's rainiest places.

Perhaps the most prestigious nature documentary filmed in Hawai'i was the 1991 National Geographic Special *Hawaii: Strangers in Paradise*. Paul and Grace Atkins of Honolulu-based Moana Productions won two Emmys and several other major film awards for the program. Kaua'i provided a diversity of scenes, including aerial footage of Na Pali Coast, goats running along the cliffs of Waimea Canyon, a "pet" feral pig rooting up the Koke'e forest, 'i'iwi birds feeding on Lobelia flowers, erosion flowing into the ocean off Kekaha, an over-the-lip view of Wailua Falls, and a trip into the Alaka'i Swamp in search of the endangered (perhaps extinct) 'ō'ō'a'a bird.

The Atkins' success, an expression of their unrelenting drive for capturing images beyond the ordinary, is exemplified by the footage of innumerable waterfalls along the cliffs below Mt. Wai'ale'ale. Instead of filming on a nice sunny day, they were on-call for thunderstorms so they could capture the "World's Rainiest Place" in all its glory, as they succeeded in doing.

Kaua'i has provided many locations for the *Hawaiian Legacy* series by island musician-turned-filmmaker Eddie Kamae. The mists of Kalalau, waterfalls on Namolokama, waves lapping the shore of Hanalei Bay, native birds in the Koke'e forest, and Wai'oli Hui'ia Church have appeared in Kamae's films, but perhaps most important was the Island's cultural heritage as expressed by Kaua'i musicians and composers such as Jacob K. Maka, Alfred Alohikea, and Helena Maka Santos.

—David Boynton

David Boynton talks about Kaua'i's streams with Japanese television commentator Yumi-san during the filming of *River Watching*.

Prospect Pictures of England returned to Kaua'i in the 1990s to reenact scenes from a number of feature films made on the Island.

Here, a British actor replays Indiana Jones with Kaua'i men who played headhunters in the original film.

A tree in Koke'e's rain forest provides a vantage point during the filming of *Strangers in Paradise*.

KAUA'I MOVIE MAP

1. Kipu Ranch—*Raiders of the Lost Ark, Diamond Head, The Hawaiians*
2. Hule'ia Stream—*Raiders of the Lost Ark, Beachhead*
3. Nawiliwili Harbor—*Donovans Reef, Jurassic Park/Lost World*
4. Kalapaki Beach—*South Pacific, Miss Sadie Thompson, Honeymoon in Vegas*
5. Lihu'e Airport—*Honeymoon in Vegas, Six Days Seven Nights*
6. Lihu'e—*Diamond Head, Honeymoon in Vegas*
7. Hanama'ulu Bay—*Donovans Reef, Pagan Love Song, To End All Wars*
8. Wailua Falls—*Fantasy Island*
9. Wailua River—*Outbreak, Islands in the Stream, Donovans Reef, Beachhead*
10. Coco Palms—*Blue Hawaii, Fantasy Island*
11. Wailua Beach—*Pagan Love Song, Pirates of the Caribbean 4*
12. Wailua Mauka—*Flight of the Intruder, Jurassic Park* (gates, T—Rex scene), *Tropic Thunder, Avatar, Time Machine II*
13. Kapa'a Town—*Jurassic Park* (Ramona's Cafe), *Throw Momma from the Train*
14. Valley House—*Jurassic Park* (visitors center, amber mine), *Voodoo Island*
15. Anahola—*Blue Hawaii, Raiders of the Lost Ark*
16. Papa'a Bay—*Six Days Seven Nights, North*
17. Moloa'a Bay—*Gilligans Island*
18. Pila'a—*Castaway Cowboy, None But the Brave*
19. Kilauea—*South Pacific, Jurassic Park* (Brontosaurus scene)
20. Kilauea Falls—*Just Go With It, George of the Jungle, Mighty Joe Young*
21. Kilauea Lighthouse—*Lilo & Stitch*
22. Kalihiwai—*Throw Momma from the Train*
23. Anini Beach—*Honeymoon in Vegas*
24. Princeville—*South Pacific*
25. Princeville Airport—*Dragonfly*
26. Hanalei Valley—*Uncommon Valor*
27. Hanalei Bay—*South Pacific, Beachhead, The Wackiest Ship in the Army, Bird of Paradise, Pagan Love Song, Miss Sadie Thompson, Behold Hawaii, Soul Surfer, The Descendants, Lilo & Stitch*
28. Wainiha Valley—*Dragonfly*
29. Lumaha'i Beach—*South Pacific*
30. Lumaha'i Valley—*Uncommon Valor*
31. Makua Beach—*South Pacific, Body Heat, Soul Surfer*
32. Waiakapala'e "Wet" Cave—*Pirates of the Caribbean 4*
33. Limahuli Valley—*Jurassic Park* (raptor cage)
34. Ke'e Beach—*Throw Momma from the Train, The Thorn Birds, Lord of the Flies, Behold Hawaii, Pirates of the Caribbean 4*
35. Kalalau Valley—*Millennium, To Fly*
36. Honopu Valley—*King Kong, Pirates of the Caribbean 4, Six Days Seven Nights*
37. Pacific Missile Range Facility/Barking Sands—*Flight of the Intruder, South Pacific*
38. Waimea—*Cane Fire/White Heat*
39. Waimea Canyon—*Donovans Reef, The Wackiest Ship in the Army, Lilo & Stitch*
40. Olokele Canyon—*Jurassic Park* (air tour only)
41. Hanapepe Valley—*Jurassic Park* (helicopter landing pad)
42. Hanapepe Town—*The Thorn Birds, Flight of the Intruder, Islands in the Stream* (in waters off Port Allen)
43. Wahiawa—*Uncommon Valor*
44. Lawa'i-Kai—*Donovans Reef, Last Flight of Noah's Ark, South Pacific, Honeymoon In Vegas, Lt. Robin Crusoe, Pirates of the Caribbean 4*
45. National Tropical Botanical Garden—*Jurassic Park* (dinosaur egg in tree roots), *Pirates of the Caribbean 4*
46. Kukui'ula Harbor—*Islands in the Stream*
47. Koloa Mauka—*To End All Wars*
48. Po'ipu Beach—*Lt. Robin Crusoe*
49. Maha'ulepu—*Islands in the Stream, Castaway Cowboy, Six Days Seven Nights*
50. Kipu Kai—(By air tour only) *Hook, The Descendants, Six Days Seven Nights*

KAUA'I

Makua Beach
Lumaha'i Beach
'Anini Beach Park
21 Kīlauea Lighthouse
Waiakapala'e "Wet" Cave 32
31
Princeville
Ke'e Beach 34
Hā'ena 28 30 29 27 26 24 25 22 19 Kīlauea
Wainiha Valley
Lumaha'i Valley
Hanalei
Kalihiwai
Princeville Airport
Hanalei Valley
18 Pila'a
17 MOLOA'A BAY
HANALEI BAY
16 PĀPA'A BAY

35 Kalalau Valley
36 Honopū Valley
Anahola 15

Valley House 14

12 Wailua Mauka
Keālia

37 Pacific Missle Range Facility/ Barking Sands
39 Waimea Canyon
Mt. Wai'ale'ale
Coco Palms 10 Kapa'a
Wailua River 9 13
11 Wailua Beach
Wailua

40 Okokele Canyon
8 Wailua Falls

Hanamā'ulu 7 HANAMĀ'ULU BAY
Līhu'e 6 5 Līhu'e Airport
Puhi
2 Hule'ia Stream
Kalapaki Beach 4
Kekaha
Waimea 38
Hanapēpē Valley
41
National Tropical Botanical Gardens
Nāwiliwili Harbor 3
1 Kipu Ranch
NĀWILIWILI BAY

Okokele
Kalāheo
Kōloa
50 Kipu Kai Beach

Hanapēpē 42
43 Wahiawa
43 47
49 Maha'ulepu Beach
Port Allen
44 Lawai Kai
46 48
Kukui'ula Harbor Po'ipū

DRIVING GUIDE TO MOVIE LOCATIONS

Kaua'i's movie locations are in many cases difficult to see. Many locations are away from paved roads, and most are on private property. Except for specific landmarks—the Hanalei Pier for example—it is best to be satisfied with finding the general location and knowing "the film was made near here." A helicopter ride is often the only way to see a number of Kaua'i's movie locations, especially those deep in the Island's interior.

Following is a list of where major Hollywood feature films and network television shows were made on Kaua'i. Movie locations visible from accessible roads have specific driving instructions. Remote locations are described by referring to nearby landmarks.

General directions common in Hawai'i refer to places being *makai* or *mauka-makai* being towards the sea and *mauka* towards the mountains. One main road makes a huge "U" on Kaua'i, ending past Kekaha on the west side and at Ha'ena on the north shore; this road is named Kuhio Highway (State Highway 56) north of Lihu'e, and Kaumuali'i Highway (State Highway 50) south and west of Lihu'e.

LIHU'E-NAWILIWILI

A number of films have been shot in and around Lihu'e. *Honeymoon in Vegas* featured the ticket counters and Lihu'e Airport, and the Lihu'e Police Department's former headquarters on 'Umi Street. Kalapaki Beach, fronting the Kaua'i Marriott Resort, is where Mitzi Gaynor and Ray Walston put on their stage show in *South Pacific*. Rita Hayworth drives up to an old general store set at Kalapaki in *Miss Sadie Thompson*. In *Six Days Seven Nights*, Anne Heche and David Schwimmer first encounter Harrison Ford in the old Lihu'e Airport Terminal, now used to service private jets and fixed wing airplanes.

Nawiliwili Harbor, between the breakwater and the docks, is where John Wayne paddled out to greet director John Ford's yacht *Araner* in *Donovan's Reef*, in *Jurassic Park* you can catch a glimpse of the breakwater with huge hurricane-driven waves crashing over it, filmed by Steven Spielberg's crew during Hurricane Iniki.

Coming out of Lihu'e Airport, turn right on Ahukini Road and drive until the road ends at what was once Ahukini Landing, on the southern end of Hanama'ulu Bay. Until about 1950 a bustling port stood here and was used in *Pagan Love Song* to replicate a boat day scene at Papeete, Tahiti. The beach park at Hanama'ulu Bay, which you can see mauka from Ahukini Landing, is accessible by driving north on Kuhio Highway from Lihu'e and turning *makai* on Hanama'ulu Road. Here John Ford and John Wayne filmed outrigger canoe scenes for *Donovan's Reef*. An opening scene of *To End All Wars*, where Japanese troops fake shooting blindfolded POWs, was filmed at the Ahukini Pier site.

For a look at main *Raiders of the Lost Ark* locations, drive along the harbor at Nawiliwili about three-quarters of a mile to the Menehune (Alekoko) Fishpond Lookout. Though you can't see it, inland of the fishpond is a pasture where Indiana Jones was pursued by headhunters. Indy escapes from the headhunters aboard a seaplane that began taxiing *mauka* of the Alekoko Fishpond, and took off near the mouth of the Hule'ia Stream, near Nawiliwili Harbor.

Diamond Head and *The Hawaiians*, both starring Charlton Heston, featured locations at the Rice family's Kipu Ranch, which is not open to the public. The rural ranch is marked by a long row of Norfolk pines *makai* of Kaumuali'i Highway, several miles south of Lihu'e. Just *makai* of Kukui Grove Shopping Center, off Nawiliwili Road, is the old plantation manager's house used as Heston's home in *Diamond Head*. Over the Ha'upu Range (the mountains to the south of Lihu'e) is secluded Kipukai, a beautiful, isolated beach and valley used in *The Descendants*, and as a model for Peter Pan's Never-Never Land in *Hook*.

WAILUA/KAPA'A

The gates to Jurassic Park, and the crash scene in *Flight of the Intruder*, were filmed near a spot known locally as the "Blue Hole." This semi-circular valley was carved out by the towering waterfalls, cascading down from Wai'ale'ale mountain and is visible in the distance from Lihu'e; the location is on generally inaccessible lands.

Turn *mauka* up Kuamoʻo Road off Kuhio Highway, at the traffic light just north of the Wailua River, and travel to the top of the rise and the little ʻOpaekaʻa Falls overlook park, the falls are featured in *The Wackiest Ship in the Army*. Then walk across Kuamoʻo Road to the overlook above the Wailua River, below is Kamokila Hawaiian Village, the disease-ridden African village in Zaire in *Outbreak*.

Double back to Kuhio Highway. *Mauka* from the beach is the shuttered Coco Palms Resort. Here, Elvis filmed *Blue Hawaii* and Rita Hayworth played in *Sadie Thompson* at the small wedding chapel that still stands. Movie casts and crews once frequently stayed at the Coco Palms, including the entire company from *South Pacific*. Johnny Depp as Jack Sparrow was tied up to a coconut tree here in *Pirates of the Caribbean: On Stranger Tides*.

North along Wailua Beach near Lae Nani condominiums is the former location of the Horner mansion, featured in *Pagan Love Song* and *Donovan's Reef*, and a beach house once well known as "The Sinatra House" where Frank Sinatra stayed. Sinatra almost drowned here.

Continuing north on Kuhio Highway is Kapaʻa town. The plantation town is where Nicolas Cage was trying to find in *Honeymoon in Vegas*, calling from a phone booth saying "Kapa…ah… ah…ah…a." On the north side of Kapaʻa, just to the Lihuʻe side of the new Otsuka Store, is where Ramona's oceanfront café was set for *Jurassic Park*; the warehouse on which the colorful Ramona's sign was painted blew down during Hurricane Iniki in 1992.

The valley and white-sand beach north of Kapaʻa is Kealia. Inland is historic Valley House, a private estate that served as the location for the massive set for Jurassic Park's visitor center.

Several miles north of Kealia is the town of Anahola. You can't miss the distinctive Kalalea mountains to the northwest of Anahola's town center. Head up the hill on the highway past the post office at Anahola and look for a safe place to pull over to see the towering peak used for the opening shot in *Raiders of the Lost Ark*. The peak looks a bit like King Kong's head, and is a match for the mountain in the Paramount Pictures logo.

NORTH SHORE

The spectacular scenery along the north shore is a popular backdrop for filmmakers.

Isolated Moloaʻa Bay, halfway between Anahola and Kilauea (the first town on the north shore) is down a pot-holed road off Kuhio Highway. Here, Bob Denver and Alan Hale starred in the pilot film for *Gilligan's Island*.

Along this section of the north shore Frank Sinatra filmed *None But the Brave* at inaccessible Pilaʻa Beach, and director Steven Spielberg chose fields *mauka* of Kilauea for the scene in *Jurassic Park* where the visiting scientists see their first dinosaur.

The U.S. Fish & Wildlife's Kilauea Point National Wildlife Refuge with its landmark Kilauea Lighthouse serves as a colorful backdrop in *Lilo & Stitch*.

Keep heading north to Princeville. Princeville Airport was set as a Venezuelan Amazon airport in *Dragonfly*. An overlook on the hill down to Hanalei Valley offers a sweeping view. Taro fields in the valley just past the landmark bridge were planted with rice to become Vietnam for *Uncommon Valor*. At the end of Ka Haku Road, the main street in the Princeville Resort, is the five-star St. Regis Princeville Resort hotel. George Clooney and family stay at the St. Regis during their revenge sojourn to Hanalei in *The Descendants*.

Continue on to Hanalei town and turn right off Kuhio Highway at Aku Road, the first turnoff in the small town. Aku ends at Weke Road, so make another right and keep driving until you come to the Hanalei River. On your left is Hanalei Pier and Black Pot Beach Park. Near the pier, scenes featuring Bloody Mary and Luther Billis were filmed for *South Pacific*, plus scenes from a number of other movies. Across the blue waters of Hanalei Bay is the distinctive outline of Mount Makana, better known to film buffs as Bali Hai from *South Pacific*. On a bluff directly across from the mouth of the Hanalei River is the location for the French planter's home in *South Pacific*. On the edge of town look for the Tahiti Nui bar and restaurant where George Clooney and kids, and his cousin played by Beau Bridges, dine. Past the Tahiti Nui turn right off Kuhio Highway at Aku Road, the first turnoff in the small town. Aku ends at Weke Road. Looking east, to the right, is the road George Clooney and kids walk down in *The Descendants*. The beach Clooney walks down at Hanalei parallels Weke Road, and Weke Road ends on the east at Hanalei Pier, another landmark easily visible in the film.

Continuing west on Kuhio Highway the road rises as you pass Hanalei Bay. Around the bend, past the top of the rise, is parking for Lumahaʻi Beach. Trails here lead down to the beach and up to an overview of Lumahaʻi Beach. Near the rocky outcrop in the middle of the spectacular beach is where Mitzi Gaynor "Wash(ed) That Man Right Out of My Hair" in *South Pacific*.

Continuing north on Kuhio Highway, the road winds along the coast. About a mile past Hanalei Colony Resort is Makua Beach, or "Tunnels" Beach named for the many underwater caves along the fringing reef here. Parking in this area is now restricted. Walk down to the beach and you are at Bali Hai, or at least the location director Joshua Logan filmed as Bali Hai. Here Mount Makana is directly behind the beach. Near where tour boats load at Makua Beach is wher the village of Bali Hai was set in *South Pacific*. Kathleen Turner ended up here, too, in *Body Heat*, after getting away with murder in Florida in the film's final scene. The nearby Waikapalae "Wet" at Ha'ena is set as the entrance to the Fountain of Youth cave in *Pirates of the Caribbean: On Stranger Tides*.

The next stop beyond Makua Beach is Limahuli Valley, which was the location for the cage where a cow was fed to raptors in *Jurassic Park*. Tours of the National Tropical Botanical Garden's grounds in the privately owned valley are available. Kuhio Highway ends at Ke'e Beach. Here, Richard Chamberlain and Rachel Ward embraced on the rocks along the coast in *The Thorn Birds*, and in *Throw Mama From the Train* Billy Crystal parodied Kathleen Turner's *Body Heat* scene. Johnny Depp and crew roam Ke'e Beach in *Pirates of the Caribbean: On Stranger Tides*.

NA PALI

Beyond Ke'e Beach is over a dozen miles of uninhabited, somewhat inaccessible wilderness area featuring spectacular valleys and sea cliff pinnacles knowsn as the Na Pali Coast. You may hike the coast from Ke'e as far as Kalalau, go along it in a tour boat, or fly above it in a charter helicopter.

Kalalau Valley and Honopu Arch are where the remake of *King Kong* was filmed in 1976. The beach on the Hanalei side of the arch is where the exploration party landed, and through the arch on the beach fronting Honopu Valley is the way to Kong's valley. Johnny Depp and the cast of *Pirates of the Caribbean: On Stranger Tides* began their Kaua'i filming at Honopu Beach. Contemporary State of Hawai'i regulations prohibit landing a boat at the pristine, environmentally-endangered valley so they came aboard a helicopter and jet skis. The pirate chase scenes in *Six Days Seven Nights* were filmed in this area and at nearby Nu'alolo Kai with the aid of the Navy base at the Pacific Missile Range Facility.

KOLOA/PO'IPU

Heading south of Lihu'e, follow Kaumuali'i Highway for about five miles to the turnoff for Koloa and Po'ipu. Follow Maluhia Road (Highway 520) through the landmark Tree Tunnel down to Koloa. The McBryde Sugar Mill just outside the town became a tropical Australian mill in *The Thorn Birds*. Drive to the coast at Po'ipu from Koloa and head east to the wilderness area at Mahaulepu. Adventurous island explorers can hike along the beaches and sea cliffs here to locations used to replicate Bimini in the Bahamas for *Islands in the Stream*.

Heading back to Po'ipu, look for Po'ipu Beach Park. Just west of the park is where Dick Van Dyke washed ashore in Disney's *Lt. Robin Crusoe*.

Continuing west along the coast, head back toward Koloa town, but turn down Lawa'i Road and drive towards the Spouting Horn. Just past this famous natural blow hole is the entrance to the lush tropical gardens at The National Tropical Botanical Garden. Tours depart daily from Spouting Horn park (reservations required) and offer a glimpse of Lawa'i-Kai. Within the private garden, which was once the estate of Queen Emma of Hawai'i in the 1870s and later cultivated as a world-class botanical garden, are locations filmed for *Jurassic Park, South Pacific, Donovan's Reef, Honeymoon in Vegas*, and *Last Flight of Noah's Ark*.

WEST SIDE

Doubling back to Kaumuali'i Highway from Koloa, head west to the art gallery-lined streets of old Hanapepe town. The road through Hanapepe's main street was transformed into a tropical outback Australia town for *The Thorn Birds*, and a bar strip in the Philippines for *Flight of the Intruder*. Disney animators captured the look of a vintage Kaua'i plantation town modeled on Hanapepe Town in *Lilo & Stitch*.

Inland of Hanapepe, helicopter passengers can view Manawaiopuna Falls. Here, a concrete helicopter landing pad was built for an opening scene of *Jurassic Park*. Further west, Olokele Canyon is visible from the air as well. Young Tim in *Jurassic Park* was electrocuted and thrown from a tall high-voltage fence with this canyon as a backdrop.

Back on Kaumuali'i Highway, continue along the coast to Waimea, the town where Captain Cook first landed in 1778 to discover Hawai'i for the western world. Here, Kaua'i film buffs may see locations from the first feature film made on Kaua'i. *Cane Fire*, later renamed *White Heat*, was mostly filmed at the old Waimea Sugar Plantation just north of Waimea town. The Waimea Plantation Cottages, just north of the old Plantation site, is reminiscent of the *White Heat/Cane Fire* era of the 1930s on Kaua'i.

North of Waimea town, the beaches and buildings of the Pacific Missle Range Facility at Barking Sands have been used in *South Pacific* and *Flight of the Intruder*. Inland, and over 3,000 feet up from Waimea, is the highland forest area of Koke'e. Waimea Canyon Road leads up from Waimea. Koke'e is haven for rare Hawaiian plants and some of the rarest forest birds in the world. Film crews from National Geographic and other documentary filmmakers have traveled to Kaua'i especially to film here. Visitors to the Smithsonian's Air and Space Museum in Washington, D.C. will recall the incredible hang-gliding sequence in MacGillivray-Freeman Films' five-story-high IMAX production *To Fly*. The hang glider soared off from Koke'e to land on a beach at Na Pali.

Promoting Kaua'i Filmmaking

Kaua'i location promotional guides were first produced in the mid-1980s, and have evolved with the ever-growing number of major feature films featuring Kaua'i locations. The website FilmKauai.com is an extension of the current guide.

Director Steven Spielberg on the set of *Lost World: Jurassic Park* at Kipu Kai in 1996 with (from left) Kaua'i Film Commissioner Judy Drosd, Kaua'i Mayor Maryann Kusaka (right) and the Mayor's Administrative Aide Millie Wellington. Judy, who left Manhattan and a Home Box Office executive job for Kaua'i, greatly expanded the scope of promoting Kaua'i location filming.

Current Kaua'i Film Commissioner Art Umezu with Kaua'i location filming memorabilia in his office in Lihu'e. In 2010 film producers working with Art brought $53 million in on-island spending to Kaua'i for feature films including *Pirates of the Caribbean: On Stranger Tides, The Descendants, Just Go With It,* and *Soul Surfer.* Art has served as film commissioner since 2004 and also ran the Kaua'i film office from 1986-1988. He's been on Kaua'i since 1975 working with film and music productions from the Mainland, Hawaiian islands, and Japan.

Kaua'i casting director and location manager Angela Tillson of A Whale of A Time Productions on the set of *Tropic Thunder.* Angela has played a key role in the making of feature films on Kaua'i since the 1980s. In earlier decades local casting directors Linda Antipala and Tom Summers provided support for filmmakers.

Director Steven Spielberg with location manager Ken Levine at the base of Manawaiopuna Falls in Makaweli during the filming of *Jurassic Park* in 1992. Ken served as the first Kaua'i Film Commissioner, hired by Mayor JoAnn Yukimura in 1988. Councilwoman JoAnn Yukimura, who served as Kaua'i's mayor from 1988-1992, recalls the formation of the Kaua'i Film Commission: "My vision for the film commission was that if Kaua'i was to diversify, we should start with that which came naturally. Creating a Film Commission meant that Kaua'i County could respond to interest, help to create and nurture interest, and facilitate the shooting of movies on Kaua'i in a professional and active way. Both Judy and Ken exemplified what we were looking for: highly skilled and polished individuals who understood the film production process and who could interact with and successfully 'secure the sale'. The vision came true almost immediately. When Hurricane 'Iniki hit and tourism virtually died, the filming of *Jurassic Park* helped keep us alive on Kaua'i in those economically tenuous months and years that followed 'Iniki."

Kaua'i Film Promotion 1910s-1950s

Kaua'i Film Commissioner Art Umezu (left) brought legendary filmmaker Roger Corman (seated to right) to Kaua'i for the Hawai'i International Film Festival in 2005. Here, Corman, who has recently used Kaua'i as a location for SyFy Channel productions, presents a seminar on filmmaking to local student filmmakers.

A 50th anniversary celebration of the release of Elvis' classic Kaua'i movie *Blue Hawaii,* filmed at the Coco Palms Resort and other locations was held in September 2012. Here Kaua'i Visitors Bureau Executive Director Sue Kanoho (left), who organized the event, is joined by singer Larry Rivera (to the right of Sue) who stages *Blue Hawaii* weddings on the Coco Palms grounds, and Elvis impersonator Tim Welch, along with entertainers and visiting travel writers. *Blue Hawaii* is known as the first major motion picture to showcase Kaua'i as Kaua'i on screen. The celebration featured a *Blue Hawaii* night at the Kaua'i Marriott Resort which drew more than 600 fans and honored Coco Palms Resort owner the late Grace Guslander.

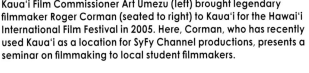

SOUND, NATURAL COLOR MOTION PICTURES OF HAWAII BEING SHOWN

"See Every Island" programs of all sound, natural color motion pictures sponsored by the Hawaii Tourist Bureau to encourage travel to all the islands, are playing to capacity houses of mainland visitors every Friday morning in Honolulu, according to word received from the capital city.

Garden Island scenes shown at the performances include the following:

Nawiliwili bay and harbor, Lihue Hotel grounds, Kukuiolono park and peacocks, flowers and flowering trees, Waimea, Hanapepe Valley, reconstructed heiau at Waialua, torch fishing, spouting horn and Lawai beach, Waimea canyon, Opaikaa Falls, sliding bathtub, banana growing, Hanalei valley, rice cultivation, Kauai coast, Napali.

The first movies filmed on Kaua'i were of scenic locations taken by visiting filmmakers to be used in promoting Hawai'i as a tourism destination by the Hawai'i Promotions Committee, the forerunner to the Hawai'i Visitors and Convention Bureau. This clipping from a 1918 news report lists the prominent sites filmed for the short films.

Lihu'e photographer and photography studio owner William J. Senda, pictured here on the set of *White Heat* at Waimea with Venezuelan actress Mona Maris, shot stills for Hollywood directors into the 1960s, most prominently for *South Pacific* in 1957. Senda movie photos were published around the globe. Charlie "Mr. Kaua'i" Fern published *The Garden Island* newspaper and was a strong proponent of attracting Hollywood filmmakers to Kaua'i both in the press and among Island business leaders and the local community.

To mark the 50th Anniversary of the Kaua'i location filming of *South Pacific* its star Mitzi Gaynor returned to Kaua'i in 2009. Mitzi reminisced about her time on Kaua'i during the talk at the Kaua'i Marriott Resort. She also was the star attraction at a private party held during the grand reopening of the St. Regis Princeville Resort. Here Mitzi (right) poses with Kaua'i Visitors Bureau Executive Director Sue Kanoho on the grounds of the St. Regis Princeville with *South Pacific* landmark Bali Hai (Mount Makana) in the background.

Acalpulco Gold • Filmed on Kaua'i September 1976. Released 1978. Marvista Productions, color. Director Burt Brinckerhoff, Producers Allan F. Bodoh and Bruce Cohn. Cast: Marjoe Gortner, Robert Lansing, Ed Nelson. Locations: Na Pali, Princeville, Hanalei. *Pirates hijack yachts and smuggle dope on the high seas off Kaua'i.*

Adventures of Captain David Grief • Filmed on Kaua'i 1957. Duke Goldstone production. Locations: Wailua. *Short-lived television show featuring South Pacific adventures of sea captain character created by Jack London.*

Avatar • Filmed on Kaua'i spring 2007. Released December 2009. 20th Century Fox Film Corporation. Director/Writer James Cameron. Cast: Sam Worthington, Zoe Saldana, Sigourney Weaver. Locations: Mauka Wailua rain forest. *Crew of landmark sci-fi computer graphics-live action linked film experienced roaming in interior Kaua'i rain forest in training for virtual scenes.*

Beachcomber, The • Filmed on Kaua'i March 1960. Producer Josef Shafel, Director Howard W. Koch. Cast: Cameron Mitchell. Locations: Wailua, Lydgate Park, Waipouli and Niumalu. *Television pilot that foreshadowed Fantasy Island set on mythical island of Amura in British Samoa.*

Beachhead • Filmed on Kaua'i July 1953. Released 1954. United Artists, color. Director Stuart Heisler, Producer Howard W. Koch, written by Richard Alan Simmons; based on the novel *I've Got Mine* by Richard Hubler. Cast: Tony Curtis, Frank Lovejoy, Mary Murphy. Locations: Wailua River, Hule'ia Stream, Coco Palms, Hanalei. *Four U.S. Marines land on Bougainville during WWII to search for planter with information on key minefield prior to massive assault.*

Behold Hawaii • Filmed on Kaua'i summer 1981. Released 1983. MacGillivray-Freeman Films, IMAX 70mm color. Director/Producer Greg MacGillivray, Screenplay Alec Lorimore. Cast: Blaine Kia, Kanani Velasco, Kimo Kahoano. 40 minutes. Locations: Hanalei Bay, Hanalei Town, Koke'e, Ke'e Beach, Wailua Falls. *Landmark first IMAX feature film with characters and plot takes Hawaiian youth back to days of old Hawai'i to face dangers and challenges in discovering his heritage.*

Between Heaven and Hell • Released 1956. 20th Century Fox, Cinemascope. Director Richard Fleischer, Producers Bill Walsh & David Weisbart, Screenplay Harry Brown, based on novel by Francis Gwaltney. Cast: Robert Wagner, Terry Moore, Buddy Ebsen, Scatman Crothers. Location: Wailua. *WWII "Hellfighters of the Pacific" fight on South Pacific island, rising above their Southern class prejudices.*

Bird of Paradise • Filmed on Kaua'i August 1950. Released 1951. 20th Century Fox, Technicolor. Director/Producer/Writer Delmer Daves. Cast: Debra Paget, Louis Jourdan, Jeff Chandler. Locations: Hanalei Bay, Coco Palms.

Frenchman tires of civilization, seeks solace in South Pacific and falls in love with Polynesian girl, breaking local taboos, resulting in her being sacrificed to volcano god. A spectacular Polynesian epic written from a popular 1911 stage play and 1932 film.

Blue Hawaii • Filmed on Kaua'i April 1961. Released 1961. Paramount Pictures, color. Director Norman Taurog, Producer Hal Wallis. Cast: Elvis Presley, Angela Lansbury, Joan Blackman. 101 minutes. Locations: Coco Palms, Wailua Beach, Lydgate Park, 'Opaeka'a Falls, Kipu, Anahola Village, Anahola Bay. *Elvis' best Hawai'i movie. Presley as rebellious son of pineapple tycoon tries to make his own way leading tours, including a trip with convertible full of co-eds on a Kaua'i highway.*

Body Heat • Released 1981. Ladd Co., TechniColor. Director/Writer Lawrence Kasdan, Producer Fred T. Gallo. Cast: Kathleen Turner, William Hurt. 113 minutes. Location: Makua Beach at Ha'ena. *Sexy Florida murderess kills her way to a fortune and escapes to paradise life on the beach at Ha'ena, Kaua'i.*

Cane Fire/White Heat • Filmed on Kaua'i September 1933. Released 1934. Seven Seas Film Corporation, B&W. Director/Writer Lois Weber. Cast: Mona Maris, David Newell, Virginia Cherill. Locations: Waimea Plantation, Wahiawa Camp. *"Authentic west side plantation scenes from 1930s highlights Kaua'i's first Hollywood feature film."*

Castaway Cowboy, The • Filmed on Kaua'i September 1973. Released 1974. Walt Disney Productions, TechniColor. Director Vincent McEveety, Producers Winston Hibler & Ron Miller. Cast: James Garner, Vera Miles, Robert Culp, Nephi Hannemann. 91 minutes. Locations: Pila'a, Maha'ulepu. *Originally titled Paniolo, this Disney family film features washed ashore Texas cowboy as savior of widow's Kaua'i potato farm, with help of novice Hawaiian cowboys. Period costumes, ranchland locations and swimming cattle to ships make for good try at capturing 19th-century Kaua'i.*

Death Moon • Released 1978. CBS Made-for-TV movie, color. Director Bruce Kessler. Cast: France Nuyen, Robert Foxworth, Dolph Sweet. Locations: Coco Palms. *Werewolves at Coco Palms!*

Descendants, The • Filmed on Kaua'i May 2010. Released 2011. Fox Searchlight, color. Director/Co-writer Alexander Payne based upon novel written by Kaui Hart Hemmings. Cast: George Clooney, Shailene Woodley, Amara Miller, Beau Bridges, Laird Hamilton. Locations: Kipu Kai, Hanalei Bay, Princeville, Tahiti Nui in Hanalei. *The Descendants is acclaimed as perhaps best film showing authen-*

tic picture of contemporary life in Hawai'i.

Diamond Head • Filmed on Kaua'i March 1962. Released 1962. Columbia Pictures, color. Director Guy Green, Producer Jerry Bresler. Cast: Charlton Heston, Yvette Mimieux, James Darren. 107 minutes. Locations: Kipu Ranch, Lihu'e, Grove Farm, Nawiliwili. *Ruthless haole plantation owner "King" Howland tries to stop marriage of his beautiful sister to a Hawaiian, while he has affair with Chinese woman; relationships come to a head creating main conflict of film.*

Donovan's Reef • Filmed on Kaua'i August 1962. Released 1963. Paramount Pictures, TechniColor. Director/Producer John Ford, Screenplay by James Edward Grant and Frank Nugent from story by James Michener. Cast: John Wayne, Elizabeth Allen, Lee Marvin. 109 minutes. Locations: Nawiliwili Harbor, Ahukini Landing, Hanama'ulu Beach, Wailua River, Waipouli, Cooc Palms, Lawa'i-Kai, Ko'olau, Waimea Canyon lookouts. *Former marine "Guns" Donovan returns to paradise in South Pacific after WWII and opens Donovan's Reef, a tropical bar. Wayne plays father for three half-Polynesian children of a war buddy-doctor who abandoned Boston and his wealthy family for the South Seas. The doctor's daughter arrives from Boston, intent on disowning her father. Instead, she falls for Wayne, and the South Seas.*

Dragonfly • Filmed on Kaua'i 2001. Released 2002. Universal Studios. Director Tom Shadyac. Written by Brandon Camp and Mike Thompson. Cast: Kevin Costner, Susanna Thompson, Joe Morton. Locations: Wainiha Valley, Princeville Airport, Kaua'i Ranch in Kealia, Wai'ale'ale Crater. *Dragonfly portrayed Venezuelan Amazon basin at Kaua'i locations. Indians from Venezuela were flown to Kaua'i for authenticity.*

Fantasy Island • Filmed on Kaua'i 1978, 1979. Broadcast January 1978 to August 1984. ABC-TV, color. Cast: Ricardo Montalban, Herve Villechaize. *Visitors travel to Fantasy Island to have their dreams fulfilled. Two segments of this hit TV series were filmed on Kaua'i. Wailua Falls featured during opening of each broadcast.*

Flight of the Intruder • Filmed on Kaua'i October and November 1989. Released 1991. Paramount Pictures, color. Director John Milius, Producers Mace Neufeld & Robert Rehme, from novel by Stephen Coonts, screenplay by Robert Dillon, John Milius, David Shaber. Cast: Danny Glover, Willem Dafoe, Brad Johnson. 115 minutes. Locations: Wailua Mauka, Pacific Missle Range Facility (Barkind Sands), Hanapepe Town. *In 1972 three U.S. Navy fliers clash over unofficial bombing of North Vietnam and personal conflicts. Crash-landing and rescue of* *crew aboard Vietnam-era Navy A-6 Intruder in Kaua'i interior set as Vietnam climaxes film.*

Forbidden Island • Released 1959. Columbia Pictures, color. Director/Writer/Producer Charles B. Griffith. Cast: Jon Hall, Martin Denny, Abraham Kaluna. *Aging 1930s–40s adventure star Jon Hall plays scuba diver searching for jewels in South Pacific shipwreck. Jungle scenes filmed on Kaua'i, underwater at Silver Springs in Florida.*

George of the Jungle • Filmed on Kaua'i summer 1996. Released 1997. Walt Disney Pictures. Director Sam Weisman. Characters created by Jay Ward. Cast: Brendan Fraser, Leslie Mann, Thomas Haden Church. Locations: Kilauea Falls.

Gilligan's Island Pilot • Filmed on Kaua'i November 1963. Broadcast 1964. Gladasya Productions, United Artists and CBS, color. Director Rod Amateau, Producer Sherwood Schwartz. Cast: Bob Denver, Alan Hale, Jim Backus. 30 minutes. Location: Moloa'a Beach. *A television pilot used to sell hit show Gilligan's Island to CBS and turn beatnik Maynard G. Crebbs into Gilligan. Kaua'i filming was done during days of Kennedy assassination.*

Hawaiian Eye • Filmed on Kaua'i November 1962. Color. Director Bob Hoffman. Cast: Troy Donahue and Bob Conrad. Location: Kaua'i Surf at Kalapaki. *Hit early-60s detective show filmed two episodes on Kaua'i.*

Hawaiians, The (aka *Master of the Islands*) • Filmed on Kaua'i August–October 1969. Released 1970. Color. Director Tom Gries, Producer Walter Mirisch. Cast: Geraldine Chaplin, Charlton Heston. Locations: Kipu Ranch, Wailua River, Kapahi. From novel *Hawaii* by James Michener, screenplay by James R. Webb. *Second part of epic movie Hawaii with Charlton Heston as Whip Hoxworth, grandson of the sea captain Rafer from the earlier film. Scenes of Queen Lili'uokalani during overthrow of Hawaiian monarchy is the only Hollywood depiction of the historic event.*

He's My Brother • Filmed on Kaua'i June 1974. Released 1974. Color. Director/Producer Eddie Dmytrk. Cast: Keenan Wynn and Bobby Sherman. Locations: Ha'ena, Hanalei. *Young man and his little brother are shipwrecked and wash ashore at a leper colony. Conflict between Christians and Hawaiian kahuna, and hang-gliding sequence, add interesting sub-plots.*

Honeymoon in Vegas • Filmed on Kaua'i 1991. Released 1992. Castle Rock Entertainment, color. Director/Writer Andrew Bergman, Producer Mike Lobell. Cast: James Caan, Nicolas Cage, Sarah Jessica Parker. 95 minutes. Locations: Lihu'e Airport, Lihu'e, Waimea, Anini, Kapa'a Town, Kapa'a Armory, Wilcox Hospital, Kalapaki. *In Las Vegas Jack loses Betsy, his fiancée, moments before their marriage to Tommy Korman. Korman takes Betsy to Kaua'i for a long weekend at Anini; Jack follows in pursuit, flies to Kaua'i, and chases Corman across the Island.*

Hook • Filmed on Kaua'i 1990. Released 1991. Amblin Entertainment, color. Director Steven Spielberg, Producers Gary Andelson and Craig Baumgarten. Cast: Dustin Hoffman, Robin Williams, Julia Roberts. 144 minutes. Location: Kipukai. *Special effects crew from George Lucas' Industrial Light & Magic filmed Kipukai for visuals used to create Peter Pan's Never-Never Land.*

Island of the Alive • Filmed on Kaua'i 1986. Released directly to video 1986. Larry Cohen Productions, color. Director/Writer Larry Cohen, Producer Paul Stadus. Cast: Michael Moriarty, Karen Black, Scott Ferguson. Locations: Lawa'i-Kai, Valley House, Nawiliwili, Ke'e Beach. *A film so bad it's almost good, with monster babies chomping searchers on Island of the Alive, better known as Kaua'i.*

Islands in the Stream • Filmed on Kaua'i 1975. Released 1977. Paramount Pictures. Director Franklin J. Schaffner, Producers Peter Bart & Max Palevsky. Based on Ernest Hemingway's book with screenplay by Denne Bart Petitclerc. Cast: Claire Bloom, David Hemmings, George C. Scott. 110 minutes. Locations: Port Allen, Maha'ulepu, Nawiliwili, Wailua River, Kuku'iula Harbor, Kipu Ranch. *Kaua'i as Hemingway's Bimini in the early days of WWII. The past and present of artist Thomas Hudson (George C. Scott) whirls around life lived on an Atlantic isle 50 miles east of Miami.*

Jungle Heat • Filmed on Kaua'i November 1956. Released 1957. United Artists, color. Director Howard W. Koch, Producer Aubrey Schenck. Cast: Lex Barker, Mari Blanchard, Miyoko Sasaki. Location: Coco Palms. *Protests raised on Kaua'i over portrayal of Hawai'i-born Japanese as spies prior to WWII in Jungle Heat gained the film notoriety. Story involves Tarzan star Lex Barker in romantic triangle and plantation strike in pre-war Hawai'i.*

Jurassic Park • Filmed on Kaua'i summer 1992. Released 1993. Universal Pictures and Amblin Entertainment, color. Directed by Steven Spielberg, Produced by Kathleen Kennedy and Jerry Molen. Cast: Sam Neill, Laura Dern, Jeff Goldblum. From book by Michael Crichton. 127 minutes. Locations: Valley House, Wailua Mauka, Limahuli, Olokele Canyon, Manawaiopuna Falls, Kilauea Mauka. *An adventure 65 million years in the making where dinosaurs are re-born thanks to high-tech tools. Cutting edge computer-generated animation and outstanding Kaua'i* *locations blended by Spielberg into the highest-grossing film of all time.*

Just Go With It • Filmed on Kaua'i May 2010. Released 2011. Columbia Pictures-Happy Madison Productions. Director Dennis Dugan. Written by Allan Loeb, Timothy Dowling. Cast: Adam Sandler, Jennifer Ariston, Brooklyn Decker. Locations: Kilauea Falls. *Comic Sandler, cast and crew went to great expense to move production company from Maui to Kaua'i to use Kilauea Falls location for adventure tourism scene.*

King Kong • Filmed on Kaua'i February–March 1975. Released 1976. Paramount Pictures, color. Director John Guillermin, Producer Dino De Laurentiis. Screenplay by Lorenzo Semple Jr. from original story by Merian C. Cooper. Cast: Jeff Bridges, Charles Grodin, Jessican Lange. 135 minutes. Locations: Honopu Beach and Honopu Arch, Kilauea, Kalalau Valley. *Updated remake of classic King Kong tale, set this time on mysterious island north of Indonesia and Twin Towers of Manhattan.*

Last Flight of Noah's Ark, The • Filmed on Kaua'i June 1979. Released 1980. Walt Disney Productions, TechniColor. Director Charles Jarrott, Producer Ron Miller, from story by Ernest K. Gann. Cast: Genevieve Bujold, Elliott Gould, Ricky Schroder. 97 minutes. Locations: Lawa'i-Kai, Port Allen. *Charter pilot reluctantly flies lovely missionary, children, and animals to South Pacific mission. Crash on desert island brings about Swiss Famiy Robinson situation and love for the disparate couple.*

Lilo & Stitch • Scenes for animation scouted on Kaua'i 1999. Released 2002. Walt Disney Pictures. Directors/Writers Dean DeBlois and Chris Sanders. Cast voices: Daveigh Chase, Tia Carrere, Jason Scott Lee. Locations animated: Hanapepe town, Kilauea Lighthouse. *Colorful tropical animated backdrops based on actual Kaua'i locations captures beauty and spirit of the Island.*

Lord of the Flies • Released 1990. Castle Rock Films, color. Director Harry Hook, Producer Ross Milloy. Americanized version of novel by William Golding, screenplay by Sara Schiff. Cast: Balthazar Getty, Chris Furrh, Danuel Pipoly. 90 minutes. Location: Ke'e Beachh. *Planeload of young boys crash-land on island and soon turn to savagery around campfire at Ke'e.*

Lost Flight • Filmed on Kaua'i November–December 1968. Released 1969. Universal Studios (TV pilot film). Director Leonard Horn, Producer Paul Donnelly. Cast: Lloyd Bridges, Anne Francis, Billy Dee Williams. Locations: Lumaha'i Beach, Manini Holo (Dry Cave) at Ha'ena. *"Naked City laid in an island jungle, concerning the problems of a group of people trying to survive," was how the* Honolulu Star-Bulletin *described this film.*

Lost World: Jurassic Park • Filmed on Kaua'i December 1996. Released 1997. Universal Studios. Director Steven Spielberg. Based upon Michael Crichton novel. Cast: Jeff Goldblum, Julianne Moore, Richard Attenborough. Locations: Kipu Kai, interior rain forest. *Short opening Kipu Kai scene ties film to original Jurassic Park blockbuster Kaua'i-made film.*

Lt. Robin Crusoe, U.S.N. • Filmed on Kaua'i August 1966. Released 1966. Walt Disney Studios, color. Director Byron Paul. Cast: Dick Van Dyke, Nancy Kwan, Akim Tamiroff, Floyd the Chimp. 91 minutes. Locations: Po'ipu Beach, Lawa'i-Kai, Lydgate Park. *Dick Van Dyke—at the time a hit on TV in his own show—goes native as Robin Crusoe, finding his girl Wednesday, rather than man Friday, for friendship.*

Making of Jurassic Park • Filmed on Kaua'i 1994. Released 1995. Media Arts, color. Narrator James Earl Jones. 50 minutes. *Intriguing documentary on the landmark computerized techniques used to bring the dinosaurs of Jurassic Park to life.*

Might Joe Young • Filmed on Kaua'i 1997. Released 1998. Walt Disney Pictures. Director Ron Underwood. Based on 1933 Merian C. Cooper film. Locations: Kilauea Falls.

Millennium • Released 1989. Gladden Enterprises, color. Cast: Kris Kristofferson and Cheryl Ladd. Location: Red Hill leading into Kalalau Valley. *People from a dying earth of the future go back in time to snatch passengers from airliners on the verge of crashing. The passengers are used to repopulate remote, safe locations—such as Kaua'i's Kalalau Valley.*

Miss Sadie Thompson • Filmed on Kaua'i May 1953. Released 1953. Columbia Pictures, TechniColor. Director Curtis Bernhardt, Producer Jerry Wald, written by Harry Kleiner based on a story by W. Somerset Maugham. Cast: Rita Hayworth, Jose Ferrer, Aldo Ray. 91 minutes. Locations: Coco Palms, Hanalei, Kalapaki, Kuku'iula, Wailua Beach, Lihu'e. *Remake of* Sadie Thompson *(1928) and* Rain *(1932) feature Rita Hayworth in role made famous earlier by Gloria Swanson and Joan Crawford. Nightclub singer (prostitute in Maugham story) enroute to New Caledonia crosses paths with muscle-bound U.S. marines, and ends in tragedy over deadly encounter with fallen missionary.*

Naked Paradise/Thunder Over Hawaii • Filmed on Kaua'i August–September 1956. Released 1957. Sunset Productions, Wide-Vision Color. Director/Producer Roger Corman. Cast: Richard Denning,

Beverly Garland, Lisa Montell. Locations: Coco Palms, Haʻena, Hanalei. *New York businessman, girl Friday, and two Bronxite sidekicks cruise into trouble in the Islands. Made back-to-back with* She Gods of Shark Reef *by low-budget genius Roger Corman.*

None But the Brave • Filmed on Kauaʻi May 1964. Released 1965. Warner Brothers, color. Director Frank Sinatra, Producers Frank Sinatra and Howard W. Koch, story by Kikumaru Okuda with screenplay by Katsuya Susaki and John Twist. 106 minutes. Cast: Frank Sinatra, Clint Walker, Tommy Sands. Location: Pilaʻa Beach. *Interesting experiment by Sinatra in combining American and Japanese cast, crew, and screenplay in study of warfare and comradeship. Made during* Manchurian Candidate *stage of Sinatra's career.*

North • Filmed on Kauaʻi 1993. Released 1994. New Line Cinema/Castle Rock Entertainment, color. Director Rob Reiner, Producers Rob Reiner and Alan Zweibel. Cast: Elijah Wood, Keone Young, Lauren Tom. 87 minutes. Locations: Lumahaʻi, Haʻena, Papaʻa Bay. *Boy decides to travel world to find new parents, stops on Kauaʻi to try out sympathetic Hawaiian governor and his wife. Filmed on north shore near home of Reiner's high school pal and Kauaʻi radio personality Andy Melamed.*

Outbreak • Filmed on Kauaʻi November 1994. Released 1995. Punch Productions, Inc./Warner Brothers, TechniColor. Director Wolfgang Petersen, Producers Gail Katz, Arnold Kopelson, Wolfgang Petersen. Cast: Dustin Hoffman, Rene Russo, Morgan Freeman. 127 minutes. Locations: Kamokila Village on Wailua River, Kipu Ranch. *Kauaʻi doubles as viral disease-plagued Africa in tropical scenes of film. Island's African-American community featured as extras.*

Pagan Love Song • Filmed on Kauaʻi April–May 1950. Released 1950. Metro-Goldwyn-Mayer, TechniColor. Director Robert Alton, Producer Arthur Freed. Cast: Howard Keel, Rita Moreno, Esther Williams. 76 minutes. Locations: Haʻena, Wainiha, Hanalei, Keʻe Beach, Ahukini Landing, Waipouli, Wailua Beach, Coco Palms, Lydgate Park, Valley House. *Dreamy, romantic movie with Kauaʻi as Tahiti. Beautiful half-Tahitian, half-American woman bored with island life is ready to split. She changes mind after arrival of handsome Ohio schoolteacher who inherits rundown coconut plantation and falls for her, unaware of her sophisticated side.*

Paradise Hawaiian Style • Filmed on Kauaʻi 1964. Released 1965. Paramount Pictures, color. Director Michael Moore, Producer Hal Wallis. Cast: Elvis Presley, Suzanna Leigh, James Shigeta. 91 minutes.

Locations: Princeville, Lihuʻe Airport. *Elvis and a local buddy bet it all on a tour aircraft business in the Islands. With a girl in every airport, Elvis runs into trouble, but finds happiness on Kauaʻi.*

Pirates of the Caribbean: On Stranger Tides • Filmed on Kauaʻi summer 2010. Released 2011. Walt Disney Pictures. Director Rob Marshall. Screenplay by Ted Elliott and Terry Rossio. Cast: Johnny Depp, Penélope Cruz, Ian McShane. Locations: Keʻe Beach, Honopu Beach, Lawaʻi Kai, Coco Palms, Waikapalae Cave at Haʻena. *Blockbuster film sets Kauaʻi scenes at Caribbean Island Fountain of Youth sites.*

Raiders of the Lost Ark • Filmed on Kauaʻi September–October 1980. Released 1981. Paramount Pictures, color. Director Steven Spielberg, Producer George Lucas. Cast: Harrison Ford, Karen Allen, Denholm Elliott. Locations: Kipu Falls, Kipu Ranch, Huleʻia Stream, ʻAliomanu (near Anahola), Kalalau Valley (footage not used in film). *Indiana Jones rips through a 1930s world of adventure battling Nazis for legendary biblical Ark of the Covenant. Final location shooting for* Raiders *took place on Kauaʻi, though the scenes appear first in the production.*

Sangra Ari • Filmed on Kauaʻi January 1962. Released 1962. Director Zenso Matsuyama. Cast: Hideko Takamine. *Story of Japanese laborers who came to Hawaiʻi in the early days of plantation immigration, of their work on sugar and pineapple plantations, and of their Nisei descendants. Early 60s peace movement theme.*

Seven • Filmed on Kauaʻi May 1978. Released 1979. Director Andy Sidaris, Producer David J. Cohen. Cast: William Smith, Christopher Joy, Ed Parker. Locations: Na Pali, Princeville, Hanalei. *Low-cost adventure film with lots of Kauaʻi scenery and tongue-in-cheek humor. Seven men hired by Feds to slaughter group of professional criminals.*

Seven Women from Hell, The • Filmed on Kauaʻi June 1961. Released 1961. Associated Producers, color. Director Robert D. Webb, Cinematography by Floyd Crosby, Written by Jesse Lasky Jr. Cast: Cesar Romero, Richard Loo, Franz Terborch. Location: Wailua. *Kauaʻi plays New Guinea in the early days of the WWII Pacific campaign as the Japanese Army invades in this low-budget action film.*

She Gods of Shark Reef • Released 1958. American-International Pictures. Director Roger Corman, Producer Ludwig H. Gerber. Cast: Don Durant, Lisa Montell, Bill Cord. Locations: Hanalei, Haʻena. *"Beautiful maidens in a lush tropical paradise ruled by a hideous stone god." Two American brothers on the lam are shipwrecked on an island inhabited by lovely pearl divers.*

Six Days Seven Nights • Filmed on Kaua'i 1997. Released 1998. Touchstone Pictures. Director Ivan Reitman. Screenplay by Michael Browning. Cast: Harrison Ford, Anne Heche, David Schwimmer. Locations: Lihu'e Airport, Papa'a Bay, Kipu Kai, Na Pali Coast, Aliomanu. *Interesting use of multiple Kaua'i locations for romantic comedy backdrop set as French Polynesia.*

Soul Surfer • Filmed on Kaua'i March 2010. Released 2011. Sony Pictures - TriStar. Director/Writer Sean McNamara. Cast: AnnaSophia Robb, Dennis Quaid, Helen Hunt. Hanalei Bay, Makua Beach at Ha'ena, Hanalei town. *Unique for telling actual Kaua'i story using Kaua'i locations, though most of film shot on O'ahu.*

South Pacific • Filmed on Kaua'i July–August 1957. Released 1958. 20th Century Fox, TechniColor. Director Joshua Logan, Producer Buddy Adler. Cast: Rossano Brazzi, Mitzi Gaynor, Juanita Hall, Ray Walston. 150 minutes. Locations: Princeville, Hanalei Pier, Makua Beach at Ha'ena, Kilauea, Lawa'i-Kai, Barking Sands near Mana and Polihale. *From book by James Michener and Broadway play by Rogers and Hammerstein. Spectacular South Pacific WWII musical that made Makaha mountain on Kaua'i's north shore into mythical Bali Hai.*

Sunny Travels in Hawaii/Hawaii Chindochu • Filmed on Kaua'i June 1954. International Theatrical Company, color. Cast: Chiemi Eri and Yoshio Tabata. *A post-war Japanese comedy.*

Thorn Birds, The • Filmed on Kaua'i 1981. Television mini-series, released 1983. Warner Brothers Production for TV, color. Director Daryl Duke, Producers David L. Wolper and Stan Margulies. Cast: Bryan Brown, Richard Chamberlain, Rachel Ward. 486 minutes. Locations: Ke'e Beach, McBryde Sugar Mill, Koloa, Hanapepe Town, Lawa'i-Kai. *Island's beaches, cane fields and plantation-era towns become outback tropical Australia in ten-hour mini-TV series based on Colleen McCullough's best-seller. Richard Chamberlain and Rachel Ward romance with Kaua'i as a backdrop before millions of TV viewers.*

Throw Mama From the Train • Filmed on Kaua'i June–July 1987. Released 1987. Orion Pictures Corp., Color by DeLuxe. Director Danny DeVito, Producer Larry Brezner. Cast: Danny DeVito, Billy Crystal, Anne Ramsey, Kate Mulgrew. 88 minutes. Locations: Ke'e Beach, Kalihiwai, Kapa'a Town, Nawiliwili. *Wife steals ex-husband's manuscript and it becomes a best-seller for her. Husband mistakenly makes Hitchcockian deal with mother-dominated mystery writer to kill ex while she takes a Kaua'i vacation.*

To End All Wars • Filmed on Kaua'i spring, summer 2000. Released 2001. Argyll Film Partners, Gumshoe Productions, Integrity Partners. Director David Cunningham. Cast: Kiefer Sutherland, David Carlyle Clarån McMenamin, Mark Strong. Locations: Mauka Koloa, Ahukini Pier, Hule'ia Stream. *Koloa field is set at WWII Thailand Japanese Army railroad construction POW camp. Use of Grove Farm narrow-gauge locomotives highlights Kaua'i ties to film.*

Tropic Thunder • Filmed on Kaua'i 2007. Released 2008. DreamWorks/Paramount Pictures. Director Ben Stiller. Screenplay by Justin Theroux. Cast: Ben Stiller, Jack Black, Robert Downey Jr. Locations: Mauka valley owned by Grove Farm Land Co. *Big, big budget film movie within a movie black comedy tale of war film crew who stumble into actual war zone.*

Uncommon Valor • Filmed on Kaua'i August 1983. Released 1983. Paramount Pictures, color. Director Ted Kotcheff, Producers Buzz Feitshans, Ted Kotcheff, John Milius. Cast: Gene Hackman, Robert Stack, Randall 'Tex' Cobb, Patrick Swayze. 105 minutes. Locations: Hanalei Valley, Lumaha'i Valley, Wahiawa Camp, Hule'ia Stream, Lihu'e. *Vietnam War buddies from California return to rescue MIAs years after war ends.*

Voodoo Island (Silent Death) • Filmed on Kaua'i October–November 1956. Released 1957. A Bel Air Production through United Artists, B&W. Director Reginald Le Borg, Producer Howard W. Koch. Music by Les Baxter. Cast: Elisha Cook Jr., Boris Karloff, Beverly Tyler, Murvyn Vye. 76 minutes. Locations: Coco Palms, Valley House. *Zombies! The Bridge of Death! Resort developers disappear trying to exploit Pacific Island that's home to voodoo worshippers and chauvanistic woman-eating plants.*

Wackiest Ship in the Army, The • Filmed on Kaua'i May 1960. Released 1961. Columbia Pictures, color. Director Richard Murphy, Producer Fred Kohlmar. Cast: Ricky Nelson, Jack Lemmon, Chips Rafferty. 99 minutes. Locations: Hanalei Bay, Kalalau Lookout at Koke'e, Waimea Canyon, Hule'ia Stream, Nawiliwili, 'Opaeka'a Falls. *On Japanese-held South Pacific island. Lt. Rip Crandall is hoodwinked into taking command of the "Wackiest Ship in the Army"—a funky sailboat with a crew of misfits who don't know how to sail.*

Yoake No Futari (Rainbow Over the Pacific) • Filmed on Kaua'i spring 1968. Released 1968. Shochiku Co. of Japan, color. Director Yukio Hashi. Cast: Yukio Hashi, Walter Omori and Etsuko Ikuta. *Love story of a young Japanese photographer who falls for an Island sensei woman. Film commemorates Meiji Centennial.*

SURFING MOVIE FACTS

A FILM BY GREG MACGILLIVRAY AND JIM FREEMAN

FIVE SUMMER STORIES

THE LAST SURFING MOVIE. "Five Summer Stories" is Greg MacGillivray and Jim Freeman's last surfing film. It is the culmination of a ten year celebration in celluloid that includes the classics "Free and Easy, Waves of Change, and The Sunshine Sea." In "Five Summer Stories" Greg and Jim give us five-plus exciting, controversial and beautiful stories about surfing. From these stories comes a perspective on surfing that warms of the future while it warms the present. SUMMER: NOT A SEASON, BUT A STATE OF MIND.

FINAL SCREENINGS.

BALI HIGH

A NEW SURFING FILM BY STEPHEN SPAULDING
Featuring the incredible tube riding of Peter McCabe, Tommy Carroll, Larry B and others, in a dazzling array of exotic wave frontiers including Java, Bali, Hav and the Mysterious "Isle of Kong."

Da Bull—Search For Surf • by Greg Noll: Filmed on Kauaʻi Fall 1957. Famed big wave rider Greg Noll, Dewey Weber, and pals travel from Oʻahu's north shore to Kauaʻi to ride Hanalei. Probably the earliest footage of surfing on Kauaʻi. The footage is part of a "Best Of" compilation taken from Noll's 1950s and 1960s movies now available on video.

Barefoot Adventure • by Bruce Brown: Filmed on Kauaʻi 1960. Filmmaker Bruce Brown of *Endless Summer* fame struck out looking for hot waves on Kauaʻi. Available on video.

Gone with the Wave by Phil Wilson: Filmed on Kauaʻi 1963. An all-Hawaiʻi production featuring surfing at Pakala on the west side and Kealia Beach on the east side.

Inside Out • by Dale Davis: Filmed on Kauaʻi 1965 or 1966. A taxi trip in an old Chevy takes longboarding surfers to Kalihiwai and Hanalei. Sequence is short. Available on video.

Free & Easy • by Greg MacGillivray and Jim Freeman: Filmed on Kauaʻi 1966. MacGillivray and Freeman captured beautiful footage of great waves at Hanalei, Polihale, Kekaha, Nawiliwili and Kalihiwai. Bill Hamilton and Mark Martinson ride longboards in the film, which was shot about a year before the short-board revolution hit surfing. No video release scheduled.

World of Waves • by Nick Beck and Gaylord Wilcox: Filmed on Kauaʻi 1969. Joey Cabell rides a thick, turned-up nose shortboard at Cannons in this rarely seen film. The footage comes at the end of a round-the-world surfing expedition undertaken by Beck, Wilcox, plus their wives and children. Interesting footage of Mauritius, South Africa, Bob McTavish riding Noosa Heads in Queensland during the V-Bottom era, Portugal and Biarritz and other surf locales.

The Islands • by Paul Witzig: Filmed on Kauaʻi Spring 1970. Aussie filmmaker Witzig captured Kauaʻi's north shore during the days of idealistic soul surfing in the early 1970s.

Five Summer Stories • by MacGillivray-Freeman Films: Filmed on Kauaʻi 1972. Hang-gliding footage from Kalalau Valley was the only Kauaʻi scene in this landmark film. Available on video from Surfer Magazine.

Island Magic • Jimmy Lucas and Joey Cabell rip Hanalei in 1972.

The Forgotten Island of Santosha • by Larry and Terry Yates: Filmed on Kauaʻi 1975. To complement footage of a surfing trip to exotic, elusive Santosha (Mauritius) Kauaʻi residents Larry Yates added shots of Pakala, Acid Drop, and PKs.

Bali High • by Stephen Spaulding: Filmed on Kaua'i 1979. Carmel-based filmmaker Steve Spaulding named Kaua'i "Kong Island" to hide the location of Ha'ena's Tunnels. Terry Chung and Titus Kinimaka are featured.

Totally Committed • by Stephen Spaulding: Filmed on Kaua'i 1983-85. Steve Spaulding returned to Kaua'i to capture footage of Cannons and Kalihiwai.

Insanity • by Bill Ballard: Filmed on Kaua'i 1995. Cannons and other Kaua'i surf spots featured in this surf video by husband of champion Kaua'i surfer Rochelle Ballard. Features Keala Kennelly.

Secret Kaua'i surfing spot.

Killer babies from *Island of the Alive*.

South Pacific tete-a-tete.

Outbreak mercenaries.

Acapulco Gold—Lucky 13 Cult Collectibles
Avatar—20th Century Fox
Beachhead—MGM Video&DVD
Behold Hawaii—Unreleased
Between Heaven and Hell—Fox Home Video
Bird of Paradise (1951 version)—Unreleased
Blue Hawaii—Fox Home Video
Body Heat—Warner Bros. Home Video
Cane Fire/White Heat—Turner Movie Channel*
Castaway Cowboy, The—Buena Vista Home Video
Descendants, The—Fox Searchlight
Diamond Head—Columbia Tri-Star Home Video
Donovan's Reef—Paramount Home Video
Dragonfly—Universal Studios
Forbidden Island—Unreleased
Flight of the Intruder—Paramount Home Video
George of the Jungle—Disney Home Video
Gilligan's Island Pilot—Columbia House Video
Hawaiians, The—MGM Limited Edition Collection
Honeymoon in Vegas—New Line Home Video
Hook—Columbia Tri Star Home Video
Island of the Alive—Warner Home Video
Islands in the Stream—Paramount Home Video
Jungle Heat—MGM
Jurassic Park/Lost World/Jurassic Park III—MCA Universal Home Video
King Kong—Paramount Home Video
The Last Flight of Noah's Ark—Buena Vista Home Video
Lord of the Flies (1990)—Orion Home Video
Lt. Robin Crusoe, U.S.N.—Buena Vista
Making of Jurassic Park—Media Arts
Mighty Joe Young—Disney Home Video
Millennium—Gladden Enterprises
Miss Sadie Thompson—Columbia Home Video
Naked Paradise/Thunder Over Hawaii—Unreleased
None But the Brave—Warner Bros. Home Video
North—Columbia Tri Star Home Video
Outbreak—Warner Home Video
Pagan Love Song—MGM Home Video
Paradise Hawaiian Style—Fox Home Video
Perfect Getaway—Universal Studios
Pirates of the Caribbean On Stranger Tides—Disney
Raiders of the Lost Ark—Paramount Home Video
Seven—Live Home Video
Seven Women From Hell—Unreleased
She Gods of Shark Reef—Loon Video
Six Days/Seven Nights—Touchstone Home Entertainment
Soul Surfer—Sony Pictures Entertainment
South Pacific—Fox Home Video
Thorn Birds, The—Warner Home Video
Throw Momma From the Train—Orion Home Video
Time Machine—Dreamworks Video
Tropic Thunder—Paramount
Uncommon Valor—Paramount Home Video
Voodoo Island—MGM
Wackiest Ship in the Army, The—Sony Pictures Entertainment

AFTERWORD

As the photographer for *The Kauai Movie Book*, I've roamed Kaua'i over the past several months, following the tracks from six decades of movie-making. Time and again, I've been thrilled by the incredible beauty that is packed into this "small island with epic locations." It's no surprise that the "Garden Island" is Hawaii's premier destination for filmmakers.

Looking back, my most vibrant impression is not so much the classic settings of films from the past, rather it is of the untapped wealth of locations that have never appeared on film: hidden beaches, coves, and caves; wind-blown dunes and crumbling stone ruins; narrow twisting canyons and silky streams amidst forests from around the world.

And beyond that, I'm continually impressed by the diversity that one place can have, be it a westside beach such as Polihale, a lookout over the Na Pali Coast, or a Hanalei taro field. I will never be bored by a place that has more moods than a school room full of adolescents.

The ruddy cliffs of Waimea Canyon, for example, are the stock of tourist postcards and guidebooks. But take a look at dawn and you may see silhou-etted hillsides fading into a misty pink haze, or later in the morning shadowed cliffs of a deep blue green that change to a monotone Chinese brush painting when afternoon clouds gather amidst pinnacles and knife-edged ridges. Heavy rains bring forth swatches of greenery spattered across ochre canyon-scapes, yet within weeks the foliage has taken on the dried and tanned look of a harsh western desert.

Kaua'i is an island awash in a sea of visual opportunities, often intensi-fied in the special glow of early morning or evening light. Even after 20 years of living here, camera in hand, I never cease to be surprised and inspired by her magnificent beauty.

–David Boynton

PHOTO CREDITS

PG	DESCRIPTION	SOURCE
4-5	*Outbreak* filming	Warner Bros.
9	John Kerr	David Penhallow
	David Penhallow	
	Pagan Love Song poster	DeSoto Brown & Metro-Goldwyn-Mayer
10	Maureen West	Maureen West Morrison
	& Howard Keel	
	South Pacific	The Samuel Goldwyn Company
	Pagan Love Song party	David Penhallow
11	*Jurassic* gates	Amblin Entertainment/Universal Pictures
14	Koko Kaneali'i	Kaua'i Film Commission
	Mayor Bernard Carvalho	Kaua'i Visitors Bureau
15	Tahiti Nui	Kaua'i Film Commission
	Weke Road	Andy Melamed
	Beau Bridges	Fox Searchlight Pictures
	& George Clooney	
16	Laird Hamilton	Joel Guy Hanalei Grass Shack Productions
17	Kipu Kai	Luis Reyes Archives
18	*Pirates* crew	Kaua'i Visitors Bureau
	Fountain of Youth	Walt Disney Productions
	Makauwahi Cave Reserve	Angela Tillson, A Whale of a Time Productions
19	*Pirates* location stills	Walt Disney Productions
	Pirates casting	Kaua'i Film Commission
20	Lava rock	Kaua'i Film Commission
21	*Just Go With It* poster	Kaua'i Film Commission
	Waterfall	Angela Tillson, A Whale of a Time Productions
	Sabra Kauka	Angela Tillson, A Whale of a Time Productions
22	1980s Kilauea Falls	Chris Cook Collection/Kaua'i Historical Society
23	Thailand group	Mark Nakatsukasa
	Raising a Soul Surfer book	Hamilton Family
	Heart of a Soul Surfer DVD cover	Becky Baumgartner Hamilton
	Soul Surfer clap board	Chris Cook
24	Bethany Hamilton	Noah Hamilton Photography
	& AnnaSophia Robb	
	Soul Surfer poster	Hamilton Family
25	Surfers ready to go out	Noah Hamilton Photography
26	Makua Beach	Noah Hamilton Photography
	Church group	Chris Cook
27	Stream in Wailua	Angela Tillson, A Whale of a Time Productions
28	Landscape	Chris Cook
29	Payton Hough, Sr.	Chris Cook
	Grove Farm Co. aerial	Michael Grimm
	Telecommunications array	Telecom Kaua'i Film Commission
30	*Tropic Thunder* Jeep	Kaua'i Film Commission
	Kukui Grove premiere	Kaua'i Visitors Bureau
31	Venezuelan Amazon Basin Indians	Angela Tillson, A Whale of a Time Productions
	Princeville Airport	Chris Cook
32	Village scenes photos	Angela Tillson, A Whale of a Time Productions
33	*Jurassic Park* "Hero Boat"	Angela Tillson, A Whale of a Time Productions
34	*Mighty Joe Young* poster	Kaua'i Film Commission
	Jurassic Ranch	Angela Tillson, A Whale of a Time Productions
35	Stunt man waterfall leap	Angela Tillson, A Whale of a Time Productions
36	*Lilo & Stitch* stills	Walt Disney Productions
	Kilauea Lighthouse	Kaua'i Visitors Bureau
38	Jimmy Bodrero caricature	Chris Cook
	White Heat lobby card	Christine Fayé Kaua'i Museum
	Virginia Cherrill & Robert Stevenson still	W.J. Senda/Chris Cook collection
39	*To End All Wars* poster	Kaua'i Film Commission
	Sakae Ito still	David Cunningham
40	*To End All Wars* stills	David Cunningham
41	*To End All Wars* cast & crew	Courtesy Anthony Sommer
	To End All Wars still	David Cunningham
42	Airplane stills	Steve Stafford Studio Wings Inc.
43	*Six Days Seven Nights* actors	Chris Cook
	Six Days Seven Nights T-shirt	Chris Cook
44	Gag sign	Chris Cook
	Jacqueline Obradors & Steve Stafford	Steve Stafford Studio Wings Inc.
45	*Six Days Seven Nights* press kit	Touchstone Pictures
	Pancho Graham	Pancho Graham
46	Art Umezu	Chris Cook
	Kaua'i location promotional guides	Kaua'i Film Commission
	Steven Speiberg & Mayor Judy Drosd	Judy Drosd
	Angela Tillson	Angela Tillson, A Whale of a Time Productions
	Ken Levine & Steven Spielberg	Ken Levine
47	Roger Corman	Kaua'i Film Commission
	Elvis group	Kaua'i Visitors Bureau
	Mitzy Gaynor & Sue Kanoho	Kaua'i Visitors Bureau
	Newspaper clipping	*The Garden Island* newspaper
	William J. Senda & Charlie Fern photos	W.J. Senda/Chris Cook Collection
	Group photo	*The Garden Island* newspaper archives
48	*Kaua'i Aloha* title screen	David Talisman
49	Waterfalls	Kaua'i Visitors Bureau
50	Cousins/students	Haunani Seward/Ke Kula Ni'ihau O Kekaha Learning Center
	Waimea Valley cave	Chris Cook
51	*Kaluaikoolau* book	Kaua'i Historical Society
	Kalalau Lookout	Kaua'i Visitors Bureau
55	*The Hawaiians* stills	United Artists Pictures
57	Diamond Head stills	Columbia Pictures & DeSoto Brown
58	*Raiders* hostages	Tom Summers
60	*Raiders* poster - slide	Lucasfilm Ltd./Paramount Pictures
	Magnum PI print	Tom Summers
	George Lucas & Steven Spielberg	Lucasfilm Ltd./Paramount Pictures